BLACKNESS AND VALUE
Seeing Double

Blackness and Value investigates the principles by which "value" operates and asks whether it is useful to imagine that the concepts of racial blackness and whiteness in the United States operate in terms of these principles. Testing these concepts by exploring various theoretical approaches and their shortcomings, Lindon Barrett finds that the gulf between "the street" (where race is acknowledged as a powerful enigma) and the literary academy (where until recently it has not been) can be understood as a symptom of racial violence.

The book traces several interrelations between value and race, such as literate/illiterate, the signing/singing voice, time/space, civic/criminal, and academy/street, and offers relevant and fresh readings of two novels by Ann Petry. Whereas commonly approaches to race and value are examined historically or sociologically, this intriguing study provides a new critical approach that speaks to theorists of race as well as gender and queer studies.

Lindon Barrett is Associate Professor in the Department of English and Comparative Literature and the Program in African-American Studies at the University of California, Irvine.

Books in the series

BLACKNESS AND VALUE

Seeing Double

Lindon Barrett

CAMBRIDGE
UNIVERSITY PRESS

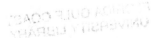

PUBLISHED BY THE PRESS SYNDICATE OF THE UNIVERSITY OF CAMBRIDGE
The Pitt Building, Trumpington Street, Cambridge CB2 1RP, United Kingdom

CAMBRIDGE UNIVERSITY PRESS
The Edinburgh Building, Cambridge CB2 2RU, UK   http://www.cup.cam.ac.uk
40 West 20th Street, New York, NY 10011-4211, USA   http://www.cup.org
10 Stamford Road, Oakleigh, Melbourne 3166, Australia

First published 1999

Printed in the United States of America

Typeset in Baskerville 10.5/12.5 pt, in QuarkXPress™ [RF]

*A catalog record for this book is available from
the British Library*

Library of Congress Cataloging-in-Publication Data
Barrett, Lindon
Blackness and value : seeing double / Lindon Barrett.
p.   cm. – (Cambridge studies in American literature and
culture)
Based on author's thesis (Ph. D.) — University of Pennsylvania.
Includes bibliographical references and index.
ISBN 0–521–62103–8
1. American literature – Afro-American authors – History and
criticism – Theory, etc.   2. Literature and society – United States –
History – 20th century.   3. Petry, Ann Lane, 1911–   – Political and
social views.   4. Violence – Social aspects – United States.   5. Race –
Social aspects – United States.   6. Afro-Americans in literature.
7. United States – Race relations.   8. Social values – United States.
9. Violence in literature.   10. Racism – United States.   11. Race in
literature.   12. Duality (Logic)   I. Title.   II. Series.
PS153.N5B296   1998
810.9'896073 – dc21   97-52757
                                                          CIP

ISBN 0-521-62103-8 hardback

For Dorothy Barrett,
with much love and respect

CONTENTS

ACKNOWLEDGMENTS

This project began as my dissertation at the University of Pennsylvania and received in those early stages of its development generous fellowship support from the Social Sciences and Humanities Research Council of Canada and the Mellon Foundation through its Program for Assessing and Revitalizing the Social Sciences (PARSS). Over the intervening years, the project has been supported by a Faculty Career Development Award and sabbatical leave from the University of California, Irvine, as well as a Resident Fellowhip at the University of California Humanities Research Institute (UCHRI). Debra Massey and the staff at the UCHRI deserve mention for their extreme efficiency. Portions of Chapter 1 have appeared in *Callaloo* 13.4 (Fall 1990) and *SubStance* 67, 1992, and an earlier version of Chapter 3 has appeared in *Cultural Critique* 25 (Fall 1993).

While at the University of Pennsylvania, I was fortunate to have the opportunity to work with David DeLaura, Betsy Errkila, Marjorie Levinson, Sandra Pouchet Pacquet, and especially John Roberts. In addition to being perceptive, Sandra Pouchet Pacquet is one of the most gracious people I have ever met. John Roberts was an indefatigable reader and supporter of my work and the most invaluable intellectual resource and friend a graduate student could have. I also had the immense good fortune at this time to meet, work with, party with, and become lifelong friends with Elizabeth Alexander, Jennifer Brody, Kim Hall, Nicole King, Amy Robinson, Laura Tanner, and James Krasner. In the intervening years, I have been able to add to this list Dwight McBride, Saidiya Hartmann, Farah Griffin, Phillip Brian Harper, Kim Dillion, Arthur Little, Kobena Mercer,

Marceyliena Morgan, Valerie Smith, and Robyn Wiegman. Charles
Rowell of *Callaloo* has been a longtime supporter of my work and a
close friend. In southern California, I have found many talented and
supportive colleagues: Rae Linda Brown, Rey Chow, Emory Elliot,
Robert and Vivian Folkenflik, Abdul JanMohamed, Lillian Manzor-
Coats, J. Hillis Miller, Harryette Mullen, Jane Newman, Leslie Ra-
bine, Gabriele Schwab, Patrick Sinclair, John Smith, and Richard
Yarborough. I must single out three colleagues in particular: Thelma
Foote, with whom I have an intellectual camaraderie; Steve Mail-
loux, who has probably read more of my work than any person on
the planet; and John Carlos Rowe, who is a person of vast intellect
and unimpeachable integrity. I have also learned much from the
graduate students I have worked with at UC, Irvine; UCLA; and UC,
San Diego; and I must recognize a series of undergraduate and graduate research assistants who have worked with me over a period of
several years: Catherine Allan, Wilson Chen, Michael Miklos, Keta
Miranda, Connie Razza, and Alonia Rose. Stuart Jay and Farid Matuk
have enriched my time in southern California with their earnest
interest in the life of the mind and their friendship. Eric Sundquist
was instrumental in bringing this project to Cambridge University
Press, and Wahneema Lubiano was a highly instructive reader of the
manuscript. I am also grateful to Anna Sanow and the editorial staff
at the Press. Certainly, for me, the intellectual example of Hortense
Spillers has been immense; it seems to me that long ago she was
already ten years ahead of the rest of us. Still, despite this abundant
generosity and whatever examples I may have taken in the writing
of this study, I am – needless to say – solely responsible for the
weaknesses of the study, its faults of presentation and thought as
well as scope and organization. I only hope they are not as overwhelming as I sometimes fear.

Beyond these forms of institutional and individual support, I have
more personal debts to acknowledge. My family and my mother (to
whom this book is dedicated) have been and are a constant source
of reassurance and encouragement. Dorothy Barrett has taught me
perserverance, laughter; to dance, to sometimes scream when you
dance; and devotion. John Roberts, Elizabeth Alexander, Jennifer
Brody, and Thelma Foote bear mention again. Last, but certainly
and by no means least, I must express my love and gratitude to
Harmon "Skip" Spruill, Lance Avington, Melvin White, and Barry
Copilow, fabulous friends who sometimes make sitting down in front
of a computer or a book an all too arduous task for me.

INTRODUCTION: "IN THE DARK"

Seeing Double is a suggestive subtitle for this study for several reasons. First, duality suggests the binarism by which the concept of value most routinely attempts to present itself. To "see" value is in some sense to "see" double. Another sense of the phrase "seeing double" implies a state of impaired, unreliable, or faulty perception, and this sense of the phrase is captured by the yoking of racial blackness with the concept of value, as the title suggests. In the U.S. polity and cultural imagination racial blackness is most often far from being taken as a term of value. To make such a proposal is most often to leave oneself open to being perceived as having impaired, unreliable, or faulty judgment. The aim of this project, however, is precisely to see double in these ways.

In considering value, this study attempts to formulate answers to three questions: In what ways does an interrogation of value as an abstract principle bear productively on the anatomization of the violence and oppressive force of racialization? In what specific ways can a critical discourse on value reveal peculiarities of race? In short, does value redact race, and vice versa? Indeed, this congress of an anatomization of value with considerations of the "racial" presuppositions of U.S. doxa reiterates one of the central premises of the study, which is that in U.S. cultural logic the abstract entities "value" and "race" keenly reflect one another, even to a point at which they might be considered isomorphic. At its simplest, value is a configuration of privilege, and, at its crudest, race is the same. Insofar as value, as a theoretical dynamic, promotes one form(ation) to the

1

2 INTRODUCTION

detriment of another (or others), race proves a dramatic instantiation of this principle.

Blackness and Value, in elaborating this thesis, is divided into six chapters, which are, in turn, presented in three sections – "Violence and the Unsightly," "Reasonings and Reasonablenesses," and "Scopic and Phonic Economies" – and their trajectory can be codified as follows: Part One elaborates a theoretical model of value and employs it in reading the cultural dynamics of a "racialized" African American presence in the United States; Part Two employs this model in relation to the cultural dynamics of the dominant "racial" position, whiteness; Part Three repeats the exercise by more openly considering the dynamics of these two configurations in tandem.

As will quickly become evident, the theoretical orientation toward value undertaken in this project grows in important ways out of a longstanding appreciation of the work of Barbara Herrnstein Smith. Smith, most especially in *The Contingencies of Value*, outlines meticulously the systemicity and transactional nature of value, ineluctably rendering it contingent despite its best efforts to appear otherwise. Nonetheless, despite the very plain fact of my debt to Smith's work, equally evident are substantial differences existing between the purview of her critical concerns and that of those pursued here. That is, at the same time *Blackness and Value* attempts to engage the sensibilities of Smith's investigations, it aims also to provide an account of those paramount figures of racialization fixed in U.S. cultural logic as "blackness" and "whiteness."

In addition to the neopragmatism of Smith, I call on a variety of criticism and critical schools to elaborate this position. My considerations, although certainly not Marxist, begin in part with Baudrillard and his reading of Marx on value; Mary Douglas's structuralist anthropology and its reconfiguration in the literary and cultural work of Peter Stallybrass and Allon White provide another initial interpretative framework. The central intellectual tradition, however, within which these analyses fall (but that they do not simply recapitulate) is the type of *poststructuralist* critical analysis following from Jacques Derrida's *deconstructive* philosophizing, as set out in formative, or earlier, productions of his career like *Speech and Phenomena, Writing and Difference, Of Grammatology*, and *Dissemination*. It is very important to note that this characterization presupposes an accountable distinction between the terms "poststructuralist" and "deconstructive": "Poststructuralism" is taken as a broader (and untidy) rubric not limited to but encompassing the permutations of deconstruction proliferated by a variety of class and racial critiques, feminisms, and queer theories, whereas "deconstruction" assumes a stricter concern with the complications of linguistic, philosophical, and textual unravelings that seem, above all, to return energies of inquiry to themselves as primarily abstracted – rather than culturally embodied – phenomena.

In this understanding, one paradigm lends itself more easily and fluidly to cultural analyses, and the other remains more clearly phenomenological. And my hope is that, given this distinction, if moments of the forthcoming analysis may resemble the phenomenologically indebted postures of Derridean derived deconstruction, they finally resolve themselves in an enterprising return to the culturally embodied scrutiny this study aims to articulate. Summarily put, the intellectual tradition most reflected in this work is the strand of deconstructive cum poststructuralist thought earnestly interested in disclosing the dysfunctions of an Enlightenment legacy both riddled and clarified by its inescapable aporias. The work shares with traditional poststructuralist theorizing a preoccupation with the antinomian and its irruptions within Enlightenment traditions of reason and culture.

In terms of interventions into African American literary and cultural criticism, the primary intervention made here is into a line of thought dedicated to conceptualizing the relation between literacy and African American subjectivity – perspectives instructively put forward by William Andrews, Henry Louis Gates, Jr., Ronald Judy, Harryette Mullen, James Olney, Valerie Smith, Robert Stepto, and Alice Walker, for instance. In various ways all these critics ask, What are the overarching terms for the production of an African American expressive presence? My wish is to join them and others in this inquiry, even though the substantial and recent investment of African Americanist critical discourse in U.S. cultural studies is not reflected here. In fact, insofar as there is any such investment, it is not in the concerted juxtaposition of expressive textual phenomena with a local historical fabric but, rather, in the attentiveness of cultural studies to the exigencies of power and powerlessness and their sublte, pervasive insinuations.

It is important to note further that, in addition to a close engagement with the work of Barbara Herrnstein Smith and other poststructuralist discourses, this study grows out of a long-standing admiration for the fiction and narrative vision of Ann Petry. Until recently, Petry has most routinely been considered a writer within the Richard Wright "orbit"; however, that description seems inadequate given her very different and considerable skills. Above all, Petry is a visionary of narrative architecture and complexity. She constructs narratives that convene and interweave the actions and lives of a broad array of characters, a feat accomplished not necessarily by bringing this array of characters into direct contact or conversation with one another but by pursuing the ways their lives affect or speak to each other through the relaying wakes of their actions in a populous narrative world. Working within traditional rather than experimental narrative forms, Petry deftly negotiates the logistics of intesecting movements and plots, as well as powerfully drawing the separate but redounding psychological intensities of a number of her characters. The marvellous effect is that what first seems the routine unraveling of a seamless plot becomes, extraordinarily, an expanding, rippling account increasingly exceeding the terms of linearity.

These impressively complex narrative architectures keenly broach the eccentricities of racialization. They provide subtle and provocative canvases on which to trace out the most intricate or compelling nuances of the U.S. cultural logic of blackness and whiteness in their "racialized" diacriticism. They provide revealing canvases on which to detail the theoretical observations elaborated at some length in these pages. Yet, moreover, they provide equally rewarding opportunities to read the critical theoretical traditions deployed in this study against their own grains, returning to these traditions a critical scrutiny made possible precisely through considering the conditions of African American cultural production. In a phrase, I hope by their congress the value of theory and the value of Petry's novels might be mutually revised in enabling ways.

The first section, "Violence and the Unsightly," elaborates the workings of value from its underside or deprivileged side; the second section, "Reasonings and Reasonablenesses," undertakes a similar elaboration from the opposing side of configured privilege. Both entertain various (yet isomorphic) ways of formulating the schism between the valueless and the valuable: "black" and "white," the "aliterate" and the "literate," the "singing" and the "signing," the "street" and the "academy." Each of these binarisms, the claim is, serves as a concomitant site of racialization and value; each documents ways in which the meaning of race as a value proliferates at overlapping cultural points related to apparatuses of narration and dissemination.

"Violence and the Unsightly," concerned primarily with the first terms of these several pairs, stakes out speculative territory afield, then, of points of U.S. culture considered valuable. The vantage of its discussion is that of the devalued racial category of blackness, its three chapters both rehearsing and querying a cultural logic that draws general lines of equivalence between these terms: "black," "aliterate," "singing," the "street."

Chapter I provides an account of the generation of value (and inevitably valuelessness) in which violence is posited as the subsequently occluded origin of value. This model understands value as a principle of order that concertedly overlooks its forceful, initial intervention into what it constructs as "disorder," a principle that subsequently sublimates its ineluctable violence through the fetishization of boundaries. Both this violence and its sublimation are read in the concerns of nineteenth- and twentieth-century African American texts, particularly Billie Holiday's *Lady Sings the Blues*. Chapter II examines the way in which the investment of African American cultural expressivity in musical production (redacted as the "singing" voice) authors competing formations of value to those of the dominant U.S. culture, which understands itself as "white." The "singing" voice challenges the primacy and exclusivity of literacy, the indominable point of concern for Western bourgeois value whether civic, legal, or individual. Drawing on deconstructive theorizing, ethnomusicology, some historizations of the origins of market society, as well as Adorno's cultural critique of jazz, this chapter troubles the dominant cultural authority of value invested in individual abilities to decipher and produce cursive script. Chapter III provides a protracted reading of Ann Petry's 1946 novel *The Street* in the service of a textual elaboration of the theoretical perspectives broached so far. It examines the ways in which the fortunes of Lutie Johnson, Petry's protagonist, can be productively charted by close readings of the symbolic weight and structural pressure the value of the singing voice brings to bear on the plot and narration of the novel.

"Reasonings and Reasonablenesses," turning to the situation of the dominant racial perspective, pursues an alternate but related trajectory. It extends the consideration of the exigencies of value not by principally examining the obverse of privileged articulations of value and the disturbances these obverse forms generate, but by examining the guileful processes by which privileged articulations emerge and are maintained. It regards its speculative territory as the latter terms of the binarisms: "white," the "literate," the "signing," the "academy." Indeed, in the same way the singing voice is taken as an esteemed form of countersignificant African American cultural expressivity, so the humanist literary academy in its stewardship, accounting, and disseminating of a dominant cultural legacy is understood as an important point of valuable cultural articulation. According to the broad outlines of U.S. logic, the literary academy, like the singing voice, proves an important index of what these divergent cultures possess as well as represent. They, of course, are not the only such indices but do speak meaningfully to the situation of each other, precisely because the operations of cultural "value" make them seem such disparate formations. The academy and the African American singing voice are understood as radically opposed counterparts, one representing the height of reason, and the other its seeming nadir, which is to say, the intensity of ludic dissipation.

Chapter IV, the single chapter comprising this section, examines the overwhelming influence of New Criticism in establishing the protocols and values of the twentieth-century literary academy, protocols and value that until late in the twentieth century are exceedingly effective in exiling the "racial." The chapter interrogates how New Criticism effectively masks its strong ties with the social and racial ideologies of the Southern Agrarians and Fugitives – which does not amount to claiming these protocols as somehow *inherently* oppressive or racially inflected but, instead, amounts to scrutinizing the circumstances out of which these protocols arise and the historically particular needs and silences they address for those championing them. How does race figure, this chapter asks, in the new configuration of institutional value that is the formative U.S. literary academy?

The final section, "Scopic and Phonic Economies," foregrounds the claim that the very strict divisions and distinctions value aspires to establish and manage are never strictly enforceable nor entirely stable. This premise is, of course, a commonplace of poststructuralist theorizing – the indeterminacies of boundaries, borders, and frames. This section more openly contemplates the interdependencies of the competing values rehearsed so far, their inevitable converse, and the mutual information they share. For each, in effect, continually announces a crisis for the other. There are two chapters in this final section, which bring together the focuses on the "street" and the academy established separately in "Violence and the Unsightly" and "Reasonings and Reasonablenesses." In doing so, they also draw together important strands of the earlier analysis by proposing scopic and phonic priorities as further indices of the racialized field of value known as "blackness" and "whiteness" in U.S. contexts.

Chapter V continues to examine the protocols of the U.S. literary academy; however, in this instance from the vantage of ascendant poststructuralist theory, since the currency of poststructuralism establishes the primary critical consensus in the post-1960s academy. Nonetheless, it demonstrates that, regardless of this change in critical fortunes, notwithstanding the apparent radical turn to Otherness, the critical and institutional formations poststructuralism represents reiterate articulations of value that do not even *theoretically* challenge the matrix of race and value assumed by its institutional predecessors. This irony is uncovered in a reading of the exemplary poststructuralist debate of Jacques Lacan, Jacques Derrida, and Barbara Johnson, in which all of these celebrated poststructuralists remain so beguiled by economies of visual exchange they overlook the crucial production of sound by which Poe's "The Purloined Letter," their object of analysis, actually resolves itself. Chapter VI returns from academic formations and debates to the "street," understood as a metaphorical site of blackness in its exile from privileged forms of race and reasonableness. This chapter focuses on Ann Petry's 1953 *The Narrows* in order to elaborate the way in which sight and sound, scopic and phonic orientations, are profoundly implicated in the racial antipathies "black" and "white," the "aliterate" and the "literate," the "singing" and the "signing," the "street" and the "academy" already pursued throughout the study.

As one easily recognizes, the originality of this project does not arise from any of its basic assumptions – which are, in fact, heuristic points of departure long recognized in a humanist academy that has both embraced and resisted various stages of escalating structuralist and poststructuralist thought. Neither the diacritical relation of terms posed as binary opposites nor notions of the instability of the boundaries assigned to regulating these relations are novel points of critical departure. Nevertheless, what is original in the forthcoming speculations, I contend, is an elaboration of the way these principles aid in rethinking the network of relations constituting the world of value implicit in the U.S. logic of race, in particular the network of relations that would put into conversation such an unlikely pair as the street and the academy. What possible cogent relation could the ragged improvisational melismas of African American vocal performance and the balanced deliberations of New Critical protocols bear to one other? What mutual information could possibly pass between them? In what ways could meditations on the curiosities of academic protocols be aligned with the vivid, racially tense worlds of Ann Petry's novels? This study attempts to answer these questions by pursuing a trajectory from the street to the academy, and vice versa. And, just as the originality of the answers presented here does not inhere in the presuppositions on which they may be based, neither does it inhere in pointed historical renditions of varying U.S. formations of "blackness" in the nineteenth and twentieth centuries. This type of work is done admirably by various other studies and only in the broadest of strokes in *Blackness and Value*. The heart of the matter lies instead, I hope, in adequately approaching what appears to be a cultural constant of "blackness" – however much historically contingent – that holds fast those within the designation as if "joined together by the memory of the music and the dancing" (Petry, *The Street* 226).

PART ONE

VIOLENCE AND THE UNSIGHTLY

1

FIGURES OF VIOLENCE: VALUATION, AUTHORIZATION, EXPENDITURES OF THE AFRICAN AMERICAN, AND OTHER WAYS OF TELLING

Within the first few pages of her autobiography *Lady Sings the Blues,* Billie Holiday (with William Dufty) recounts an entrepreneurial enterprise she undertakes at the age of sixteen. The enterprise brings Holiday quickly to the point of a confrontation, one in which she learns to negotiate the complexities and ritual importance of boundaries and borders to her advantage. Sixteen-year-old Holiday, rather than scrub neighborhood steps for a nickel, buys her own supplies and demands an exorbitant fifteen cents for each set of steps she would scrub. Her demands are met with incredulity, but Holiday is fortified with the understanding that

> [a]ll these bitches were lazy. I knew it and that's where I had them. They didn't care how filthy their damn houses were inside, as long as those white steps were clean. Sometimes I'd bring home as much as ninety cents a day. I even made as high as $2.10 – that's fourteen kitchen or bathroom floors and as many sets of steps. (10)

Holiday, big for her age, "with big breasts, big bones, a big fat healthy broad, that's all" (9), keenly understands and exploits the paramount significance given to markers setting off inside from outside, as well as her position in relation to such markers. Across the boundary – the set of steps – that she will scrub and maintain "white," Holiday faces her adversarial benefactor and plays upon her own intuitive knowledge of both the significance attributed to the boundary and the relative positions she and her adversary occupy in relation to the boundary, one inside and one outside.

The boundary is not crossed; rather, it is apparently reinforced. Accounting and counting upon its significance, Holiday "works" to maintain the relative positions of herself and the one she faces across it. It is her "laboring" over the boundary and recognition of its ritual significance that ensure her success – her ability to exact the exorbitant price of her labor and her relative identity, a price she will not forgo. She understands that the maintenance (and, therefore, observance) of the boundary or border takes precedence even over that which lies within it, and, gauging her success accordingly, she tallies the $2.10 she might earn in a day as "fourteen kitchen or bathroom floors and as many sets of steps." Not only by her physical presence but by her intuitive negotiations as well, Holiday embodies the problems that inhere in all matters of value, whether value is understood primarily in regard to the dynamics of distinction or of exchange.

Holiday's sly deliberations and actions are instructive because they begin to illuminate the usually secreted agonisms of value. This is to say, despite a strict "form"-ality and apparent singularity, the phenomenon of value is on the contrary indiscrete and eccentric and remains so precisely to the extent that it struggles to appear a hypostasized, singular, fixed, centered phenomenon – in other words, precisely to the extent that it struggles to appear to be anything but eccentric. The project of Marx, the West's most celebrated and influential modern theorist of value, is well understood in these terms. Both the preeminence of the position given to Marx as well as the eccentric operations he goes so far in illuminating are well summarized by Jean-Joseph Goux:

> Marx, then, was the first to lay the foundations of a *science of values* . . . the story of a universal process: the accesson to power of a *representative* and the institutionalization of its role. This process (in its diachrony) and the functions of the representative (in their synchrony) lead us to a pivotal structuration, in which sociohistorical organization may be discerned in its entirety: the genealogy of its values, the formative phases of its economy, its successive overall modes of the exchange of vital activities. (12)

Understood at its simplest, value is an arbiter among disparate entities – however, an arbiter seeking to naturalize its very processes of arbitration to the point of sublimation and fetishization. Marx with his materialist agenda aims to expose as false and pernicious the overly subtle mystifications of sweeping capitalist instantiations of value; Marx exposes, for instance, "the binary internal structure of the commodity" (Levin 15) – the essential and cathected node of modern political economy that presents itself as anything but binary. Like the very phenomenon of value itself (or "value-effect," to borrow a term from Goux) to which it is so closely related and that it so much resembles, the commodity masks itself as unitary and self-involved. It masks the social relations to which it is inevitably tied and that it equally redacts. Scholarly commentary on Marx's project is, of course, endless and reiterates the importance of the exposures at the center of his project. Some recent characterizations bear noting: Michael Ryan, aiming in *Marxism and Deconstruction* to present coimplications of the two broad intellectual projects, writes: "Capitalist ideology presents capitalism as a homogeneous entity; Marx's text is deconstructive of that ideology in that it demonstrates the fissured structural and historical origin of the system. Any stasis that it attains is merely the provisional stabilization of a differential of antagonistic force" (88). Gayatri Spivak observes in *In Other Worlds*: "In opening the lid of Money as a seemingly unitary phenomenon, Marx discovers a forever-seething chain in the pot: Value – Money – Capital. . . . [T]he definition of Value in Marx establishes itself not only as a representation but also as a differential" (157–8). It is this differential nature that value most successfully secrets when it most fully seems itself. The phenomenon of value – like its particular instantiations in political economy: the commodity, capitalist ideology, money – is most fully exposed in terms of acknowledging its occluded differential economy, the circuit of displacement, substitution, and signification that value is always struggling to mask by means of a hypostasized "form." In short, both the ideal referent and confirmation for value are the forms it is in the process of seeking to substantiate.

As it has become pro forma in theoretical considerations of value to recognize the premier position of Marx and his analyses, similarly provocative insights have emerged from attempts to outline and supersede the limitations of the classic Marxist project as Marx himself understood it. The trajectory of Jean Baudrillard's critical thought provides a significant case in point:

Marx gives priority to exhange value (the given economic formation). But in doing so, he retains something of the *apparent movement of political economy*: the concrete positivity of use value, a kind of concrete antecedent within the structure of political economy. He does not radicalize the schema to the point of reversing this appearance and revealing use value as *produced by the play of exchange value.* We have shown this regarding the products of consumption; it is the same for labor power. The definition of products [and labor] as useful and as responding to needs is the most accomplished, most internalized expression of abstract economic exchange. (*Mirror* 24–5; emphasis in original)

Put differently, Marx's critique of capitalist political economy leaves untroubled – and, hence, reiterates – foundational terms of the system.[1] Baudrillard suggests that Marx fails to recognize fully the positive terms or the positive pattern of the system under scrutiny and, as a result, takes up unexamined some of the very *forms of value* he aims to demystify and anatomize; he remains blind to the fact that the apparent solidity and apparent groundedness of use value prove merely more convincing points of hypostasis than the free floating play of exchange value:

In concrete labor man gives a useful, objective end to nature; in need he gives a useful, subjective end to products. Needs and labor are man's double potentiality or double generic quality. This is the same anthropological realm in which the concept of production is sketched as "the fundamental movement of human existence," as defining a rationality and sociality appropriate for man. (*Mirror* 32)

Although Marx undermines only the "form"-ality, or positive terms, of materialist instantiations and modes of production of capitalist political economy, he ironically respects forms of value he can least afford to respect, given the aims of his analysis.

Galvanized by this insight into Marx's unintended "universalization of th[e] system's postulates" (*Mirror* 33), Baudrillard is determined not only to expose Marx's failure, but to repeat it in no form at all, and his own error vis-à-vis an analysis of value lies precisely in this determination, in his attempt to think himself *out of* rather than through the paradoxical problem he sees plaguing Marx: "[Marx] changed nothing basic: nothing regarding the *idea* of man *producing* himself in his infinite determination, and continually surpassing himself toward his own end" (*Mirror* 33; emphasis in original). By positing the notion of symbolic value, Baudrillard attempts to get outside "the logic of value" to a site at which

> man has "need" of nothing. What is neither sold nor taken, but only given and returned, no one "needs." The exhange of looks, the present which comes and goes, are like the air people breathe in and out. This is the metabolism of exchange, prodigality, festival – and also of destruction (which returns to non-value what production has erected and valorized). (*Critique* 207)

Baudrillard seeks a space of formlessness that would belie the possibility of value itself. However, beyond the obvious problems raised by a troublesome Western anthropological nostalgia, Baudrillard's notion of symbolic value repeats the oversight attributed to Marx himself. Baudrillard here thinks solely in terms of a materialism that blinds him to more subtle forms, play, and reappearances of value. "The social wealth produced [in the Marxist and capitalist model] is *material*; it has nothing to do with *symbolic* wealth which, mocking natural necessity, comes conversely from destruction, the deconstruction of value, transgression, or discharge" (*Mirror* 43; emphasis in original). The move to imagine a complete scission between the material and the symbolic is naive and, indeed, contradicts Baudrillard's own program and his reproval of Marx. Even as he criticizes the Marxist and capitalist modes for the materiality of their focus, Baudrillard overlooks the fact that the value produced (or not produced) by the type of exchange he privileges need not be material, which is to say, need not be primarily located in the disposition (destruction, discharge) of the material object(s) in question. Ironically, he refuses to relinquish a focus on the material object(s), in the same way Marx seems, paradoxically, unable to relinquish the notion of use value. Baudrillard merely proposes a practice of nonuse in opposition to *use* so that, in effect, the grounds of the debate do not change, and that move amounts to the same charge he brings against Marx. Rather than gaining a place outside value, Baudrillard reconstitutes the very play and the enduring *form* of value itself, since value always declares such a scission in order to substantiate, privilege, hypostasize a particular form or "positive term."[2] Value inheres in all claims to discretion and integrity, the upshot of which is always a bounded, posit(ed)(ive) form – regardless of how hard that form is to specify with the exactitude to which materiality so often lends itself. In other words, it makes no difference in this case that the positive term is a negative conception poised against the notion of value as a positivity, for this negativity supposedly outside "the logic of value" claims a scission and integrity no different from those claimed by the opposing positivity (so mistakenly identified here exclusively with materiality). Baudrillard merely positions one form of value against another and in doing so formalizes, rather than examines, the scission or antagonism between them, an antagonism crucial to the dynamics – and, therefore, the analysis – of value.

Boldly but unsuccessfully, Baudrillard tries to move beyond the *bounds* of value. The attempt is inevitably unsuccessful because, from our perspective within the play of value, value will reconstitute and intrude itself endlessly. This play will color everything one sees, even when what is sighted reportedly lies outside "the logic of value." In effect, Baudrillard's misstep alerts us more than ever to the subtleties of interrogating value. One cannot move beyond the *limit of value*, because the very notion of value is intimately tied to the notion of limits. To invoke or imagine one term is implicitly to invoke or imagine the other. Limits and boundaries prove the "essential" matter of value, because they delineate the point of and, therefore, instate the need for the arbitration undertaken by value in the first place. Limits and boundaries prove points of reckoning and ambivalence at which difference is formally reiterated or reconstituted by the operations of value. Although not necessarily material, value is necessarily formal – deeply implicated in the points of division and convergence signaled by limits and boundaries. For these reasons, it makes sense to understand Baudrillard's misstep as the attempt to think himself out of, rather than through, the paradoxical problem he sees plaguing Marx.

There is no region – to speak of – beyond the "the logic of value." Rather, the crux of the matter seems to be those negotiations undertaken precisely at points of difference – negotiations that do not result in radical difference (absolute scission) but, more interestingly, in the coherence of system. The difference of the terms arranged along formalized boundaries by the operations of value constitutes the basis of the systemic relation of those terms and, from the perspective of my investigation, never losing sight of this differential play, even as it may be masked by form-ality and hypostasis, is crucial to the anatomizing of value. Some observations by Jean-Joseph Goux support this position:

Now as long as the domination of the . . . value effect by formal and dynamic structuration is not acknowledged, as long as the value effect dissimulates as appraisal or assessment[,] the dialectical syntax that decides which values reign and how they rule through the mediation of concrete equivalents, the axiology[,] cannot be written. (11)

In brief, the "dialectic syntax" that is always characteristic of value is often obscured and, hence, unrecognized. The investment of value in matters of limits, form, and system is an investment made in the service of conferring privilege; the hypostasization, singularity, and fixity of value are tied to the configuring of lesser and greater status or worth. Value is fundamentally relational despite all appearances to the contrary. Indeed, the inaugural moves of Marx's *Das Kapital* confirm this. After defining the commodity and its ties to both labor and use as registers of value, Marx presents what seems the most definitive or socially consequential instantiation of the commodity and of value:

The simplest value relation is evidently that of one commodity to some other commodity of a different kind. Hence the relation between the values of two commodities supplies us with the simplest expression of the value of a single commodity. (17)

Even though the commodity itself suggests fixity, limit, or form, perhaps the most widespread and powerful conceptualization of the commodity depends upon the terms of substitution, exchange, fluidity, relation. Its signification depends inevitably on a boundary or boundaries – "that which serves to indicate the bounds or limits of anything, whether material or immaterial: also the limit itself" *(OED)*. Value always signifies the form-ality of one or more precincts. To recognize value fully one must, at least, see double.

   The promiscuous relations of value underscored by Holiday's actions and recollections are theorized in different discursive and disciplinary frames by Mary Douglas in *Purity and Danger* and Peter Stallybrass and Allon White in *The Politics and Poetics of Transgression*. Fetishized boundaries, all of them suggest, are sites not only of separation but also of influential yet often surreptitious traffic and exchange. As inexorable sites of arbitration, these boundaries are, once examined from certain vantages, also inexorable sites of violence. Violence is taken here to mean the forcible altering of Otherwise established forms, and, as discussed by the historian Joel Williamson in *Rage for Order*, for example, the U.S. ritual of lynching as a process securing the fetishized boundary between racial blackness and whiteness documents this relation between value and violence in hyperbolic fashion. Still, the violence perpetrated in processes of value – in elaborating a binarism of valued and devalued – is not always or merely played out in physical terms. The promiscuous play and violence of value may be also immaterial, as suggested by the autobiographical subject in its rhetorical and textual struggle for a dissembling unity. Indeed, the notion of the sign itself, as rehearsed by Ferdinand de Saussure, might be taken as an emblem of this more attenuated form of the forcible altering of Otherwise established forms. And, like *Lady Sings the Blues*, other African American texts are also suggestive for disclosing these matters. Frederick Douglass's *Narrative* and Harriet Jacobs's *Incidents in the Life of a Slave Girl* provide signal examples of the attenuated peculiarities of the autobiographical subject and, moreover, by their new found status in the academy also provide signal examples of these dynamics within the institutional formations of U.S. literary study. The series of transactions ultimately allowing these two texts to be embraced within an institutional site from which they were long excluded may recall in provocative ways the curious, sly machinations of a young Billie Holiday across the marble steps of Baltimore.

The inaugural claim here, then, is that Billie Holiday's negotiations across the steps profoundly illuminate the coimplication of value, boundaries, and privilege. Her negotiations engage the terms of inside and outside, high and low, up and down, clean and dirty, mistress and maid, the commanding and the commanded. Indeed, the solicitous Holiday not only remains the agent by means of which these bounded oppositions – bounded by reciprocal ratification – are set in place but embodies, furthermore, the set of problems that scramble the integers, or values, so clearly set in place. Holiday's adversary remains inside, while Holiday is outside. Her adversary is high, while she literally stoops low on the steps. One is clean, the other dirty. One mistress, one maid. One commanding, one commanded. The boundary and Holiday's ritual observance of it engender these configurations; however, at the same time, Holiday transgresses the boundary by (re)configuring the integers to her own ends. She exacts from the inside, the high, the up, the clean, the mistress, the commanding, an exorbitant confirmation of herself beyond the boundary as much as she capitulates to an aggrandizing recognition of the boundary that confirms those within it. As the success of her outlandish scheme suggests, she is both the principle and the principal of the integers set in place. Her "originary" labor that affirms the site (sight) of the valued and the not-valued, the inside and the outside; her antinomian presence on the boundary and, finally, within the house – primarily kitchens and bathrooms, architectural sites of inside meeting outside – maintain the value of the valued. Insofar as Holiday is outside, the low, down, dirty, maid, the commanded, the not-valued, she is also a source of value, as her knowledge that she "ha[s] them," if not the success of her scheme, upholds. Holiday both knows and demonstrates that value is never radical but always relative, that all boundaries have an Other side.

Holiday understands that boundaries only make sense and only maintain significance if they are surreptitiously crossed. Holiday scrubs the steps and observes the ritual importance of boundaries in order to engineer an exchange that takes place across them. Boundaries separate, but they also mark places of exchange and crossings. Although she joins those inside the boundary in their fetishization of it, and although she becomes the means by which it is symbolically and materially maintained, Holiday nonetheless neglects the boundary in order, immoderately, to take from within it that which is within her reach to take. Holiday respects and reinforces the boundary only in order to cross it.

As does the mindful Holiday, value operates by fashioning and refashioning relationships across boundaries and borders. Oddly, it proves both calculus and symbol, calculating a boundary then signifying itself in terms of that boundary. It specifies a relation defined above all by diacritical marks (or remarks), yet occludes that relation in order to figure itself in the singular and discrete terms of the boundary. There are multiple perspectives from which to view every boundary; yet, in signifying itself by means of the apparent singularity of a boundary and the singularity of an accompanying narrative, value attempts to occlude or, at least, overmaster those multiplicities on which it is premised.

Value denotes domination and endurance in a space of multiplicity. Its presence and performance entail the altering, resituating, and refiguring of the Other, or many Others, in margins, in recesses – indeed, paradoxically, outside a self-presence (defined by a fetishized boundary) that nonetheless aspires to be everywhere. Except willfully by those situated without the boundary (as demonstrated by Holiday), that which lies beyond the boundary is never accounted. From the dominant perspective of value, that which lies without the boundary is seen as "offend[ing] against order"(2) – to employ a phrase from Mary Douglas's 1966 *Purity and Danger*. Value extends surreptitiously into the domains of that which it rejects, domains it attempts to fix in a relation it overmasters, and, for these reasons, Mary Douglas's landmark "analysis of the concepts of pollution and taboo," the subtitle of *Purity and Danger*, stands in many ways as a profound study of value, for Douglas investigates how "dirt involves reflection on the relation of order to disorder, being to non-being, form to formlessness, life to death" (5), indeed, the *relative* domain of value.

The chief claims set out by Mary Douglas as she elaborates her understanding of dirt also hold true for an understanding of value. "Dirt," Douglas writes, "is never a unique, isolated event. Where there is dirt there is system. Dirt is the by-product of a systematic ordering and classification of matter, in so far as ordering involves rejecting inappropriate elements. The idea of dirt takes us straight into the field of symbolism and promises a link-up with *more obviously* symbolic systems of purity" (35; emphasis added).

It is this arrangement that Billie Holiday, at sixteen years old, understands to her advantage and begins to negotiate. From the domains of dirt – the routinely occluded domains of purity – as well as from the occluded domains of value (domains I choose to describe as left "in the dark"), "link-up[s] with *more obviously* symbolic systems" often appear as violence.[3] Mary Douglas approaches such a conceptualization when she broadly defines culture as follows:

> Culture, in the sense of the public, standardised values of a community, mediates the experience of individuals. It provides in advance some basic categories, a positive pattern in which ideas and values are tidily ordered. And above all, it has authority, since each is induced to assent because of the assent of others. (39)

However, from vantages in the dark, the "*more obviously* symbolic systems," which determine "pollution behaviour," amount merely to "th[os]e reaction[s] which condemn[] any object or idea likely to confuse or contradict cherished classifications" (36).

The reification and the symbolics of value are categorical, in both senses of the word – positive and classificatory; yet, as much as value and its correlate authority prove categorical, effecting a widely ac-

knowledged and widely organized presence – "a positive pattern" –
value and authority remain at the same time arrant. They compel
and coerce an unknown absence. As much as they are affirmative,
value and authority are at every point oppressive, from absent or
unknown vantages. For value "negativity is a *resource*,"[4] an essential
resource. The negative, the expended, the excessive invariably form
the ground of possibilities for value. Mary Douglas makes analogous
remarks in her discussion of the "anomalous":

> Any given system of classification [value] must give rise to
> anomalies, and any given culture must confront events which
> seem to defy its assumptions. It cannot ignore the anomalies
> which its scheme produces, except at risk of forfeiting confi-
> dence [among other things]. This is why, I suggest, we find in
> any culture worthy of the name various provisions for dealing
> with ambiguous or anomalous events. (39)

A chief premise of this discussion of value is that, like Douglas's
"purity" and "the sacred," value is always a social formation that
more or less openly comprises conflicting social practices in a carefully arranged hierarchy. Value must concern itself with the rejected
and the anomalous and, compromising the very boundaries on
which it relies to specify the rejected, and the anomalous, a significant, but necessarily unremarked, element of these "dealing[s]"
must occur "in the dark," in that which is designated as dirt. Recall
again that in the opening pages of *Lady Sings the Blues* Holiday profitably affirms the value of the fetishized white steps of Baltimore by
acknowledging and addressing herself to their dirt, to their anomalous condition, fully equipped with numerous instruments of purity, "a brush of my own, a bucket, some rags, some Octagon soap,
and a big white bar of that stuff I can't ever forget – Bon Ami" (9).
It is the necessary convergence of the pure and the unclean, the
high and the low, the up and the down, that is the key to the anecdote. The steps, the boundary marking the outside and the inside,
also prove the point of the greatest commingling of the outside and
inside.

Along with its largely concealed and only ostensibly insignificant
"negativity," Holiday elucidates the relativity of value, and, equally,
Mary Douglas illustrates the ineluctable interaction between dirt or
defilement and the positive structure to which it bears a concealed
relation.[5] Such concealment remains a deliberate and fundamental
part of the agenda of value. Douglas displays a primary concern with

such concealment, as do Peter Stallybrass and Allon White some twenty years later in *The Politics and Poetics of Transgression*, a study openly indebted to *Purity and Danger*. Elaborating "a nexus of power and desire which regularly appears in the ideological construction of the low-Other" (5), Stallybrass and White trouble hierarchies of the high and the low and pursue uncharted yet indispensable interactions between them. In a broadly literary and historical study, they delineate at the sites of "the human body, psychic forms, geographical space, and the social formation . . . dependent hierarchies of high and low" (2). These hierarchies prove akin to Douglas's designations of the pure, or sacred, and the polluted. It is fair to say the work of Stallybrass and White extrapolates many of Douglas's insights in the field of symbolic anthropology into the field of literary preoccupations.

The Politics and Poetics of Transgression more expressly probes the essential relation between the high and the low, the clean and the unclean, as well as the promiscuous and transgressive nature of that relation. Defining transgression by reference to Barbara Babcock's notion of symbolic inversion (17–18), the authors uncover again and again at the four sites that they examine in both isolation and convergence a "recalcitrant Other . . . troubl[ing] the fantasy of an independent, separate, 'proper' identity" (148), an "identity" that might be understood as analogous to the "positive structure" posited in Douglas's analysis. Aiming to disclose the complex falsity of standard high/low dichotomies informing bourgeois identity as well as various literary formations, Stallybrass and White observe:

> The point is that the *exclusion* necessary to the formation of social identity [i.e., the "positive structure," value] at level one is simultaneously a *production* – at the level of the Imaginary, and a production, what is more, of a complex hybrid fantasy emerging out of the very attempt to demarcate boundaries, to unite and purify the social collectivity [i.e., the upshot of the "positive structure," value]. (193; emphasis in original)

The efficacy and symbolics of boundaries are never as nearly settled as they first seem, nor as they are reported to be. With this insight in mind, Stallybrass and White, from their transgressive analytical stance, attempt to specify and revise in their project a "cultural identity [that] is inseparable from limits[;] it is always a boundary phenomenon and its order is always constructed around the figures of its territorial edge" (200).

In the same way that *The Politics and Poetics of Transgression* in some measure translates the insights yielded by *Purity and Danger* into the field of literary concerns, the aim of this consideration of value is to bring similar notions to bear on a theoretical anatomization of value and, insofar as it is illuminated by this model of value, to the course of the twentieth-century U.S. literary academy as inflected by the concerns of race and gender. Granted that negativity is an indispensable resource of the "positive structure," "proper" identity, or value, it is clear that African American women and men (as well as other racial Others) constitute a great negative resource of the "positive structure," a "proper" identity, and value within the U.S. landscape whether within or without the academy. African Americans are those designated and understood as without a fetishized boundary – as polluted or unclean, the objects of restriction and "pollution behaviour," in the terms of Mary Douglas's analysis; the low-Other, in the terms of Stallybrass and White; that which is not valued, in terms of my discussion. "[F]igures of [the] territorial edge" of value – of the U.S. imagination generally, and of the U.S. imagination as it undertakes and determines literary critical discourses – African Americans, in both the literal and figurative senses of the phrase, remain "beyond the pale."

Vividly making this point, Billie Holiday, in the second chapter of her autobiography, "Ghosts of Yesterday," briefly rehearses her experience as a maid. Continuing to provide a vitae of her adolescent employment, Holiday recounts a time when, having moved beyond entrepreneurial forays with her own scrubbing equipment and Bon Ami, she is employed full time, like her mother, to clean the inside of houses:

> This great big greasy bitch [the woman for whom Holiday worked] didn't do a thing all day until about fifteen minutes before her old man was due home for dinner. Then she would kick up a storm. I didn't know my way around her fancy kind of joint. Instead of telling me what she wanted me to do, she'd get excited because her husband was waiting, start hollering at me and calling me "nigger." I had never heard that word before. I didn't know what it meant. But I could guess from the sound of her voice. It was weird, that house – filled with crazy furniture and junk that just collected dust – and pillows all over. How she used to dog me about those pillows. (22)

Even though at this point Holiday works inside the house, she remains outside a fetishized boundary. Holiday, in the eyes of the "great big greasy bitch" for whom she works, not only is in the house to attend to the dirt, but amounts apparently to a part of the dirt. The epithet "nigger," with which Holiday claims she is unfamiliar, categorically marks her as an anomaly within the house. Never knowing her "way around [the] fancy joint," Holiday is confirmed in her categorically alien status by the alien appellation. Her affront to the "positive structure," "proper" identity, or the valued, is marked additionally by "the great big greasy bitch" insistently "dog[ging]" her about the most characteristic and intimate furnishings of the house, those "pillows all over": the pillows, no doubt, soft, ample, and constructed of cloth as are the dusting and cleaning rags used by Holiday, stand – in light of the privileged attention they receive – in polar opposition to a girl who in another time would have known "how it felt to be a slave, to be owned body and soul by a white man who was the father of her children" (8). In their ornate way, the pillows strewn throughout the inside of house bear the symbolic burden of the "positive structure," the proper identity, the value that Holiday by her alien presence confirms.

The boundary in question no longer remains the site (sight) of an inanimate and inconsequential physical structure – white marble steps, for instance. Very differently, the boundary in question is the very site (sight) of Holiday's animate and particular physical structure. Because her relatively valueless status without the boundary is marked by the conspicuousness of her own flesh – the very site (sight) of her – Holiday seemingly can never cross this more punctilious and more highly symbolic boundary. Holiday, like all "niggers," is visibly insignificant; she is visibly and categorically relegated to the domain of those left in the dark.

Notwithstanding her relative position beyond the boundary without which all "niggers" stand, Holiday understands and undermines the categorical significance of the boundary: Forgoing the condemnatory efficacy of sight, Holiday is apprised of the full extent of her *relatively* valueless position ("nigger") by "the sound of [the] voice," the medium she will learn to value, master, intensify, and privilege so well. Later in the autobiography, Holiday writes of her work as a singer and of the improvisational genius of Basie and his musicians: "[e]verything that happened, happened in the ear" (62). Since monopolized sight cannot account the significance (or counterview, to use a term of Stallybrass and White) of Holiday's position and point of view "in the dark," sound proves, instead, of primary and eventually thrilling instrumentality. One might say the physical boundary of the steps of "[the] fancy joint" is transgressed by Holiday's necessary and ironically purifying presence within the house. In the same way, one might claim that the more momentous boundary specifying Holiday's insignificance in the unalterable terms of her flesh is transgressed (symbolically inverted, according to Stallybrass and White's use of Babcock) by Holiday's flippant and antinomian recounting of the significance of the incident. This attribution of significance in Holiday's version is flippantly *sounded out.*

Indeed, "in the dark," where sound must be given primacy, the significance of the fetishized boundary is read Otherwise. Holiday's final pronouncement on the incident is "I figured there had to be something better than this" (23). This reading is transgressive and countersignificant, because Holiday's final pronouncement on the incident, and equally the cultural efficacy later attained by her voice, represents what might be called a performance of value where value is not. If value, the "positive structure," a "proper" identity, is the fabrication of a community, which "commits men and women to [the] norms [of the community]" (Douglas 92), then the transgressive reading of value, the performance of value where it is not, is the fabrication of value by those not committed to the norms of the valued, the "positive structure," a "proper" identity. It is the fabrication of those who Otherwise figure that "there ha[s] to be something better than this."

Gayatri Spivak notes:

> I wrote above that the will to explain was a symptom of the desire to have a self and a world. In other words, on the general level, the possibility of explanation carries the presupposition of an explainable (even if not fully) universe and an explaining (even if imperfectly) subject. These presuppositions assure our being. Explaining, we exclude the possibility of the *radically* heterogeneous. (*In Other Worlds* 105; emphasis in original)

One might say, to phrase the matter in terms of Spivak's observations, that "the desire to have a self and a world," although never fully accounted or accredited "in the dark," nonetheless presides "in the dark." One understands – despite all appearances to the contrary – that the "*radically* heterogeneous," on which value is routinely presupposed, is never more than the *relatively* heterogeneous.

Exploring this relativity compels one to recognize further that boundaries operate equally as points of crossing, points at which the integers of value distress as much as confirm the calculus.

Recall that Mary Douglas's investigation ultimately addresses itself to culture as "a set of assumptions by which experience is controlled" (128), assumptions informing rituals of the polluted and the unpolluted. Stallybrass and White look upon "what one might call the rock bottom of symbolic form" (3). In both accord with and revision of such investigations, Holiday's commentaries suggest the complementarities of race, value, and violence, which is to say – if one were to reconsider and value Otherwise the phrase of Stallybrass and White "the [black] bottom of symbolic form," the "[black] bottom" of value, a "[black] bottom" into which one is profoundly plunged by Holiday's autobiography. Understanding the place at which she is fixed by value, as well as understanding the value of Baltimore's famous white marble steps, the youthful Billie Holiday anatomizes and elucidates value from its Other side, its occluded side, the side without the boundary, the side of indiscrete performances and seeming formlessness. She negotiates and describes value in both its patency and its concealments, in the open and in the dark. Billie Holiday, the performer, analyzes the performance of value. Acknowledging Holiday's vantage, one begins to see everything double. One is invited to see that, like "a singer [who] is only a voice, and a voice is completely dependent on the body" (171), value enters the world in a performance. More accurately: Value enters the world in concomitant performances.

The relationship between the import of Holiday's recollections and the dynamics of Anglo-American literary criticism might not be immediately apparent; however, as with all value, literary value invariably begins with excess. It engages, as Holiday invites us to see in very different circumstances, the problematics of many Others and, as marked by the course of twentieth-century literary theory, proves increasingly embattled. Particularly in the past twenty-five years or so, the values of literature and literary critical activity find themselves scrutinized, theorized, and historicized to the point where they are defined in part by matters, peoples, and cultures to which they were once set in explicit contradistinction. For example, whatever they might be, when they are first published in 1845 and 1861, respectively, *Narrative of the Life of Frederick Douglass* and *Incidents in the Life of a Slave Girl* are not understood as literature; nor are they so understood for more than a hundred years after their

publication. Only as twentieth-century Anglo-American critical discourse and society at large (re)theorize themselves in response to
menacing fissures in a once stable cultural design do institutional
discourses recognize, against their will, as it were, the narratives of
Douglass and Jacobs as literature – literature taken here as the object
of an honorific critical appraisal and as the site of professionalized
and specialized processes of reading and dissemination.

Despite the frequency and confidence with which the term
"value" is used in the sound-byte rhetoric of contemporary U.S.
politics, the problematics of value remain increasingly intricate and
arresting in a century heir to the consequences of the abolition of
chattel slavery. The abolition of African slavery in the New World is
an act of revolutionary proportions, which at the very least one historian names the most dramatic and far-reaching of the many
revolutions of the nineteenth century.[6] The release of African Americans from the muteness and illegality of chattel slavery – however
partial, intermittent, and hard won – marks the (re)emergent visibility of an excessive and residual Otherness long essential to the
normative enterprises and the dominant orders of the U.S. landscape. The extent of this revolution is not yet entirely seen, and to
imagine its limits is to think for a moment of calling into question
and making reclamations upon resources, labor, and economic and
cultural designs long overshadowed by "the notion of democracy at
the core of 'traditional' American" (Christian "But What" 70)
thought.

To phrase the issue in the terms of an anatomizing pronouncement on value, one might say that both within and without the
academy, the conditions of dominance and exorbitance prove the
characteristic conditions of value. Always presupposing contingency,
competition, and convergence, value proves merely form – a normative design – forcefully emergent from and provisionally triumphant over a relative parataxis of Others. No matter how
convincingly it proposes "the claim of certain norms, standards, and
judgments to objective validity, which is to say the demonstration of
the noncontingency of the contingent" (Herrnstein Smith 54),
value is characterized foremost by force and promiscuity – indelible
traces of its contingency. No matter how overwhelmingly value
seems to impose itself as a normative design, a noncontingent form,
a singular objective validity, it nonetheless reserves for itself an
Other – a negative resource – and, from the perspective of the reserved Other, the force and promiscuity of value are, with equal

invariability, dis-covered. Invariably and paradoxically, value reserves for itself an Other perspective from which "value as form" bursts forth as "value as force."

Jarring in thought or deed, the violence of the process of the dis-covery of value (dis-covery of its reserved Other) – of the *solicitation* of value, in the Derridean sense of the word[7] – mirrors the *soliciting* activity of value in the first place. In short, violence, the forcible disrupting and altering of Otherwise established forms,[8] betrays the original instance of all value. First, value is an impeachment of the Other, the willful expenditure of the Other in an imposing produc-tion of the self. The perspective of the Other thus reveals the rela-tivities of value as ratios of violence; the discovery of value from the perspectives of the Other reveals the exorbitant foundations and overdeterminations of value. Violence – to emphasize the point – is the opening that allows value. It remains the original mechanism by means of which valuation initiates, then resists, change. Yet it would be a mistake to believe that value and violence are coterminous. Rather, it is imperative to recognize that value introduces itself by way of a violent agency that it subsequently seeks to deny. To quote again Jean-Joseph Goux:

> In certain points of condensation, value seems to gather, capitalize, centralize itself, investing certain elements with a privileged representativeness and even with a monopoly on representativeness within the diverse set of which they are members. The mysterious genesis of this privilege is effaced, leaving their monopoly absolute, *absolved*, exempt in their tran-scendent role as standard and measure of values. (Goux 10; emphasis in original)

Value is a twofold action or structure, a presentation and re-presentation, a performance riddled by the dialectic nature of its coming into being and, more than merely dialectic, categorically disjunctive in its binarism. In its latter and most visible form, value is a representation of an "object(ive)" design; however, as a result of its dialectic nature, value in this latter, objectified appearance is inexorably discovered as revising promiscuous interest in an under-privileged and displaced Other. Always inherent in value is the trace of an original, violent expenditure. Value is violence and, more to the point, value is violence disguised or dis-figured. This duplicitous structure or movement of value can be imagined as the staging of two separate, but only glancingly separate, appearances – the second appearance an attempt to eclipse the first. "Value as force," the first appearance of value, is overcome by the latter objectification it sustains. Because "value as force" is a misdemeanor or atrocity that "value as form," as overinvested object or design, will not tolerate, value masquerades both its violence and the revisionary impulses of its belated self-representation by means of the symbolics of a boundary. Presenting a boundary solely as a barrier, solely as a visible and inviolate demarcation (rather than also a site of crossing and exchange), "value as form" secures itself the site (sight) of value. By means of the visible and fetishized boundary, value attains its too apparent form, confers upon itself *visibly* immanent distinction, and, thereby, re-covers itself. To borrow the sociologist Pierre Bourdieu's appositive definition of taste, a related entity: Value takes the boundary as "the uncreated source of creation" (11). From an arguably uncreated position, boundaries create.

The valorizing efficacy imputed to boundaries is briefly and graphically discernible, for example, in the discussion of the ritual aspects of lynching undertaken by Joel Williamson in *A Rage for Order*, a 1986 treatise on race relations in the postbellum U.S. South. Williamson, in his chapter "In Violence Veritas," emphasizes what he calls "the ritual of lynching" (124) as a public spectacle, an act performed in and at the site (sight) of the public: "Ordinarily, there were hundreds and sometimes thousands of spectators. It was not uncommon for railroads to run special 'excursion' trains to the site" (124). As much as it is an act of violence – an act of torture and murder – lynching proves a representational act:

> Now and again the lynchers would halt their proceedings and pose with their victim so that photographs could be taken or, sometimes, stand aside so that the victim could be photographed alone. Such discipline suggested recognized leadership, understood procedures, and concerted purpose. (125)

Such discipline reveals as well the deliberation and histrionics that mark highly representational acts. One might argue that beyond putatively meting out "justice," lynching spectacularizes the deformation, fragmentation, and disfiguration of Other boundaries, the "boundaries" of devalued black bodies. Insofar as "the ritual of lynching" proves an act of the (re)affirmation, (re)production, and (re)creation of esteemed boundaries and values, the boundaries and values of a dominant white regime, it is conversely an act of disrupting those neither esteemed nor fully recognized. Holding as much importance, if not more, as painfully inducing the death of the victim is the ritualized disposition (dis-position) of the African American victim's wracked body:

> Fingers, toes, ears, teeth, and bones were common souvenirs. A pro-lynching governor of South Carolina, Cole Blease, received the finger of a lynched black in the mail and planted it in the gubernatorial garden. In 1906, in Salisbury, North Carolina, several Negroes were hanged and their bodies riddled with bullets, allegedly for committing a set of horribly brutal ax murders. There is a story that the next day, a thoughtful friend brought a female relative, the person of the "little old lady" image, in his car to see the remains and, doubtless, to relish the sweets of revenge. The woman descended from the vehicle, gazed up for a time at the still swinging bodies, opened her purse, took out a knife and cut a finger from the hand of one of the victims. She put the knife and the finger in her purse, closed, [sic] it, climbed into the car again and was driven away. (124–5)

The twofold movement or structure of value is evident in unusually graphic detail in this instance: Recall or imagine a photograph of the broken and ruined body or bodies of African American victim(s) of lynchings. These bodies are mutilated and grotesque forms surrounded by the smiling, intact, and communally united forms of their white persecutors. Such photographs too vividly underscore the thesis that the valorizing process, which is to say the formalizing of value, the instatement of the valued, relies in the first place upon violence as well as on the conversion of that violence into novel significance, into a renewed recognition of a privileged form.

In an article in which she catalogues various scenes of lynching in notable works of twentieth-century African American literature, Phyllis R. Klotman writes, "[T]hat that macabre ritual has been replaced by other more modern and subtle forms of control exercised by a society still unable to live up to its claims that the 'American Dream' is more than a nightmare for black people" (63). Nonetheless, this fetishized boundary between black and white need not always be recognized or understood as representing the value of whiteness. Klotman's statement suggests the important duplicity of all boundaries and all established value. The highlighted opposition between the terms "dream" and "nightmare" suggests that boundaries routinely crossed in one direction may be re-crossed and reimagined from the Other vantage, the vantage of those whom the boundary marginalizes and subordinates as Other. In *A Rage for Order* in a chapter subsequent to "In Violence Veritas," Williamson similarly characterizes the processes of valorization animating the act of lynching:

> Race, in brief, is a problem of the mind and not of the body. It also assumes that, overall, white people have the power to make scapegoats of black people, to manage them sufficiently to create the illusion that they want to see.... The uses to which white power put black people in this fashion [are] virtually limitless. Once the game started, the Negro could be made the scapegoat for any number of ills, either of the body or of the mind. Indeed, from the white point of view, one might say that the Negro-as-scapegoat has been one of the nation's most valuable renewable resources. (199)

African Americans, in sum, remain the negative resource of valuable white Americans.

Nevertheless, the difficult task of anatomizing the intricacies of value remains more complex than simply specifying this agonism between a privileged form and its negative resource. Not only must one specify the integrity of the object of value and the Other of value, but, additionally, one must specify the vertiginous internal relationships of the twofold structure or movement of value. Value not only produces a binarism of sorts but is produced by a binarism of sorts. Displaced in the formalizing of value – like the Other of value, the Other without the boundary – are the originary and enabling violences of value and the relation they bear to the more perceptible hierarchy of the privileged and underprivileged terms of value. For instance, if in the U.S. landscape those bearing white skin are the formalized of value and those bearing dark skin are the violated of value, then, within this scheme, the perceptible and almost imperceptible activities both *determining* and *unsettling* this dualism may be interpreted as the occluded violence of the original moment of value. The binarism of the valued and the devalued as well as the positions in which they are fixed relative to one another remain more easily perceptible than the violences that produce that binarism as well as the relativity of the positions in which the elements of that binarism are fixed. In a phrase, within the twofold structure or movement of value there is a further twofold structure or movement. Within the duplicity of the valued and the not valued, value as force is underprivileged to the promiscuous value as form.

Value as form overdetermines two relationships – its relation to the Other of value and its relation to value as force. It is fair to say that inasmuch as value as force originally displaces an Other in deference to value as form, it is itself displaced in deference to value as form. The agency of the expenditure of the Other, value as force is overwhelmed in turn by the fetishized and formalized boundary of value as form. It is this valorizing re-covery of the violences of value as force that realizes the form of the privileged object. These violences, large or small, amount to realizations of form that dispel, disrupt, and disfigure those forms with and *upon* which the realized terms of value as form are contingent – the requisite excess out of which value as form materializes. When value as form materializes, the priority of the boundary occludes even the violences of value as force and renders them more imperceptible than the requisite excess of value. Value as force, the violence of value, the forcible disrupting of Otherwise established forms, is the secreted – even *unthinkable* – third term of the dialectic of value. It appears, then, that "force creates value but has no value; it is excluded from the world of values" (Goux 61) as value itself would have it.

Monstrously, the problematics of value are the problematics of many Others, of monstrous conditionals, of monstrous permutations. The troublesome structure and movement of value are dizzyingly self-reflexive.[9] In addition to Othering the Other, processes of valorization render Other the very processes by which they undertake Othering the Other. Processes of valorization render Other the violences they perform upon the Other. Vexingly, then, value can invest itself everywhere and in everything, so that even inside itself – insofar as value has an inside and an outside – value is ceaselessly in operation. Within the concentric vertigo of processes of valorization, value as force becomes itself a displaced Other, at the same time it effects a displaced Other. To return to the racialized dynamics of the United States, for example, established value would have it appear that there is nothing white Americans *do* to secure their relatively superior, collective situation. Established value would have it seem, rather, that there is a boundary, *visible* and fixed in terms of complexion, that presents itself as and remains the unsolicited and unsolicitous arbiter of the issue; it proposes a boundary symbolized in terms of skin complexion as the immanent and singular issue.

To summarize this anatomization of value: The forceful and the formal constitute the twofold structure or movement of value. However, value as force is ultimately underprivileged in relation to value as form in a way similar to that in which the Other of value is underprivileged in relation to value as form. Accordingly, any attempt at an analytical recognition of value reveals extreme promiscuity, since value is perpetually at war with itself. The valued and that which is not valued and "value as form" and "value as force" and the intermural and the intramural relations they bear to one another compose the complexities and the perplexity of value.

In order to imagine this perplexity more completely, conjure a surreal television or movie camera that, by focusing on the background, distorts images in the foreground of its purview, and vice versa, as do all cameras. The coming into focus of an object pushes out of focus many Other objects. Imagine further the true agency of this flux as an invisible hand indistinguishable from its delicate movements that create the changes in focus. If, further, this camera–hand could, after each manipulation, embody itself as the object brought into focus, it would be the equivalent to value. The work of the camera–hand at its simplest seems twofold: exertion and masquerade. Furthermore, however, this camera that is a hand can register immaterial or invisible objects, so that even its own vicissitudes from exertion to masquerade might become an object of its vision. In short, this camera – hand sees the work of seeing the work of seeing the work of seeing itself.

Still, in the end, despite the precariousness of isolating and grooming it completely, value always emerges, *traces itself*, spirals dizzily, proliferates as a compound entity, a compound fiction, a twofold memory, a twofold dream. Both initiating then resisting change, value remains in perpetual contestation with violence, its earlier self, as well as with the Other produced by its earlier violating self; in effect, value remains in perpetual internal and external contestation. Value is violence, then it is not. Value is violence, then it is form. Value courts violence, then, in an immediate second appearance courting form, tries to belie its Other and Othering past.

Only when value as force begs attention – as the result of its magnitude, or as the result of special circumstances – is the surprising, forcibly transformative nature of all value noticed. Aversion might, of course, be one such circumstance. Shock might be another. Awe another. Intellection another. Aversion, for example, at the fact that "[i]n all regions, when black people in large numbers have become relatively assertive in pursuit of a fair share of [the economies of the U.S. imagination and fiscal 'free marketplace'], white people have proved themselves ready for violence" (Williamson 285): shock, awe, or intellection concerning the same. In such instances, a revolution of value occurs. The formalized and fetishized boundaries of value are recrossed and reimagined from an Other vantage. They are transgressed, and in this moment

> [t]ransgression carries the limit [or boundary] right to the limit of its being; transgression forces the limit to face the fact of its imminent disappearance, to find itself in what it excludes (perhaps, to be the more exact, to recognize itself for the first time), to experience its positive truth in its downward fall. (Foucault *Language* 34)

Transgression is necessarily allied with the valorizing processes of the Other. It remains the *unthinkable* trace of the Other of value, unthinkable because when value as force is recognized in spite of the camouflaging influence of value as form, its discovery is disarming. It is always disarming to discover promiscuity where none is suspected. When this transgressive exposure occurs, value is confounded, as is the one perceiving the exposure. Value becomes tentative, questioned, suspect, uncertain, all the things value cannot be. It becomes devalued, violated, *not* value, *not* itself.[10] And just as the effort to hold the thought of value so de-formed that it is no longer value is somewhat anguished and troublesome, so too the person who sees value in its nakedness, in its devaluation and violation, is restive.

The reason for this restiveness resides not merely in the fact that the violent motivation of value denied by its formal guise might be repellent but, equally, in the fact that value is revealed as arbitrary. It becomes clear that there is no founding principle for value, no principle without contrary and insinuating value(s) that selects those forms valued. There is no surpassing or paramount principle governing who sites (sights) what or who sites (sights) whom in the *name* of value. Thus, it is both the violence and the promiscuity, a masked indiscreteness, that together are disarming. The perceiver is confounded because, rather than occupying exclusive ground, value occupies the identical ground to that of its forcibly displaced Others. At the site (sight) where incontrovertible identity should be found – where, at least, *any* principle should be found – the perceiver discovers instead a relation of violence to the Other as well as the unsettled and unsettling self-reflexivities of this violence. The fact that any principle might occasion value is equivalent to the fact that *no* principle occasions value. In the stead of incontrovertible identity, one finds only competition, contingency, expenditure, and excess. If the problematics of value begin in this way with excess, and excess in turn responds in unlimited arbitration,[11] then unlimited arbitration provides value with a ground that is unadmittingly groundless. Value rests on an unlimited and always *soliciting* groundlessness, a groundlessness marked, however surreptitiously, by forms of violence.

Exposed and therefore not itself, value, beside itself, finds itself if only for a moment in the place of an Other, who or which is always *without* value. This transgression and disclosure of the groundlessness of value play an important thematic role, as already demonstrated, in the autobiography of Billie Holiday. However, upon examination, the same is true for the "the metaphysics of subjectivity" (Watson 57) characteristic of the genre of autobiography itself. In the reflective activities of autobiography, one finds a striking illustration of the anatomization of value outlined here: An undermining and undermined formalized identity, or ipseitic form, provides the central drama of the genre.[12] Examples are abundant in *The Confessions of St. Augustine,* one of the earliest autobiographies claimed by the Western tradition. Particularly to the point is the conclusion of the seventh chapter of book I, in which Augustine attempts to dismiss his infancy from the record of himself:

> So then, Lord, as to this period of my life, which I cannot remember having lived, which I take on the word of others, and which, however reliable the evidence may be, is still a matter of conjecture from the behavior of other infants, I am reluctant to count it as part of this present life of mine which I live in the world . . . so far as the darkness of forgetfulness is concerned, it is just the same as the period of life which I spent in my mother's womb. But if I *was shapen in iniquity, and in sin did my mother conceive,* where I beseech you, my god, where Lord, or when was I, your servant, ever innocent? But, see, I will pass over that time; for what have I to do now with it, considering that there is not a trace of it that I can recall? (24–5; emphasis in original)

The dissemblance involved in Augustine's attempt to deny any resemblance between his infantile and his present selves is highly ironic. Initially, Augustine is dismissive of infancy because he learns of his earlier life only through the report of Others and therefore only knows it mediately. However, the very act of defining himself in opposition – or in any relation – to this mediated Other is an act of incorporating that Other, for this mediated Other alerts him to himself, by showing him who he is by showing him who he is not. His infancy is a "darkness" into which he cannot see; yet, by being so, it marks and outlines what he can see. Moreover, even the invocation of the anterior embryonic self re-marks the self that Augustine claims he presently is: As an unborn child he lives in sin, and this selfhood of sin aids, during its rejection, in delineating the boundaries of the present, pious Augustine.

The final moment of the passage is the most patently ironic: "For what have I to do now with it, considering that there is not a trace of it that I can recall?" writes Augustine. Yet, he has much to do with it, and he does, in fact, have much of it to trace, as shown by the measured expenditure of his text, or self-inscription, in order to retreat from the infancy. In the sixth chapter of the autobiograhy, his infancy is a death that transports him to his present life; in the seventh chapter, in the passage considered here, it is – mostly because of its inherent iniquity – dismissed; and, in the eighth chapter, the antithesis of his infancy to his present self is illustrated in particular: "By making all sorts of cries and noises, all sorts of movements of my limbs, I desired to express my inner feelings, so that people would do what I wanted: but I was incapable of expressing everything I desired to express and I was incapable of making everyone understand" (25). Augustine's dismissed self intrudes to retrace and uphold the self that is inscribing itself. Augustine discharges his infancy from himself, but only to the margins of his maturity, from which it inexorably returns.

As in all autobiography, the self itself writing fails to control as it wishes the self being written about. Just as with Augustine's dismissal of his infancy – which, unwanted, appears for a time as the defining trope of himself – the self writing, or valorized, is never entirely that which it claims to be, because this self is also that which it effaces and, by doing so, records. Whereas the autobiographical text purports to rehearse and yield a singular self, critics of autobiography now generally begin their deliberations with the recognition that the autobiographical text inevitably yields a plurality of selves:

[A]utobiograpy is not simply a recapitulation of the past; it is also the attempt to and the drama of a [person] struggling to reassemble himself [or herself] in his [or her] own likeness at a certain moment of his [or her] history. Thus delivering up the earlier being brings a new stake into the game. (Gusdorf 43)

Similar insights can be drawn from an autobiographical text recently (re)discovered by the academy, Frederick Douglass's *Narrative of the Life of Frederick Douglass*, in which the climax of the narrative draws its force from the nadir. The climax is the ultimate moment of self-proclamation within the prolonged self-proclamation that constitutes the book; however, in order to establish this zenith Douglass must recall the imposed self-denunciation of U.S. slavery he has suffered, and that it is his task in turn to denounce. Douglass undertakes this task by always considering closely the issue of knowledge. His narrative begins as follows:

By far the larger part of the slaves know as little of their ages as horses know of theirs, and it is the wish of most masters *within my knowledge* to keep their slaves thus ignorant. I do not remember to have ever met a slave who could tell of his birthday. They seldom come nearer to it than planting-time, harvest-time, cherry-time, spring-time, or fall-time. A want of information concerning my own was a source of unhappiness to me even during childhood. (21; emphasis added)

The early admission of knowledge – in this case quite literally the phrase "within my knowledge" – in this representation of a prior state of lacking knowledge prefaces the confounding of self more clearly evident in Douglass's climactic moment of self-proclamation in the final chapter:

We owe something to the slaves south of the line as well as to those north of it; and in aiding the latter on their way to freedom, we should be careful to do nothing which would be likely to hinder the former from escaping from slavery. I would keep the merciless slaveholder profoundly ignorant of the means of flight adopted by the slave. (106)

By withholding information concerning his means of escape from slavery, Douglass appropriates the central power of the white Amer-

ican slaveholder over the African American slave, the power to determine what is known and what is not and by whom it is known
and by whom it is not. The roles of the possessed and the dispossessed of knowledge are startlingly reversed. The self-present autobiographical self of Frederick Douglass, making its ultimate
self-proclamation, eclipses the earlier, ignorant self; nonetheless,
this self-proclamation depends entirely upon the excess, the past
expenditure, of Douglass's prior and Other self. It is the earlier, ignorant self, presently belied by the self writing itself, that produces
the possibility of Douglass's climactic withholding of knowledge. In
a phrase, *Narrative of the Life of Frederick Douglass* depends upon that
which it ultimately dismisses: Douglass must reconstruct his present
self, the self writing itself, by recalling the self that his book proclaims he no longer is and that he never should have been in the
first place – himself as a slave. Indeed, in the one hundred and
twelve pages of Douglass's autobiography, the "I" of the text does
not in earnest become the focus of the text for some twenty-two
pages. Foregrounded in the first twenty-two pages are the "she, he,
it" of slaves and slavery. Douglass rehearses his former life as a
slave in order to create himself as the "free" man presently so useful to William Lloyd Garrison and the Massachusetts Anti-Slavery
Society, and, thus, the rehearsal is self-riddled. Douglass, in order
to represent the exemplary nature of his present self in the pre–
Civil War North, must represent himself as a slave in the antebellum South.

Beyond the illusion of a singularly unfolding unity, one recognizes an Other repeatedly broaching the site of the center of the
text from which it is expended with equal repetition. This is yet
another way of stating that value always begins disputatiously. Yet,
these examples from *The Confessions of St. Augustine* and *Narrative of
the Life of Frederick Douglass* provide nearly insensible, hard to grasp,
hard to make tangible examples of the settling and unsettling of a
dispute, for the type of dispute delineated by these excerpts takes
place within "a complex of linguistic acts in a discursive field" (23
Andrews). Accordingly, the violence of these disputes is not often
thought of as violence, since the spectacle of value returning to
violence is much more easily physically perceived.

Still, it is important to understand that the integral interaction of
value and violence occurs in all instances of value, even those instances taking place within "a complex of linguistic acts in a discursive field":

What is distinctive about *verbal* actions is . . . their radical dependence on social dynamics and, indeed, social economics,
for their effect. For it is in the very nature of verbal actions
that they can have appropriate consequences for the performer
– that is, can serve his [her] interests and enable him [or her]
to obtain and achieve what he [or she] desires – only to the
extent that they affect and control the behavior of other people. (Herrnstein Smith *On The Margins*, 86; emphasis in original)

The coimplication of value and violence within "a complex of linguistic acts in a discursive field" may be attenuated but is not to be
overlooked.

Value confounded by itself remains violence, whether it is physical
or it is only symbolically or discursively expressive. The exceptional
circumstances of Harriet Jacobs related in her autobiography *Incidents in the Life of a Slave Girl* illustrate the point well. Persecuted
sexually by the slaveowner to whom she legally belongs, Jacobs es-
capes his assaults by feigning an escape to the North while, in fact,
never leaving the South and remaining secreted among her relatives. Jacobs confines herself in the rafters of a shed attached to her
grandmother's house and suffers there for many years the miseries
of an "atmosphere . . . so stifled that even mosquitoes would not
condescend to buzz in it" in the summer, and in the winter the
miseries of her limbs "benumbed by inaction, and the cold fill[ing]
them with cramp" (123, 125). In this place, she endures violence
that is difficult to imagine. Equally, however, this site of confinement
is the place from which Jacobs initiates a textual violence that transforms and, to some extent, controls the actions of her persecutor.
Her dissembling letters to Dr. Flint and her grandmother initiate
transformations commensurate, in their own way, with that of her
confinement: Jacobs prompts Flint to believe that she is living hundreds of miles away and to conduct himself accordingly. The words
of Jacobs's letters bespeak, as if Jacobs had made the journey as well,
a distance that only they have traveled. The letters are actually taken
to New York by a "seafaring person," return to the house of Jacobs's
grandmother, and fall inevitably into the hands of Flint as fictional
testimony of Jacobs's presence in the North. This beguiling achievement is not lost on Jacobs, who writes, "This was as good as a com-
edy to me" (133).

All this is to say there is no denying that the pressing and the repressing of the physical on the physical are the most immediately grasped of all instances of value and violence, the competitive pressing and repressing that can take place between the physical and the immaterial a greater struggle for the eye,[13] and still moreso the pressing and repressing of the immaterial upon the immaterial, violence least discernible to the eye – the forcible altering of Otherwise established forms within "a complex of linguistic acts within a discursive field," for instance. Nonetheless, one such highly organized and specially valorized discursive field is literary critical theory, in which the forcible altering of Otherwise established forms is often not easy to specify. In *The Body in Pain*, Elaine Scarry remarks the difficulty of specifying even the instance of physical violence and claims it is only the presence of the weapon that expresses most comprehensibly and most permanently the occurrence and potential occurrence of physical violence. Embodying the "expressive potential of the sign" (17), the weapon gives shape by means of its presence to the pain experienced diametrically by victim and assailant. "[O]ccupying a primal place in the original moment of transformation" (172), the weapon stands as the sign of the injury, as the emblem of both the agency of the injury and the sensate outcome of the injury.

If material violence is thus inadequate to the task of recording itself, the same is true to a much greater degree of nonphysical, intellectual, or cultural violence, violence taking place within "a discursive field." The originality and instantiation of these violences are necessarily less immediate than the violences of the bullet, the blade of the knife, the fist, the whip. These forcible alterings of Otherwise established forms are characterized by the same insensibility as the texts of St. Augustine and Frederick Douglass. It is imperative to see, however, that the forms of these violences and the ratios they bear to violence remain no less valuable for their insensibility. They are registered in more abstract and abstruse forms in

> process[es] by which different kinds of meaning are produced and reproduced by the establishment of a mental set towards the world in which certain sign systems are privileged as necessary, even natural, ways of recognizing a "meaning" in things and others are suppressed, ignored, or hidden in the very process of representing a world to consciousness. (White 192)

Needless to say, it proves more difficult, but not impossible, to locate the complexities of violence that inevitably constitute such forms of value.

It is not correct to say that nonphysical, intellectual, or cultural violence does not possess a sign of its own – does not possess "the expressive potential of the sign of the weapon" in Elaine Scarry's terms (17). On the contrary, in such instances, the performances of value as form and value as force are reflected in the performance of the linguistic sign itself, as the sign has come to be understood since the investigations of Ferdinand de Saussure. The claim here is that the sign (or weapon) of cultural violence is the sign of signific“ation itself. Mediated self-presence and dialectical self-difference constitute the linguistic sign as much as they do the moment or structure of value. As with value, the sign is not an entity coextensive with itself but, as it is understood after de Saussure, an entity that comes into being only in relation to that which it exceeds. It is important to note that de Saussure is very careful in *Course in General Linguistics* to make an emphatic distinction between signification, which he sees as "the counterpart of the sound image" (115), and value, which he describes as the ground taken up by the sign in relation to and under the pressure of other signs within the same system. The resemblance pursued does not necessarily abrogate this distinction; differently, the matter pursued is the relational dynamics that both value and signification, at bottom, share. Signification and language depend on principles of alignment, correspondence, and occlusion. Like value, the sign comes into being only as a result of diminishing, in its moment of self-display, that which it is not. Accordingly, de Saussure understands *relative* difference as the ultimate fact of the sign, of its larger presence as language, and of all signification:

> [I]n language there are only differences. Even more important: a difference generally implies positive terms between which the difference is set up; but in language there are only differences *without positive terms.* (120; emphasis in original)

The sign takes its ground in relation to and as a result of the displacing pressure it exerts on Other signs around it; only in this way does it attain status qua sign, gain meaning, and hold value. To quote de Saussure again: "Everywhere and always there is the same complex equilibrium of terms that mutually condition each other.

Putting it another way, *language is a form and not a substance*" (122; emphasis in original).

One should not be misled by de Saussure's use of the term "equilibrium," because equilibrium exists in signification only provisionally. In order for the sign to become operative, equilibrium must be dispelled. Only by disparaging those Other possible signs not operative does the sign in effect become itself. Nor should one be misled by the comparison being drawn here between the structure or movement of value and the structure or movement of the sign. This is not a proposal calling for one to see a coincidence of the elements of value and the elements of the sign. The signifier and signified of de Saussure's sign are not somehow imagined to correspond to the valued and devalued elements of value, nor de Saussure's referent to be somehow the counterpart of the original violence of value as form.[14] The coincidence remarked here involves the acts of displacement or expropriation characteristic of both. One might say that, just as the sign is a form without substance, value is a form but not a substance.

These characteristic acts of displacement and expropriation might be schematized in another way in order to conceive further of the likeliness of the sign and of value. The sign is as internally disjunctive as is value. It aspires not only to take the place of those terms with and *upon* which it is contingent but, as it were, to replace and represent the world in itself. In addition to occluding Other signs in order to fulfill itself,[15] the sign must fragment and displace the world, although it desires – on the contrary – to reproduce or re-form the world completely. Despite its efforts, the sign can never be, as is the world, concomitantly spatial and temporal. The sign is alternately one or the Other, as is repeatedly apparent in the work of de Saussure – either *langue* or *parole,* synchronic or diachronic, paradigmatic or syntagmatic, systematic or historical. When the sign formulates itself spatially, it necessarily assumes its own displacement in a previous moment and equally risks displacement in the next, and when the sign formulates itself in a sequence, it at some point breaks with that sequence in order to speak itself. Like value, the sign, in order to come into being, must assert itself in two ways, and one way nullifies the Other. When representing the space of the world, the sign must forget the time of the world; when representing the time of the world, the sign must forget the space of the world.

Like value, signification is always attempting to wrest itself from itself, to disregard its disjunctive nature and appear as Other than arbitrary and competitive. Signification attempts to belie its own makeshift construction, its structure or movement as a momentary point of distinction dependent upon exclusion. Still, it is equally important to note that the sign, like value, does ultimately overcome the adversities of itself, or else there would be no signification, just as there would be no value if value did not overcome its confounding itself. In a phrase, both value and the sign inevitably forget themselves. By means of their self-masking amnesias, both ignore their former expenditures and achieve authority. Both achieve climaxes of self-display – authority being no more than undeniable self-display, no more than blind and strict self-sightedness.

This relational and Othering power of signification, its potential cultural violence, and its sometimes masked relation to physical violence are made clear on a more concrete level by the critic Aijaz Ahmad, who codifies the importance of signifying practices to the far-reaching projects of Western colonial and postcolonial dominations:

> [W]hen it comes to knowledge of the world, there is no such thing as a category of the "essentially descriptive"; that "description" is never ideologically or cognitively neutral; that to "describe" is to specify a locus of meaning, to construct an object of knowledge, and to produce a knowledge that shall be bound by that act of descriptive construction. "Description" has been central, for example, in the colonial discourse. It was by assembling a monstrous machinery of descriptions – of our bodies, our speech-acts, our habits, our conflicts, and desires, our politics, our socialities and sexualities – in fields as various as ethnology, fiction, photography, linguistics, political science – that the colonial discourse was able to classify and ideologically master the colonial subject, enabling itself to transform the descriptively verifiable multiplicity and difference into the ideologically felt hierarchy of value. To say, in short, what one is presenting is "essentially descriptive" is to assert a level of facticity which conceals its own ideology and to prepare a ground from which judgments of classification, generalisation and value can be made. (6)

The priority of Western forms of economic, political, and even psychological domination rests in large part with the signatory authority they can manufacture for themselves.

The process of value attaining the condition of authority should be imagined as value blinding itself and its perceiver to its relational and disjunctive nature, with authority defined here as an uncompromising and aggrandizing self-reflection of value as form.[16] In authority, value contests itself in a friendly and stalemated manner. It blinds itself to the Other so as to recognize itself (by negation) in the place of the Other, effecting an acknowledgment of itself to itself. The condition of authority – which might be called exponential value – arises when, more than violating the Other, it cites itself in the place of the Other. Value as form (dis)figures the Other in the image of itself.[17]

Authority, the sighting of the self elsewhere, refigures the potency of blindness as perception. Because the potency of blindness rests in its disabling effects, these disabling powers are directed toward the troublesome and confounding sites (sights) of the Other. In the cases of value itself blindness is directed at the very least toward value as force and in the case of the sign toward its makeshift inefficiency. Consequently, the alternate perceptions of value as form and of the sign as competent emerge. Authority, then, is a selective blindness, a vision of self premised upon blindness.

Such expositions of authority abound in African American slave narratives. For instance, in substantiating her claim that "[c]ruelty is contagious in uncivilized communities," Linda Brent describes in *Incidents in the Life of the Slave Girl* the ordeal of a fellow slave, who "gave [his master] some offence":

> He was divested of his clothes, except his shirt, whipped, and tied to a large tree in front of the house. It was a stormy night in winter. The wind blew bitterly cold, and the boughs of the old tree crackled under falling sleet. A member of the family, fearing he would freeze to death, begged that he might be taken down; but the master would not relent. He remained there three hours; and, when he was cut down, he was more dead than alive. (47)

As this brief example demonstrates – and in ways analogous to the example of the U.S. ritual of lynching – the authority of the slaveholder is fabricated and signified in the negative or, so to speak, deauthorized condition of the African American, in this case a slave. The authority of the slaveholder resides in his or her act of acknowledging elsewhere, in the dark skinned slave, the preeminence of her or his own form. When waving the gun or the knife or plying the whip, the slaveholder sees the gun, the knife, the whip and recognizes the preeminence of herself or himself inscribed in the place of the gun, the knife, the whip, and, moreover, by means of this inscription her or his preeminence inscribed in the place of the submitted victim(s).[18] This transaction involves a sleight of hand but, nonetheless, a highly profitable one well illuminnated by Elaine Scarry's penetrating analysis of what she terms the "language" or structure of physical torture:

> While torture contains language, specific human words and sounds, it is itself a language, an objectification, an acting out. Real pain, agonizing pain, is inflicted on a person; but torture, which contains specific acts of inflicting pain, is also itself a demonstration and magnification of the felt-experience of pain. In the very processes it uses to produce pain within the body of the prisoner, it bestows visibility on the structure and enormity of what is usually private and incommunicable, contained within the boundaries of the sufferer's body. It then goes on to deny, to falsify, the reality of the very thing it has itself objectified by a perceptual shift which converts the vision of suffering into the wholly illusory but, to the torturers and the regime they represent, wholly convincing spectacle of power. The physical pain is so incontestably real that it seems to confer its quality of "incontestable reality" on the power that has brought it into being. It is, of course, precisely because the reality of that power is so highly contestable, the regime so unstable, that torture is being used. (27)

Less material forms of authority and its violence are marked by similarly peculiar acts of substitution. Intellectual authority, textual authority, cultural authority construe themselves in the same way, and de Saussure's anatomized sign stands as the emblem of this more rarefied violence. De Saussure's anatomized sign, in other words, is equivalent to the *significant*, material weapon; it proves the most comprehensible and permanent record of the occurring or potential rarefied violence, as is the material weapon in the instance or threat of physical violence. The sign, the weapon of cultural violence, the violence of "a complex of linguistic acts in a discursive field," authorizes the supremacy of whoever controls it just as the physical weapon authorizes the supremacy of whoever controls it. Importantly, however, precisely like the confounding of value, this assumption of supremacy has no founding principle and, therefore, also resides in arbitration.

To recapitulate the entire matter, as the confounding or disintegration of value is the arbitrary collapse of value into itself, authority is value arbitrarily and exponentially arising from itself. Authority amounts to value that becomes most fully valued, confirmed, certain, unsuspected, formalized, objective, and, concomitantly, also most fully devaluing, violating, deforming, and subjectifying (from the vantage of the Other). The invisible violence of value becomes all the more intense for its denial. Indeed, there appears to be no replaced Other because the preeminent form of value remarks itself manifestly in the place of the Other. Removing itself from its vicissitudes, value appears stable and singular; the masquerade of the camera–hand most completely outwits and denies its undeniable exertions.[19]

Equally, as they are exemplary of the confounding of the self or value, autobiographical texts prove exemplary of the authorization of the self or value. Despite their self-anticipatory and self-remembering moments – its secret violences – autobiographical texts often manage to represent the self writing itself as adequately controlling the self being written about. Like most narratives, autobiography sustains a convincing argument for singularity and unity. To return to the instance of *Narrative of the Life of Frederick Douglass*, at the climax of his narrative, Douglass takes particular and beguiling care to emphasize the self-command of the self writing itself. The act of withholding pertinent information – an empowering stipulatory act of the narrative – blinds the self writing itself and the reader (on a casual reading) to the earlier self, the enslaved self, which is the motive force of the self-proclamation of the narrative. Emphasizing the desire to keep "the merciless slaveholder profoundly ignorant" (106), Douglass writes of his escape from Maryland:

> It required no very vivid imagination to depict the most frightful scenes through which I should have to pass, in case I failed. The wretchedness of slavery, and the blessedness of freedom, were perpetually before me. It was life and death with me. But I remained firm, and according to my resolution on the third day of September, 1838, I left my chains, and succeeded in reaching New York without the slightest interruption of any kind. How I did so – what means I adopted, – what direction I travelled, and by what mode of conveyance, – I must leave unexplained, for the reasons before mentioned. (110–11)

Douglass glosses all factual specifics of the episode, and these omissions patently reiterate the startling reversal of who constitutes the possessed and the dispossessed of knowledge. In addition, Douglass glosses all imaginative specifics of his escape – so that only the date of his escape rehearses this central episode in any particular way. Punctuated by the specificity of "the third day of September, 1838," these omissions of fact and imagination effectively belie the immediacy and uncertainty of an earlier, Other, less self-possessed self. Rather than any competition between that earlier self and the self writing itself, there singularly emerges the reassured, successful, reflective, and self-possessed self writing itself. Matter-of-factly, the announcement of "the third day of September, 1838" appears to mark the severance of Douglass's present self from his former enslaved self. Representing an incontrovertible boundary between the selves, the appearance of "the third day of September, 1838" resolves the cursory, suggestive antithesis between the uncertainty of the phrase "the most frightful scenes" and the certainty of "But I remained firm," and between the phrases "perpetually before me" and "without the slightest interruption of any kind." The date also resolves the antitheses between the pairs "the wretchedness of slavery, and the blessedness of freedom" and "life and death." In brief, the appearance of "the third day of September, 1838" guarantees the disappearance of these antitheses in the subsequent certainty of success. However, the uncertainty of the disappearance of the antitheses is precisely the point of their appearance. The antitheses are simply faint, discounted, and immediately recuperated registers of uncertainty, which is to say, simply inverted, unostensible registers of certainty. The appearance of "the third day of September, 1838" abruptly resolves that irresolution in accordance with the situation of the later self writing itself, as does the brief acclamation "I left my chains," much more potently than the antitheses mark any irresolution. The self writing itself refigures these antitheses – glancing representations of the presence of an Other self – in singular confirmation of itself.

Visibly inscribing the supremacy of itself upon an Other self, the self writing itself controls the signification of the autobiography, the signs of the autobiography. To function as author is to function as authority. For, as Foucault again and again reminds one, the self is always produced *in* authority. Analogously, value is always produced *in* authority, namely, at a remove from itself. This remove is emblematized by the boundary, and the aim of value and authority is, above all, to site (sight) themselves in terms of this boundary. However, the Other is both critical for and critical of value, authority, and the boundary. To the perplexity of value, of authority, and of the boundary, the Other remains the source and resource of their removes; the calling into question of value, of the boundary of value, and of the authority of value is a crisis inevitably arising from this troubling presence of the Other of value.

Put differently, the calling into question of established value is an inevitable consequence of the formation of value. It is never an activity foreign to any instantiation of value and, accordingly, is not new to the established values of literary critical discourse. Nevertheless, the recent and ongoing questions of value asked within literary critical discourse and of literary critical authority are framed in an unusually explicit and (confoundingly) forthright manner. What is more, they are framed by those never fully permitted to pose such questions before. The transformations that have taken place in the field of U.S. literature over the past twenty-five years or so are emblematic. In a 1992 assessment of the field, Richard H. Brodhead recognizes the implementation of what he calls "the scheme for a completely reconstituted way in which Americans could be represented by their literature, a scheme that only became thinkable within fairly recent historical memory and that long remained an outsider's hope" (62). In terms of both textual and professional representation, the positions of women of color, African Americans, Chicanos, Latinos, Asian Americans, and gays and lesbians generally constitute open points of debate and analysis as never before in the academy. Indeed, inasmuch as the study of African American literature appears to be at an unprecedented premium in the U.S. literary academy (insofar as it makes sense to speak of blackness in terms of priority), it is reasonable to say that issues and reconsiderations of literary critical value are also at a premium.

Gerald Graff and Michael Warner, in their introduction to *The Origins of Literary Study in America,* note that "from their beginnings, academic literary studies were held together not by any shared definition of literature or of the discipline, but by tacit social agreements that enabled incompatible principles to coexist in an uneasy truce" (2). In recent times this "uneasy truce" has come to a point at which it seems much more uneasy and much less of a truce than ever before. The tacit social agreements, and particularly the boundary defining that which is traditionally acknowledged as within and without the purview of literary critical discourse, exist under increas-

ing scrutiny and increasingly revisionary pressure. Of remarkable
currency in the present scheme is the view that "critical practice is
occasional, that is, positioned within sets of discursive and institutional formations that are parts of larger constellations of cultural
and political power" (239). This statement by Paul Bové succinctly
rehearses the exceptionally troublesome insight of twentieth-century
literary critical discourse that is in large part responsible for what
many contemporary commentators have called its crisis. Bové observes and plainly articulates the integral interaction of the literary
and the extraliterary. Increasingly perceived, theorized, and acted
upon is the fact that the boundary of the literary is as questionable
and routinely transgressed as it is fetishized. Now long open to serious debate is the position – to name only one very celebrated
advocate – undertaken by René Wellek, who in the essay "Criticism
as Evaluation" in his tellingly titled *The Attack on Literature* proposes
that "a work belongs to literature at least in the sense of imaginative
literature, of *belles lettres*, because the aesthetic value is dominant"
(51; emphasis in original). He appeals further to notions "that there
is a common feature in all art which we recognize . . . [and] a common humanity that makes all art, however remote in time and place,
accessible to us" (63). The certainty and clarity of such a realm of
a discrete "aesthetic value" in which one discovers a "common feature" of all art and the precepts or grounds of "common humanity"
have long served as a standard presupposition of literary critical
pragmatics. They have authorized a long unarticulated arbitration
of whose interests are celebrated within the bounds of the literary,
a long unarticulated policing along the lines of race, gender, sexuality, and class, to name four broad categories.

It is the place, function, and estimation of this long unarticulated
boundary effecting the demarcation of the literary and the extraliterary (the valued and nonvalued in these circumstances) that prove
most crucial to the revolution remarked by both Bové and Brodhead. For once this boundary was reimagined, as it unabashedly was
by the mid to late 1980s, critical attention could earnestly turn to
what Samuel Weber in *Institution and Interpretation* terms "*the ambivalence of demarcation*" (138; emphasis in original) and to the position in which, as phrased by Frank Lentricchia, literature is understood as

> all writing considered as social practice, all writing viewed in
> its material circumstances and in its purposiveness. It is power

as representation. The literary is all around us, and it is always doing its work upon us. It bears the past in many complex ways, but it does its deed, makes its mark, marks, here and now. (157)

One upshot is the allowance in the profession of both criticism of texts and critical practitioners never before fully imagined within the circle of the literary.

Holiday, her text, and those who would take up her text as an object worthy of literary investigation and study stand newly within the circle of the literary academy. For, in the customary elaborations of value in the U.S. landscape and Western culture, the contours of African and African American features and bodies are routinely dismissed, as documented, for instance, by Jan Nederveen Pieterse in *White on Black: Images of Africa and Blacks in Western Popular Culture.* However, the "grotesque" nature of these bodies resides not only in their status as peculiar artifacts but also in their status as agents of cultural influence. Journalistic trepidation and even hysteria at African American cultural influences form a regular feature of U.S. popular history. Reactions to the emergence of jazz and jazz culture early in the twentieth century provide a case in point:

> Of all the cabaret activities, the public character of dancing aroused the bitterest and most prolonged attacks. To reformers, the close physical contact and body expression connoted loss of self-control. The lifting of legs, the jerking of shoulders represented an unreserved demeanor on the part of youth and womanhood in general. The fact that respectable women danced forms originating among inferiors, sensual blacks and Latins, moved critics to envision the enshrinement of undisguised sexuality and lower-class behavior. (Erenberg 81)

In the view of the dominant culture, grotesque African Americans and their cultural influence undertake productions of value *without the site (sight) of value,* and much of these productions has to do with resourcefully relinquishing the sight (site) by which they are condemned. As already remarked in the earlier discussion of *Lady Sings the Blues,* of the primary senses of sight and sound, one does best to rely upon sound from our vantage "in the dark" – from our vantage where sight is condemnatory. As already noted, Billie Holiday writes among her autobiographical observations that "[e]verything that happened, happened by ear. For the two years I was with [Basie's] band we had a book of a hundred songs, and every one of us carried every last damn note of them in our heads" (62). From Holiday's vantage inscribed in sound and by the singing voice and by its metonyms of music and dance, the site (sight) *without boundaries* and the site (sight) *of boundaries* are rendered very differently from costumary prescriptions in the United States:

> I found out the main difference between [black] uptown and [white] downtown was people were more for real up there. They got to be, I guess. Uptown a whore was a whore; a pimp was a pimp; a thief was a thief; a faggot was a faggot; a dike was a dike; a mother-hugger was a mother-hugger.
> Downtown it was different – more complicated. A whore was sometimes a socialite; a pimp could be a man about town; a thief could be an executive; a faggot could be a playboy; a dike might be called a deb; a mother-hugger was somebody who wasn't adjusted and had problems. (86)

In order to undertake an Other production of value (without boundaries and outside value), one must forgo the acknowledged significance of *site (sight)*, which amounts to the fancy and the medium by means of which boundaries are most faithfully determined. At their most respected,

> [b]oundaries are established to separate and distinguish entities one from the other, but by the very same process, they link the delimited entities together. As a boundary is traced, it defines the integrity of each entity in terms of and in opposition to the others; it establishes where it begins and ends. A boundary therefore should be clearly marked or posted with visible signs in order to function as a boundary. When one crosses it, one should know immediately that one is in a different place where a different language is spoken, and different laws, rules, and procedures are followed. Because boundaries mark areas and limits, they assure us that we are where we think we are, and that wherever we are, we are on safe familiar ground – for each area has been charted and defined, made recognizable and mastered before our arrival there. (Gearhart 3)

However, "it does not function this way. It is more open than closed, more often displaced than fixed, as much within each field as at the limits of each" (3). These observations are made by Suzanne Gearhart in her study of the French Enlightenment undertaken in terms of the "open boundary" delimiting the disciplines of history and literature, yet the larger point Gearhart overlooks is that it is not only this disciplinary boundary that never operates in "an unproblematic, unequivoal manner" (3); indeed, all boundaries do. Having come to a point at which it reluctantly embraces the textual as well as professional presence of African Americans, the literary academy witnesses those boundaries delineating traditional, privileged sites of textuality as they undergo notable reform sometimes as dramatic as the countersignificant characterizations of uptown and downtown remarked by Holiday.

The reformation has much to do with specifying, examining, and attempting to alter the little considered intersections of – not boundaries between – literary and extraliterary authority or, in other words, textual, cultural, and political authority. Since the disposition of African Americans in the New World forms a paramount drama of textual, cultural, and political power and powerlessness in the U.S. landscape, a signal aspect of these reformatory activities proves an investigation of literary textuality in relation to the disposition of African Americans in the New World. The institutionalized literary critical order and its established values are in significant ways analogous, even identical, to various extraliterary orders and values authorizing and more or less rationalizing *signs* of privilege in the U.S. landscape mediated in terms of an African American inclusion by exclusion, an African American *present absence*. Any understanding of literary critical discourse as "sets of discursive and institutional formations that are parts of larger constellations of cultural and political power" (Bové 239) can by no means ignore the issue of power and powerlessness as it is played out in terms of relegating African Americans as Other – as "beyond the pale" of value. Textuality – the *sign* of privilege and value over which the discipline of literary studies presides – is reconceived along unorthodox and formerly unimaginable lines, antinomian lines. One can well imagine that the settling of African Americans in recognizable numbers into the professoriat and academic propagation of literary critical discourse represents an extension of an already "disturbing" presence in the United States.

Nevertheless, liberations (intellectual or otherwise) are not all assured, or even fully promised, simply by the posing of urgently contested questions of value. To interpose no alternative value in the theoretically neutral moment of calling value into question remains equivalent to strengthening and reincarnating reified, dominant value. Frederic Jameson, when he directly considers the issue of value in *The Political Unconscious,* clarifies this shortcoming of a strictly interrogative approach to questions of value: "[T]he study of value is at one with nihilism, or the experience of its absence" (251). The calling into question of established value presupposes a nihilism of value, a moment or situation in which all value is in abeyance. But, of course, in point of fact, such a moment never exists and, therefore, such a moment can never remain an end in itself. Assuming the prodigality of ceaselessly calling value into question amounts to an act of no consequence, and as she would have it in her autobiography, Holiday can never afford and never indulge in this prodigality. She must *sound out* new signs, new significations, and new values that one "get[s] . . . the hard way" (176). She and her voice revise and remeasure the "positive structure," the "proper" identity.

Speaking to the situation of the literary academy and, for a moment, solely in terms of language, E. D. Hirsch in *Cultural Literacy* notes, "[t]he monolingual nation as we know it developed alongside a new kind of social and economic organization – the industrial nation state" (72). Therefore, one might surmise, to speak solely in terms of language is entirely impossible. Against the grain of the project he shares with other cultural commentators like William Bennett, Allan Bloom, and Dinesh D'Souza, Hirsch in this observation reconfirms that issues, questions, sounds of value ineluctably lead where one would least expect; this is an insight that by the mid-1980s the literary academy had profoundly recognized. This insight also forms the intuitive knowledge Holiday plays upon, early in her life, across the white marble steps of Baltimore; it seems no accident that the episode in which she garners as much as "$2.10 – that's fourteen kitchen or bathroom floors and as many sets of steps" introduces Holiday's reader to her first notation of the *singing voice,* very plainly in this instance, one sign of *the value of the Other outside value.*

The anecdote amounts to much more than an autobiographical recollection. Holiday explores the limits and countersignificance of value in ways revealing for situations far removed from her own – even formerly unimaginable discussions of and within literary critical discourse that animate a post-1970s literary academy in earnest. Throughout *Lady Sings the Blues,* Holiday highlights the significance of the singing voice as it remeasures and re-moves established and valued determinations of signs and the signing voice. It might be fair to say that, accordingly, from the vantage of those valuing and evaluating African American cultural productivity, the disordering of institutionalized literary critical speculations and praxis in a post-structuralist academy signals what might be termed the intervention of traditionally unmeaning "singing voices" into a carefully re-stricted economy of signs. Holiday demonstrates, then, by means of these disorderings, and by means of seeing double, how one under-takes the establishment of the value of important lives and voices Otherwise dismissed.

2

FIGURING OTHERS OF VALUE: SINGING VOICES, SIGNING VOICES, AND AFRICAN AMERICAN CULTURE

An examination of value within the terms of its quotidian, cultural specifics remains as involved an undertaking as its theoretical anatomization, and, as one might imagine, the exercise proves even more intriguing. Particularly at issue here is the way in which the disjunctive dynamics of value as force and value as form illuminate the socialities of *race*, a term that the literary critic Dana D. Nelson defines provocatively as "the arbitrary enforcement and institutionalization of Anglo superiority in United States history" (21). Forgoing notions of race as an "essence" or as a primarily individual experience, Nelson's definition suggests, to my mind, just how profoundly race (the preeminent "New World"[1] *value?*) and racialized practices are caught up in the agonisms of violence and form already outlined. Race, as it is made a priority in the New World, amounts to a series of actions and transactions never represented as such, but represented as formal essences instead. Nelson's pairing of "enforcement and institutionalization" captures this tension well.

Still, what exactly does it mean to pursue an understanding of race (as a value) in these terms – as both fluid and hypostasized, as concomitantly a series of transactions and the representation of a formal essence, as agonistically systemic? One might begin by highlighting the appropriateness of the term "transaction." The word brings to mind in its most popular sense the dynamics of sales and purchases, and the New World institutionalization of race (vis-à-vis racial blackness) originates precisely in a system of international trading often involving, according to the historian Basil Davidson, a "morning's scene of long and earnest haggling . . . between partners

55

who knew each other well, and had long since learned to tolerate each other's peculiarities and methods of bargaining" (106). This bargaining concerns the exchange of African bodies for "rolls of tobacco, pipes of rum and firearms, or more generally [for] lengths of iron or copper or [for] 'pots and basins' of brass" (107). Blackness proves a commodity in a network of international markets. Additionally, however, beyond the legacy of mercenary Western impulses to fashion "a cheap and constant source of labor" with African bodies (Mullin 3), a further transaction concerns itself with efforts to determine African American consciousness. If the material economic transaction produces racial blackness as a phenotypical and commodifiable essence, the related transaction aims at producing blackness as a negative discursive, cultural, and psychological essence:

> From the moment that Africans arrived on the North American continent, their enslavers mounted a campaign of abuse, the goal of which was to convince them that slavery was their destiny and that white power was the only important one in their lives. By stripping Africans of their personal autonomy and basic human rights, the enslavers revealed that their objective was not merely to dominate Africans politically and physically but to redefine black identity by destroying their sense of humanity. (Roberts 141)

In a phrase, the New World arena of value, in both its materialist and idealist transactions, depends upon the expenditure of blackness. To expend the "humanity" of Africans in the profitable cultivation of staple crops (or other commodities) as well as the political and psychological contours of a privileged whiteness (defined foremost as Anglo or Western European) remains a fundamental element and an enduring legacy of the New World arena of value. Forcibly, blackness is positioned as excess in relation to a more "legitmate" and significant presence known as whiteness, a more legitimate presence invariably revising its promiscuous interests in (re)situating the black Other. Moreover, these riddled intramural relations of the *valued* form of whiteness are matched by equally unsettling extramural dynamics. In the same way that *valued* whiteness must struggle to occlude its internal mechanisms – the originary and ongoing violences that maintain its privileged status – so too it must struggle to occlude competing formations of value sponsored by and within the "excessive" communities designated as black. For, needless to say, the force and forms of dominant value in the New World are hostile and dehumanizing from African American perspectives and, therefore, cannot be easily assumed. Competing and resistant forms of value necessarily arise:

> In their daily lives enslaved Africans [and one can certainly extend the analysis to contemporary situations] turned to behaviors which allowed them to subvert the masters' authority and control. . . . Subversive behaviors became both a part of the everyday strategies of the enslaved and a primary focus [in the relating] of many personal experience stories. (Roberts 32)

Transactions and formations of dominant value are invariably and Otherwise unsettled, and it is in this context that the powerful, revisionary force of the African American singing voice becomes apparent, as documented so well by Billie Holiday in her recollections. The singing voice stands as one very important sign of the value of those lives and voices situtated in the dark. It assuredly provides evidence of ties to forms of value of a cultural past in which, as stated by John Lovell, Jr., "[t]he occasions for instrumentalizing, dancing, and singing – usually in that order – are numerous and striking" (38), but, moreover, it provides a primary means by which African Americans may exchange an expended, valueless self in the New World for a productive, recognized self. It provides one important means of formalizing and celebrating an existence otherwise proposed as negative and negligible.

The singing voice provides the allowance for African Americans to enter or subvert symbolic, legal, material, and imaginative economies to which we are most usually denied access. The vast iconic and financial successes of African Americans as performers and musicians in the recording industry (such as Holiday herself) make this observation abundantly clear. Indeed, the extreme centrality of music and its collateral activities to African American cultural practices – in terms of not simply production but, above all, reception – equally underscores the point. This central role of music in African American culture and expressivity is a characteristic of the culture widely and repeatedly acknowledged. Notable figures enumerating and elaborating this observation – whether critically or artistically – include W.E.B. DuBois, James Weldon Johnson, Jessie Redmond Fauset, Ralph Ellison, Amiri Baraka (formerly Leroi Jones), Eileen Southern, Dena Epstein, Sterling Stuckey, John Lovell, Jr., and Portia Maultsby. It seems safe to say, in accordance with these as well

as many other figures, that musical traditions form the primary legacy of African American presence in the New World, of a presence
that the materially dominant community insistently attempts to distort or erase.

Indeed, the instrumentality of the singing voice within the most
oppressive circumstances of chattel slavery makes the point acutely.
In his 1867 autobiography, for example, Sella Martin recounts an
early childhood memory of African Americans chained together into
a "coffle" so that they might be taken to the trader's block. As those
in the coffle are ordered to march, they are also ordered to sing,
and Martin explains:

> Of what heartbreaks there are in these rude and simple songs!
> The purpose of the trader in having them sung is to prevent
> among the crowd of negroes who usually gather on such oc-
> casions, any expression of sorrow for those who are being torn
> away from them; but the negroes, who have very little hope of
> ever seeing those again who are dearer to them than life, and
> who are weeping and wailing over the separation, often turn
> the song thus demanded of them into a farewell dirge. (Blas-
> singame 705)

The revisionary allowance of singing in this circumstance is plain;
the African American singers "turn" the song and, therefore, the
moment to their own purposes and against the imperatives of their
captors. The singing reflects not an alien indifference that would be
made to supplant the highly emotional state of the people chained
into the coffle but, instead, the very sorrow they are exhorted to
mask. The sly alterity of the singing voice provides Martin's community the opportunity to speak in a landscape where such activity
is either already scripted or prohibited altogether. The singing voice
proves a form of contestation and the vehicle of indirect but effective self-expression.

The singing voice in African American communities is more than
simply one sign of the "value of the Other outside value." Onc can
claim that the singing voice as well as the musical forms of cultural
expressivity for which it synedochically stands constitute the preeminent sign of the production of cultural value in African American communities. African American communities, like the African
communities from which much of African American cultural sensibilities originates, are ones in which the production and reception
of music are highly privileged forms of both communal interaction

and personal pleasure. The activities surrounding the production and reception of the singing voice prove so essential to these communities that if one accepts the premise that "whatever human rationality consists in, it is certainly tied up with narrative structure and the quest for narrative unity" (Mark Johnson 172), then, one begins to understand the significance of the singing voice to African and African American cultural sensibilities by recognizing it as a paramount site at which these dynamics between human consciousness and narrative structures are played out. The cultural site of the singing voice provides the ground for intimate acts of self-definition and for forging of reasoned relations to the world.

The preeminence of this cultural site in African and African diasporic communities is certainly not uninvestigated. Historical and cultural research documenting and accounting for social and aesthetic continuities between the cultures of continental and diasporic African peoples forms a standard part of the scholarly record. The ethnomusicologist Olly Wilson, for example, provides convincing demonstrations that "black cultural practices in America, particularly in religion and the arts, have shown an amazing ability to retain or adapt African practice to conform to the demands of the new environment" (3). Wilson charts the geography of "a black-music cultural sphere ... which includes the music of the African and African-descendant peoples [in an area] ... bounded by West Africa on the east with the northern part of South America and the Carribean Islands on the south-west and the United States on the north-west" (6). With particular attention to its North American component, Wilson charts the formal principles of this sphere. His work forms part of a body of scholarship that carefully supports the belief that African cultural formations might overwhelm great discontinuities of time and space.

However, beyond the dynamics of cultural survivals, other exigencies might account for the privileging of the singing voice in African American culture, exigencies having much to do with the circumstances of the New World arena of value. Like many other commentators on African American culture, Alice Walker recognizes as much when, in her essay "In Search of Our Mothers' Gardens," she asks, "How was the creativity of the black woman kept alive, year after year and century after century, when for most of the years black people have been in America, it was a punishable crime for a black person to read and write?" Walker immediately exhorts her reader to "[c]onsider, *if you can bear to imagine it*, what might have been the result if singing, too, had been forbidden by law. Listen to the voices of Bessie Smith, Billie Holiday, Nina Simone, Roberta Flack, and Aretha Franklin, among others, and imagine those voices muzzled for life" (234; italics added). Disclosed by Walker's question and exhortation is the impossibility of divorcing the singing voice from the existence and condition of African Americans in the New World landscape. And her particular phrasing of the issue is so effective and pointed because it underscores the fact that the erasure she cannot bring herself to imagine proves inconceivable in the same way that the thought of any socially and psychologically tyrannized population failing to find alternative means for recording and celebrating individual lives as well as the life of their culture in general proves inconceivable. As documented in the instance of one South Carolina plantation by the historian Drew Faust Gilpen, populations in these circumstances invent and reinvent individually and collectively effective ways of scoring the life of the mind and of insisting upon the urgency of their presence despite ubiquitous and confining reports of their cultural – even human – absence.

The very famous early description of slave songs in Frederick Douglass's *Narrative of the Life of Frederick Douglass, an American Slave* is one passage in African American letters often quoted in support of this point. In this section Douglass contradicts his later and equally famous unqualified privileging of literacy – a position implicit also in Walker's question and exhortation.

> I did not, when a slave, understand the deep meaning of those rude and apparently incoherent songs. I was myself within the circle; so that I neither saw nor heard as those without might see and hear. They told a tale of woe which was then altogether beyond my feeble comprehension; they were tones loud, long, and deep; they breathed the prayer and complaint of souls boiling over with the bitterest anguish. Every tone was a testimony against slavery, and a prayer to God for deliverance from chains. The hearing of those wild notes always depressed my spirit, and filled me with ineffable sadness. I have frequently found myself in tears while hearing them. . . . To those songs I trace my first glimmering conception of the dehumanizing character of slavery. . . . Those songs still follow me, to deepen my hatred of slavery, and quicken my sympathies for my brethen in bonds. (37)

Just as Walker recovers a denied artistry and creativity for African Americans invested in the singing voice, so Doulgass recovers a denied African American thoughtfulness and cognizance. They both propose that the singing voice be taken as the standard of an African American present absence in the economies of voice and mind in the United States. The singing voice superintends a moment original to configurations of voice and significance in the United States. This originality intercedes in and disturbs the dialectic of voice and silence governing American cultural production, contesting, as it does so, dominant forms of value. For one, it contests the notion that literacy – understood as the ability to read and write alphabetic script – provides the only significant means of voice for any culture and the only meaningful expression of the life of the mind, or the fundamental ties between "human rationality . . . [and] narrative structure and the quest for narrative unity" (Mark Johnson 172). Given this contradistinction to Western sensibilities and economies of voice, it stands above all as a "disturbance" of New World configurations of value, a disturbance decried by the West from the earliest moments of contact with African and African diasporic cultures:

> People from Western cultures historically have had a difficult time understanding anything African. Those who dislike African music respond to it in several ways. Some say that they are bored, that the music is so monotonously repetitive that it just dulls the sense. Others, alternatively, say that the music is so complicated rhythmically that they get confused and cannot make any sense of it. These people are likely to add that because they cannot figure out any pattern, they feel threatened that either the monotony or the confusion might take them over, and they do their best to ignore the unpleasantness. Less tolerant people have felt their sanity or their morals challenged, and in the past some of them even took the truly remarkable step of forbidding Africans to make music. (Chernoff 27–28)

The naming of the cultural expressivity of the African diasporic singing voice as a disturbance is easily traced in Western accounts of black communities settled in the New World, and the characterization can even be traced to accounts of the middle passage: In Jamaica in 1796, George Pinckard notes of Africans aboard a Guinea slave ship "bound to Savanna in Georgia" that "[t]heir song was a *wild* yell, *devoid of all softness and harmony,* and *loudly* chanted in *harsh* monotony" (Pinckard, 97–103, as quoted in Epstein, 10; emphasis added). Notations of the disturbing acoustic qualities of the diasporic singing voice often accompany the misrecognition of its cultural significance and its dismissal as a meaningful artefact. This misrecognition and dismissal, however, are often not cavalier. In New World slave societies the affront to Western aesthetic sensibilities often finds a further corollary in fears concerning the potential threat posed by the singing voice to Western sociality or polity. Some hundred and forty-two years before Pinckard makes his observations in Jamaica, "the first official attempt to suppress African dancing and instruments" had already taken place, when "the Conseil Souverain de Martinique issued an ordinance on May 4, 1654, prohibiting 'danses et assemblées de negres.' " As important as the early date of the decree is the fact that "[t]his sweeping prohibition, so contrary to the natural inclinations of the black population, apparently proved impossible to enforce" (Epstein 27). Somewhat contradictorily, the singing voice proves a disturbing announcement of the vacuity of African and African diasporic cultures but, nevertheless, also an announcement of a threat to Western societies and psyches.

In the United States' history, this characterization is reiterated again and again in the reactions of white Americans to the exuberance of the religious shout, the primary forum for the singing voice in the years when African American physical presence and discursive absence were most brutally and undisguisedly policed. In the opening chapter of his study *Slave Culture,* Sterling Stuckey presents at length testimonies of several white witnesses to the "ceremonial context" (27) of African American singing in the mid-nineteenth century. According to the accounts of the white spectators, the distinction between singing (and other *apparently aimless* utterances of the voice) and the apparently meaning-laden appropriations of the voice (or what I term signing) is not preserved in these ceremonials, but most often undone. Herein lies a great element of their disturbance. "The [African American] vocal style, encompassing charactersitics of West African traditions, is an extension of the Black preachers' style of developing sermons. Creating a cross between speech and song, the performer dramatizes his [or her] delivering with rhythmic moans, grunts, wails, shouts, glides, bends, dips, cries, hollers, vocables (words composed of various, possibly meaningless sounds), falsetto, and melodic repetition" (Maultsby 1985, 49). Put differently, during these ceremonies, the biblical "word" and "logos" itself appear strangely and originally disfigured to the spectators.

After witnessing a religious service in an exclusively black church in New Orleans, Fredrika Bremer, a South Carolina jurist, recalls:

> By degrees the *noise* increased in the church and became a storm of voices and *cries*. The words were heard, "Yes, come, Lord, Jesus! come oh come, oh glory!" and they who thus cried aloud began to leap. . . . Whichever way we looked in the church, we saw somebody *leaping* up and *fanning* the air; the whole church seemed transformed into a regular *bedlam*, and the *noise* and *tumult* was *horrible*. (as quoted in Stuckey 54; emphasis added)

Frederick Law Olmsted, also describing religious ceremonies in New Orleans, "a city noted for . . . public expressions of Africanity" (Stuckey 60), observes of another church meeting:

> The *tumult* often resembled that of an *excited political meeting;* and I was once surprised to find my own muscles all stretched, as if ready for a *struggle* – my face glowing and my feet stamping – having been affected *unconsciously*, as men often are, with *instinctive* bodily sympathy with the *excitement* of the crowd. (as quoted in Stuckey 61; emphasis added)

Olmsted writes about the singing in particular:

> I think every one joined, even the children, and the collective sound was *wonderful*. The voices of one or two women rose above the rest, and one of these soon began to introduce variations, which consisted mainly of *shouts* of oh! oh! at a *piercing* height. Many of the singers kept time with their feet, balancing themselves on each alternately, and swinging their bodies accordingly. (ibid.)

Thomas Wentworth Higginson, a colonel in the union army, finding himself in the Sea Islands of South Carolina and fascinated by the ring shout, describes those participating as

> singing *at the top of their voices*, in one of their quaint, *monotonous, endless*, negro-Methodist *chants*, with *obscure* syllables recurring constantly, and slight variations interwoven, all accompanied with a regular *drumming* of the feet and *clapping* of

the hands, like *castanets*. (as quoted in Stuckey 83; emphasis added)

Describing as well the dancing accompanying the "half bacchanalian, half devout" shouts and songs, Higginson continues:

> Some "heel and toe" *tumultuously*, others merely tremble and *stagger* on, others stoop and rise, others *whirl*, others caper sideways, all keep steadily circling like *dervishes*; spectators applaud special strokes of skill. (ibid.)

Edward Channing Gannett, writing for *The North American Review* at the conclusion of the Civil War, defines the ring shout similarly, as

> a *peculiar* service in which a dozen or twenty jog slowly round a circle behind each other with a peculiar *shuffle* of the feet and *shake* of arms, keeping time to a *droning* chant and hand-clapping maintained by by-standers. As the exercise continues, the *excitement* increases, occasionally becomes *hysterical*. Some religious meaning is attributed to it. (as quoted in Stuckey 85; emphasis added)

Driven by the frenetic union of voice and body, the peculiarity and originality of the African American religious performance disturb, in the eyes and ears of the white amanuenses, conventional notions of religious ceremony and meaningfulness. Their reports suggest an uproarous, exotic hubbub. The idiom of disturbance and confusion seems to designate activity in the absence of propriety, order, significance, and meaning. Stuckey's claim, however, and needless to say, the understanding of the African Americans participating in the religious shout, is that these ceremonies are powerfully resonant with meaning. Stuckey undertakes a rehearsal of their "orderliness" and of African "analogues" for these ceremonies, claiming for the analogues a powerful influence on U.S. culture in general. He proposes, in part, that "during and following slavery . . . the shout continued to form the principal context in which black creativity occurred" (95). He contends that the shout profoundly influences nascent jazz traditions soon to become "American" art forms. "The basis for the shout's flourishing in the North," he writes, "[is] laid by the great migrations of blacks from the South from the close of the nineteenth century to the 1940's and later. The implications of this movement are enormous not only for black religion but for American culture – a subject of great importance that awaits full exploration" (97). In short, rather than a designated absence of meaning, the religious shout and the centrally important singing voice stand as unexplored and undesignated sites of meaning. Another way of seeing this issue of undesignated meaning is to understand that, when African American spectators or participants provide reports of the interactions of the religious shout, these reports read very differently from those of Bremer, Olmsted, Higginson, and Gannett. Stuckey, for instance, points out the observations of Zora Neale Hurston and James Baldwin.

In *The Music of Black Americans: A History*, Eileen Southern explains the shout as a gathering that took place "after the regular [religious] service," which was composed of "two groups, shouters (that is, dancers) and singers. . . . The dancers participated in the singing according to how they felt. Sometimes they danced silently; sometimes they sang only refrains of the song; sometimes they sang the entire song along with the singers" (161). Southern makes clear that the shout was an occasion of varied but meaningful participation and that, although it was insistently marked by fervor, it was nonetheless an occasion defined by "strictly observed rules" (161). The shout presented enslaved African Americans with a primary respite and clearly structured retreat from the daily, extemporaneous tyrannies of enslavement in the United States and its legacy.

It is no exaggeration to state that the singing voice sounds one of the most enduring of African American testimonies to the exigencies of our presence in the Americas. This insight clearly underwrites Alice Walker's question and exhortation concerning the creative opportunities historically available to African American women, which, nevertheless, reveal an understanding of the complex ties between the singing voice as a preeminent form of African American cultural expressivity and the imposition of institutional illiteracy on African American communities during the period of their most undisguised violation in the United States. She acknowledges that the expressive importance of the singing voice in African American cultures is the upshot not only of survivals from West African cultures in which "[t]here are very few important things that happen without music" (Chernoff 34), but also of New World concepts and impositions of literacy and illiteracy understood as the ability or inability to read and write alphabetic script. Like African enslavement, a signal element of the emergence of Western modernity is a burgeoning importance assigned to literacy: "Over the last four hundred years reading and writing have been the primary skills by which Western civilization has expressed its consciousness of itself as a language-using organism" (Pattison 5). Thus, it is at the nexus of the philosophical assumptions and social practices clustered around the concept of literacy that one discovers an essential component of modernist Western programs "to redefine black identity by destroying their sense of humanity" as well as African American struggles to resist those programs. In short, from the dominant vantage, the prioritized status given literacy in Western cultural practice provides the mark of meaningfulness in relation to which the singing voice takes on its characterization as frivolous at best and meaningless at worst.

Overlooking the fact that the conditions of language-consciousness and of literacy understood as the ability to read and write alphabetic script are under no set of circumstances necessarily synonymous, the West conflates the two. Those who master literacy defined in Western terms stand within the circle of language-consciousness and, accordingly, full humanity. Those who do not, stand without. The exorbitance of this conflation in the Western mind is presupposed, it seems to me, by the phenomenon that Harvey J. Graff, a preeminent historian of Western literacy, terms the literacy myth: the belief that "[v]alue to the community, self- and socioeconomic worth, mobility, access to information and knowledge, rationality, morality, and orderliness are among the many qualities linked to literacy" (1979, xv). Innately tied to literacy, these qualities characterize, in turn, the individual and communities possessing literacy. Given this set of assumptions, great import in U.S. slave societies necessarily rests on the issue of who is and is not allowed access to this condition. The historian Janet Duitsman Cornelius in *When I Can Read My Title Clear: Literacy, Slavery, and Religion in the Antebellum South* makes the point succinctly:

> [W]hite Southerners in the late eighteenth and early nineteenth century were in a unique position: they sought to prevent enslaved African-Americans from learning to read just as mass literacy was being vigorously promoted in England and in the northern United States as a positive good, necessary for training the citizens of a republic and for accustoming the population to industrial routine. Their defensiveness at being out of step made white Southerners increasingly adamant against literacy for their own enslaved working population. (6)

However, despite a well-embedded set of cultural assumptions concerning literacy by the turn of the eighteenth century, the cultural position of the West's literacy myth is relatively new and its ascendancy clearly traceable. Three key episodes are the invention of mechanical book production in Mainz, Germany, in 1447; the Protestant Reformation of the sixteenth century, also beginning in Germany and introducing the first sweeping educational campaigns; and, two centuries later, the high cultural movement known as the Enlightenment. The Enlightenment yields, in the words of Graff, the "final ideological underpinnings for the 'modern' and 'liberal' reforms of popular schooling and institution building that established the network of educational, social, political, and economic relationships central to the dominant ideologies for the past 150 years" (1987, 14). The Enlightenment, as it does for many of its other elements, codifies for Western modernity its prevailing notion of and relationship to literacy.

A definitive Enlightenment spokesman, Immanuel Kant, provides one instance of this codification in his "Lectures on Pedagogy." In his introduction, Kant begins by citing the necessity of education to humans as one mark of the distinction between humanity and animality, for animals "employ their powers, as soon as they have any" (101), whereas humans must be trained to employ theirs properly. It quickly becomes clear that, in these meditations, Kant affords himself the opportunity to contemplate not only the situation of the individual human subject or pupil but also human capacities in general. He claims for literacy the status of a highly significant mark in the development of entire cultures; in a word, it signals the movement from barbarity to civilization: "We also find a very close adjacency to barbarity among very well civilized people in the earliest information they have left to us on record. But how much culture is already presupposed by writing! In regard to civilized people, the beginning of the art of writing can be called *the beginning of the world*" (115; emphasis added). The attainment of literacy is equivalent to the attainment of civilization, which is in turn equivalent to the gaining of proper, rational cognizance of the world. The achievement of literacy is tantamount to the attainment of (self-)-consciousness – individual and communal. One sees, then, in Kant's pronouncements that for the Western mind the belief that "[w]hatever human rationality consists in, it is certainly tied up with narrative structure and the quest for narrative unity" (Mark Johnson 172) is a belief premised on the underlying assumption that one gains *foremost* access to the rational markers of "narrative structure" and "narrative unity" through the mastery of alphabetic script.

Nevertheless, whereas Kant's formulations draw connections in abstract between "lesser" capacites of the human mind and literacy – between "savagery" and a respectable cultural awareness of the world – the French philosophe the marquis de Condorçet, also a late Enlightenment thinker, makes explicit the particulars of nation and/or race always implicit in Enlightenment thought and, accordingly, the thought of Western modernity. No matter how open or mediated, a disqualification or pathological bracketing of dark-skinned Others remains an invariable premise of both popular and learned traditions of Euro-American thought. Thus, in the final section of his 1793 "Sketch for a Historical Picture of Progress of the Mind," Condorçet asks: "Will all nations one day attain that state of civilization which the most enlightened, the freest, and the least burdened by prejudices, such as the French and the Anglo-Saxons, have attained already? Will the vast gulf that separates these peoples from the slavery of nations under the rule of monarchs, *from the barbarism of African tribes, from the ignorance of savages*, little by little disappear?" (141; emphasis added). "Africans" are placed on the other side of the gulf created by the attainment of literacy, placed without the circle of language-consciousness, without the sign that apparently marks the most fully human. Early in the nineteenth century, to the same end, in his *Lectures on the Philosophy of History* G.W.F. Hegel proposes that "[w]e must lay aside all thought of reverence and morality – all that we call feeling – if we would rightly comprehend ["the African"]; there is nothing harmonious with humanity to be found in ["the peculiarly African"] character. In Negro life the characteristic of point is the fact that consciousness has not yet attained to the realization of any substantial objective existence, – as for example, God, or Law, – in which the interest of man's volition is involved and in which he realizes his own being" (97).

It is important to consider this extreme understanding of literacy in relation to the broader contours of Enlightenment thought, a body of thought that highly esteems concepts of reason, rationality, as well as what the political theorist C. B. Macpherson in his important 1962 study codifies as "possessive individualism." The major texts of the Enlightenment appear between 1720 and the end of the eighteenth century and signal a period of intellectual activity among social theorists, philosophers, men of letters, and men of science primarily in England, France, and Germany, who undertake ambitious contemplation of the material world, human cognizance, nations and national characters, religion, civil obligation and organization, as well as what is understood as the cultured arts. As these interests imply, the paramount set of assumptions to which this period gives expression is the secularized worldview endemic to the modern West – secularization understood to denote a social, political, economic, philosophical positivism and pragmatism dependent on careful amendment of previous concepts of human subjectivity. The Enlightenment, or "age of reason," although it by no means initiates this secularization, naturalizes and instantiates its assumptions both in learned traditions and on a massive social scale (as, for example, in the French Revolution of 1789).

Very carefully qualified, democratization is an emergent principle of this period, and, because it so openly seeks to safeguard the *individual sovereignty* of members of national and social collectives, it is a revealing one, for one discerns in the principle of *individual sovereignty* a crucial element of modern Western thought, one extensively considered by Macpherson in *The Political Theory of Possessive Individualism,* his classic study of British social theorizing from Hobbes to Locke. The sweeping alteration in self-understanding and social organization Macpherson scrutinizes is the ascendency of an individual's self-proprietory relationship to the civil collective over the individual's position as the subject of externally imposed wills, whether sovereign or divine. As first theorized in the seventeenth century then codified in the eighteenth, human subjectivity is amended to reflect the idea that "[t]he essential humanity of the individual consisted in his freedom from the will of other persons, freedom to enjoy his own person and to develop his own capacities" (Macpherson 153). In other words, this reconceptualizing of human subjectivity brings into alignment three principles indispensable to the emerging market society of the West: property, self-sovereignty, and the law. To quote Macpherson at length:

[T]he individual . . . is free inasmuch as he is proprietor of his person and capacities. The human essence is freedom from dependence on the wills of others and freedom is a function of possession. Society becomes a lot of free equal individuals related to each other as proprietors of their own capacities and of what they have acquired by their exercise. Society consists of relations of exchange between proprietors. Political society

> becomes a calculated device for the protection of this prop-
> erty and for the maintenance of an orderly relation of ex-
> change. (3)

In short, *man* is postulated as having a natural right to himself protected by law, in the same way he has a natural right to property
also protected by law. Ownership of oneself (of one's potential to
labor, or to invest, and so on) becomes legally recognized property
that may be disposed of and exhanged in the marketplace.

The crux of the matter is not so simple and straightforward, however, for just as important as this initial postulation is a subsequent
intellectual sleight of hand made in deference to "the accumulation
of the means to produce wealth and the establishment of the political means to order society" (Caygill 91) around this priniciple.
This sleight of hand, which Macpherson first locates in Hobbes but
extends also to Locke, consists of reading the civil conditions of early
Western modernity back into an originary natural order or state of
natural man. To identify the natural order of things with the conditions of emergent bourgeois capitalism is to press for the validity
and inevitability of these conditions in the most powerful of ways.
That is, in the words of Macpherson, "[i]t was only in so far as the
behaviour of men in the hypothetical state of nature corresponded
to their necessary behaviour in society that deductions made from
the state of nature could have any validity for men already in (an
admittedly imperfect) society" (70). The spurious correspondence
between a distant natural condition and immediate social condition
works in the service of affirming a civil order in which "market
relations so shape or permeate all social relations that it may be
properly called a market society, not merely a market economy"
(48). Therefore, what passes in the codification of possessive individualism for human subjectivity proves merely a form of subjectivity
requisite for the orderly functioning of market societies: "As with
Hobbes, Locke's deduction starts with the individual and moves out
to society and the state, but, again as with Hobbes, the individual
with which he starts has already been created in the image of market
man" (269).

Terry Eagleton, in *The Ideology of the Aesthetic*, illuminates the necessity for this type of move in Enlightenment thought (and, of
course, also later):

> For a social order to demolish its own metaphysical foundation
> is to risk leaving its meanings and values hanging in empty

space, as gratuitous as any other structure of meaning; and how then are members of such an order to be persuaded of its authority? The urge to coopt reality by theoretical violence into one's own project may then prove well-nigh irresistible. (87)

Part of this irresistible theoretical violence consists, it seems to me, of the priority given literacy, because literacy emerges as an *instrumental* redaction of the revised human subject. Writing of the cultural meaning of the printed word in the eighteenth century, Marlon B. Ross claims, "We could say that print gradually seduced the mind into thinking of mental experience in terms of individual possession" (235). The privileging of literacy (with attendant notions of authorship and readership) strongly invites concepts of self-possession. If, by assuming the very condition of literacy, literate subjects embody and enact integral notions of communicable, commercial self-possession, which is the project of possessive individualism, then literacy becomes an important sign of a newly negotiated and exorbitant subjectivity passing for essential human subjectivity. In its capacity to tie "the private mind to public realities in a literally tangible way" (Ross 237), literacy draws into alignment – like the concept of possessive individualism itself – the three indispensable principles of property, self-sovereignty, and the law. This convergence is, of course, most glaringly evident in the form of the contract, with the sociolegal construction it places on the form of the signature. As particularly assumed in the form of the signature, literacy both becomes an instrumental redaction of "self-interested contractual relations with others" (Macpherson 275) and the visible and privileged sign of the possessive human subject.

The individual cursive script of the signature, as a redaction of literacy – which is in turn a redaction of the self-possessing subject – is a figure of special capacity in the service of the rights of property. The curious nexus of presence and absence, and of calculation and accord, known as the signature appears to represent, more than print, "the eccentricity of the individual whose steady or unsteady hand traces the marks . . . [,] marks of the soul within itself, for the hand that scripts the text marks the frailty of all flesh in the very materiality of the text" (Ross 232). Still, notwithstanding this appearance as the inalienable mark of a particular human subject, the signature remains in fact nothing more than a riddled – though widely accepted – convention. Jacques Derrida, in the famous first essay of *Limited Inc*, exposes the signature as such when he observes:

"In order to function, that is, to be readable, a signature must have a repeatable, iterable, imitable form; it must be able to be detached from the present and singular intention of its production. It is its sameness which, by corrupting its identity and its singularity, divides its seal" (20). In other words, rather than the inevitable and unquestionable mark of a singular human subject and intention, a signature is a formulaic text that must be reproducable by rote or on demand; therefore, by its very character, it is susceptible to misrepresentation or forgery. The elevating of the form of the signature and the seeming literacy of its progenitor to the status of the key repository and emblem of rational human subjectivity amounts to no more than ever so neatly equating "the beginning of the world" (Kant 115) with the dawn of civil relations, in which "[e]veryone is a possessor of something, if only of his capacity to labour [and] all are drawn in to the market [where] competition determines what they will get for what they have to offer" (Macpherson 57). Needless to say, the calculation of the beginning of the world provides the terms for subsequent rationality:

> The essence of rational conduct therefore is private appropriation of the land and the materials it yields, and investment of one's energies in improving them for the greatest conveniences of life one may thereby get for oneself. The industrious and rational is he who labours and appropriates. Such behaviour is rational in the moral sense of being required by the law of God or law of reason, as well as in the expedient sense. (233)

In brief, the interrelations among literacy and savagery and civilization proposed by Enlightenment thinkers such as Kant and Condorçet only register, in point of fact, distinctions between societies that enshrine the rights of property and those that do not. Even though presented as much broader, the claims of Kant and Condorçet are not. Their misleading and ambitious identification of human subjectivity with literacy is accomplished by means of the sleight of hand employed by Hobbes and Locke. The natural and progressive order of things is identified with the conditions of nascent bourgeois capitalism. The conditions of nascent bourgeois capitalism are read into sites and societies where they do not obtain, and, accordingly, cultural discrepencies are reconciled in the inevitable favor of the terms of bourgeois capitalism. Ethnographic tensions are translated conclusively into the terms of a simple symmetrical narrative,

and in this translation one witnesses the originary violence of formations of value. One sees that, "[b]ecause the disclosure of value
always dreams of consensus (conceived as a kind of separate peace)
it must deny not so much the reality of conflict as the *constitutive*
nature of conflict for any discourse of value" (Guillory 282; emphasis in original).

In the Western mind, the lack of literacy – understood in the
terms of the myth summarized by Graff and exemplified by Kant
and Condorçet – provides the strongest evidence of the marginal or
lesser human status of Africans and their descendants. Literacy becomes simultaneously the mark of African lack and Western mastery.
Such a configuration is sketched briefly in several essays by Henry
Louis Gates, Jr. Gates's most extensive analysis of the issue appears
in "Literary Theory and the Black Tradition." Drawing on statements by Hume ("Of National Characters"), Kant (*Observations on
the Feeling of the Beautiful and the Sublime*), and Hegel (*The Philosophy
of History*), among others, Gates outlines a Western certainty that
Africans and their descendants are excluded from the life of the
mind, a life understood above all in terms of literacy – which provides the most manifest and least ephemeral representation of the
life of the mind. He concludes that, given this state of affairs, "it is
obvious that the creation of formal literature could be no mean
matter in the life of the slave, since sheer literacy was the very commodity that separated animal from human being, slave from citizen,
object from subject" (1987, 24–25). Still, the matter never quite
addressed by Gates, but which Walker takes into account, is the notion that Western constructs of humanity and value are never wholly
untroubled either by their own dynamics or by dynamics "underwritten" by competing constructions of cultural presence and value.
The singing voice, as Walker suggests in her more penetrating formulation of the issue, remains one such alternative and powerful
construction in African American communities. Valerie Smith, with
a similar imperative in mind in *Self-Discovery and Authority in Afro-
American Narrative*, cautions those considering relations between literacy and blackness that to privilege heedlessly the notion of literacy
amounts "to pay[ing] homage to the structures of discourse that so
often contributed to the writer's oppression [and the oppression of
her or his community]" (6) in the first place. Smith admonishes
her readers that to reproduce without qualification a prioritizing of
literacy in African American responses to their oppression is simply
to reproduce ideological frameworks intended to dehumanize slave

communities, since such privileging "suggests that, without letters, slaves fail to understand the full meaning of their domination" (3). Gates's assessment, then, that "[w]e black people tried to *write* ourselves out of . . . a slavery even more profound than physical bondage" (1986, 12–13; emphasis added) provides insight into only one of many possible responses to the cultural dilemma he outlines – moreover, a response, one might argue, that most concedes the foundations of the hostile Western challenge underlying the dilemma. One might very easily imagine, instead, as does William Barlow in *"Looking Up at Down": The Emergence of Blues Culture,* that the very tensions between literacy and orality might themselves be exploited as another possible response to dehumanizing Western concepts of literacy. Barlow notes:

> The slaves' culture of resistance was articulated in their secular and sacred songs – as well as family histories, verbal games, folktales, aphorisms, proverbs, sermons, riddles, toasts, hexes, and jokes. Like the other components of the oral tradition, the songs illuminated the slaves' growing *consciousness* of their collective struggle for freedom during the antebellum period. The widespread existence of the slave songs and the "coded" messages they conveyed has been thoroughly documented in Dena Epstein's *Sinful Tunes and Spirituals: Black Folk Music to the Civil War* and John Lovell Jr.'s *The Forge and the Flame.* The evidence these books present demonstrates that spirituals and secular songs were an important part of the slave community's oral tradition and that that tradition was the engine *driving* their cultural resistance to slavery and white supremacy. (xi; emphasis added)

It is exactly this sense of a New World cultural dynamic that Walker captures so powerfully in her rhetorical interrogation of her readers.

In his recognition of the cultural significance of the question of literacy, on the other hand, Gates imagines a negotiation of the dilemma facing African Americans that in the historical moment he writes of is not available to the majority of them. His solution, ironically, excludes the majority of the population he identifies: "[w]e black people tried to *write* ourselves out of . . . a slavery even more profound than physical bondage." The "we" in Gates's formulation is a highly selective marker of nineteenth-century African American communities, so that his solution in many ways recapitulates the disenfranchisement he seeks to critique. This curious logic is extended even further by Ronald Judy in his *(Dis)Forming the American Canon: African–Arabic Slave Narratives and the Vernacular*. Even though he offers a much more substantive consideration of the cultural significance of literacy in relation to racial blackness than does Gates, Judy extends nonetheless a highly exclusive notion of an African American cultural response to the dilemma: "the humanization in writing achieved in the slave narrative" (92). Whereas Gates posits African Americans' acquiring English literacy as unsettling the racialized meaning of literacy, Judy proposes that a much greater challenge arises from "the Negro who was fluent in Arabic" because such literacy "flew in the face of the received conception of the Negro of Africa as a subhuman brute" (160), refuting the notion that learned culture "was in no way to be found indigenous in Africa" (160). Both Gates and Judy correctly imagine the assured disturbance of an African American entrance into the guarded and aggrandizing condition of literacy; however, neither poses any deep or sustained challenge to the concomitantly aggrandizing and disenfranchising notion of literacy. Neither, in characterizing African American responses to such circumstances, confronts and challenges

> the underlying assumption that where there is illiteracy there is no evidence of thought, which was one of the authoritative arguments for justifying the enslavement of Africans, an argument which runs something like: they had no literacy, therefore, could not be shown to have thought, which is an essential peculiar condition of humans, so they cannot be shown to be fully human. (104)

Conversely, from the vantage of those "in the dark" cultural sites symbolized by the singing voice provide, by standing without literacy and its apparent monopoly of meaning, a profound, widespread, and much more inclusive challenge to such assumptions. These cultural sites and the communities they represent assume and valorize alternative grounds of meaningfulness. In the terms of the theoretical model elaborated in Chapter I, these cultural sites stand as "Otherwise established forms" displaced or disfigured by the violent play and instantiation of dominant value: in this instance, the violent cultural play that conflates the terms *literacy, whiteness,* and *full humanity.* This play of dominant value would configure the singing voice and orality as negligible in official accountings of matters so that, despite its often-noted disturbing acoustics, the African American singing voice remains, more or less, a void or a space of silence in Western economies of value, voice, and mind. W. Ross Winterford, in his summation of the work of Eric Havelock, Jack Goody, and Ian Watt on literacy, characterizes as follows the modern contrast between orality and literacy:

> Oral language, said Havelock, is concrete, unsuited to abstract speculation and logic. Literacy, in contrast, not only enables abstract thought but demands it. Extending Havelock's thesis, Jack Goody and Ian Watt pointed out that written language is static – as I like to say an array in space – allowing one to scan backward and forward, to compare one utterance with another. Without this characteristic of written language, the sequentiality of logic and comparisons of one text with another to check veracity would be impossible. The logic of Aristotle, which is the basis for Western systematic thought, was the result of literacy. (15)

As an African American cultural artifact, the singing voice belies this estimation of matters and, because it openly refuses, as outlined here, "the basis for Western systematic thought," one can easily imagine its disturbance of dominant communities and configurations of value as inhering in far more than its vocal acoustics. As a central valorizing instrument of dispossessed communities, this refusal of the singing voice cannot be minimized; the singing voice is, in its own context and on alternative premises to "the basis for Western systematic thought," a site of the active production of meaning.

Yet, what is more, even as imagined by the Western mind, the standard contrast in value between oral and written cultural sites is never as strict as assumed. One is certainly led to this conclusion, for instance, by the value assigned the African diasporic singing voice in modern popular culture from its very beginnings to the present. A further way of recognizing this curiosity is to understand that, even though the boon of literacy is imagined in exceedingly broad terms by the Western imagination, the boon does not come without its price. Orality, for the modern mind, seems to possess a self-presence and immediacy regretfully forfeited by the abstract nature of literacy. Although literacy yields important social technologies and a *seemingly* greater presence of mind, it is also imagined as a second order experience only simulating an original and, hence, invariably fixing the literate mind in an indirect and alienated relationship to the natural world. This logic, neglecting the fact that "the phonic signifier is as conventional as the graphic" (Spivak, "Translator's Preface" xvii), inscribes orality within a romance of primitivism that posits orality as a sign of cultural naïveté or mindlessness akin to the undeveloped, artless, happily delusory intellectual state of childhood. Oral cultures are taken to exist, to borrow the words of Mariana Torgovnick, "in a cherished series of dichotomies: by turns gentle, in tune with nature, paradisal, ideal – or violent, in need of control, what *we* should emulate or, alternately, what *we* should fear" (3; emphasis added). In a similar vein, Walter Ong in *Orality and Literacy: The Technologizing of the Word* writes:

> A deeper understanding of pristine or primary orality enables us to better understand the new world or writing, what it truly is, and what functionally literate human beings really are: beings whose thought processes do not grow out of simply natural powers but out of these powers as structured, directly or indirectly, by the technology of writing. (78)

Orality, as a marker of lesser civilization and lesser human beings, is the object of a condescending, even if somewhat distantly envious, scrutiny.

Thus, upon close scrutiny, as with all privileged forms of value, literacy – the self-evident sign of Western mastery and African diasporic lack – appears not as a discrete noncontingency but as a powerful and deployed apparatus. In point of fact, literacy is not so removed from orality as one is often led to imagine, for "[a]ll cultures are by definition oral cultures. When [people] learn to write they do not then forget how to speak. Even with writing, much information – probably most information necessary for fundamental human activity – continues to be passed along solely by speech and held in the mind without written records" (Pattison 24). In short, literacy has more to do with the manipulation of arbitrary social bureaucracies than an elevated state of reason or rationality, and the same point can be made within the terms of various historical analyses, as Gerald Strauss's observations concerning the German Reformation illustrate:

> If there were two cultures, they interpenetrated so deeply and at so many points that neither could have flourished independently. . . . [T]he distinction between the learned and the laity was a function more of the offices to which formal eduction

gave admittance than of education itself. It was certainly not a product of literacy, which in any case was by all appearances much more widespread among the broad population than has been recognized. (96)

Literacy is not so much an innately elevating and honorific condition as, rather, a mechanism of social stratification in which powerful ideological apparatuses can be redacted – and alternately disturbed.

Considered even beyond the level of cultural production, the *singing voice* in its very physiology underscores the potential for this disturbance of matters of the *signing voice*. *Singing* amplifies generally overlooked and seemingly meaningless physical dimensions of the *signing voice*, or speech – the originary self-presence that the technology of literacy aims to recover, fix, and represent. These overlooked physical dimensions become plain as one considers that, "[w]hen not speaking, the time to inhale and the time to exhale is [*sic*] roughly equal, and this is true whether relaxing or strenuously exercising. However, when speaking, the time to inhale can be as short as one fifth of a second and the time to exhale can be as long as twenty seconds" (Handel 133). The *singing voice* foregrounds and plays upon bodily dimensions of vocal action usually taken for granted. One's relation to the production of speech is radically altered: Speech, or the *signing voice,* is emptied and reconfigured, because the apparent incorporeal immediacy of voice itself is starkly betrayed as a bodily one – not spiritual or ineffable.

On the contrary, Western thought, entrenched in what Derrida terms logocentric metaphysics, takes for granted "the supposedly *underived* immediacy of speech and presence" (Ryan 28; emphasis added). Speech is posited as the primary sign of a transcendent spirit ontologically separate from but superintending the merely secondary or supplementary realm of the body. Speech is privileged over other forms of communication because of its seemingly unique proximity to – and therefore special ability to represent – the mind and spirit from which the communication is issuing. Speech (the production of what I am calling the *signing voice*) becomes in the Western mind the "mode of spirituality" (Ryan 29), the originary mode of human presence. It is "natural, good, and original because it is the medium of the voice of consciousness in its self-presence" (27). The mind and spirit seem to find no deferral or intermediary between themselves and their communication and, given this understanding, the monopolizing of speech (and its technologies) would seem to amount to monopolizing a chief element of the most fully human, a chief element of the *exclusive* human spirit privileged over the body – and especially the most *unsightly* of bodies, African American bodies.

Because it reaffirms voice as a bodily presence, the singing voice amends immaterial conceptualizations of vocal action. It resoundingly announces vocal action in the body, a signal cultural moment and revision for those who would be confined, according to dominant wisdom, to the supplementary realm of the body. Singing in its physicality reclaims the voice for the body. It suggests that all vocalizing is deeply embedded in and profoundly affects the physiological workings of the body. For these reasons, the complexity of the physiological operations of voice are worth noting:

> During normal breathing, the vocal cords are held apart. When speaking [or singing] is about to begin, the cords are brought together. The high pressure resulting from the airflow from the lungs forces the cords apart, which allows air to move up into the vocal tract. The vocal cords still present a narrowing of the vocal tract, so the air pressure at this point is lower in the surrounding area. This creates a "suction" (the Bernoulli effect) that tends to draw the vocal cords together. . . . In addition to the Bernoulli force, the muscular tension of the cords themselves also acts to reclose the opening. Because the cords are initially together, the separation caused by the airflow induces a muscular force to bring them back together. The two forces acting in synchrony overcome the airflow pressure separating the cords, reclose the vocal cords, and the oscillation begins again. (Handel 137)

By celebrating the complex materializing of voice, the singing voice highlights the nontranscendent imperatives of speaking, and the paramount aesthetic of African American vocal performance is the insistent foregrounding of this materiality, so that the disruption and refunctioning of routine bodily activity emerge as central performatives of both its production and its reception. The propensity is to underscore the acoustic and affective materiality of all linguistic signs. Traditionally, African diasporic vocalists

> bring intensity to their performance by alternating lyrical, percussive, and raspy timbres; juxtaposing vocal and instrumen-

tal textures; changing pitch and dynamic levels; alternating straight with vibrato tones; and weaving moans, shouts, grunts, hollers, and screams into the melody. (Maultsby 1990, 92)

This revisionary allowance of the singing voice depends chiefly upon suspension of meaningfulness understood *singularly* as the fixed and static sign, a suspension readily apparent in virtually all African American vocal performances, and most especially, and most vividly, in a blues and jazz tradition in which scatting abandons meaningful speech altogether and turns freely and ludically to the charged instrumentality of voice – an Other, novel realm of meaning.[2] In the context of this tradition, the ludic corporeality of the singing voice suggests that the dominant act of monopolizing voice amounts not so much to monopolizing meaningfulness itself as the transcendent symbol of the most fully human but, instead, the monopolizing of a particular kind of bodily production – the capacity of the body and of a culture to engage in a particular kind of work that is, in turn, a particular kind of self-representation. It amounts to an attempt to monopolize no more than the power of speech and literacy as tied to a *civic* vision in which "property might be seen as the foundation and determinant of social and political personality" (Pocock 122).

For these reasons it is imperative not to conceive of the legacy of the diasporic singing voice within the terms of the romance of primitivism alluded to earlier; precisely what the circumstances of diasporic Africans emphatically preclude is living within the bounds of a cultural simplicity akin to the artless and delusory intellectual state of childhood. Early in his 1963 study of the place and meaning of music in the development of African American (as opposed to African) cultures, Leroi Jones – aka Amiri Baraka – pointedly makes this observation when he "insist[s] that the African, because of the violent differences between what was native and what he [or she] was forced to in slavery, developed some of the most complex and complicated ideas about the world imaginable" (7). The complexities and achievements of this imagination are by no means diminished simply because they do not readily resemble dominant estimations of speech and literacy, the emblems by which the modern West seeks most fiercely to imagine presence of mind and sophistication of thought. *It is not the case that African Americans are wholly precluded from meaning and the voicing of meaning – for the power of white Americans does not and cannot extend nearly so far – rather, African Amer-*

icans must pursue novel or original access to meaning, voice, value, and authority. More simply put, speaking – like Frederick Douglass, LeRoi Jones (Amiri Baraka), Alice Walker, and Sterling Stuckey of the potent meanings of African American singing voices – W.E.B. DuBois writes in *The Souls of Black Folk*: "In these songs [African-American spirituals], I have said, the slave spoke to the world. Such a message is naturally veiled and half articulate" (270).[3] By means of the singing voice, the African American articulates a "soft, stirring melody in an ill-harmonized and unmelodious land" (275), a land in which she or he is presented violently and above all with the impossibility of voice. Eileen Julien in her study *African Novels and the Question of Orality* reminds her readers of the close ties between orality, cultural authority, and power in African contexts, an alignment that challenges any oversimple equation of orality with a romance of primitivism or necessary innocence. She writes:

> We tend to think of oral traditions as universally egalitarian
> because every human being is endowed with voice and because
> writing and print are technologies that require special training
> and resources, but, in fact . . . the [African] griot is in a posi-
> tion of power. . . . His message is proffered when and to whom
> he wishes to proffer it and is designed to suit the needs of the
> authority he serves. . . . Not everyone will or can be heard. Nei-
> ther voice nor print, then, is exempt from political persuasion
> and pressure. (14–15)

Similarly, though in a very different context, the ethnomusicologist Mellonee V. Burnim, writing of gospel music, a twentieth-century development of nineteenth-century spirituals, elaborates the issue as follows: "Critics of gospel music hold the common misconception that because the predominant sound quality of gospel violates virtually every ideal associated with Euro-American vocal production, gospel music is, therefore, devoid of a rational system" (154). Burnim questions the widespread presupposition that Western systems and modes of representation monopolize rationality and mindfulness.

Abrogating this precept allows one to understand fully that the emotional or playful intracacies of African American vocality are much more than simply rude or playful, a point made about African American voices in general by James Weldon Johnson in the sober and sly preface to the seven folk sermons of *God's Trombones*. In this preface Johnson constructs a juxtaposition between commonly stereotyped "Negro dialect" and the elevated "idioms of King James English." He does so as he enumerates his reasons for not rendering the forthcoming sermons in dialect:

> The old-time Negro preachers, though they actually used dialect in their ordinary intercourse, stepped out from its narrow confines when they preached. They were all saturated with the sublime phraseology of the Hebrew prophets and steeped in the idioms of King James English, so when they preached and warmed to their work they spoke another language, a language far removed from traditional Negro dialect. It was a fusion of Negro idioms with Bible English. (9)

As it turns out, by describing a remarkable rift of language that African Americans are able to bridge dextrously and regularly, Johnson undermines the clichéd notions of African American discourse and primitivism obstructing his project. As do the eloquence and vision of the prayer and seven sermons following his preface, Johnson empties oppressive expectations and dominant configurations of speech in the U.S. landscape in order to introduce "another language" usually dismissed as merely unsophisticated and rude; he credits this other language with forging an intricate, unrecognized "fusion" that he forces his reader, at least, to consider. He accomplishes this task by avoiding dialect altogether and, thereby, the risk of its condescending dismissal by his reader. He champions the notion that the heightened voice of the engaged preacher succeeds at a task neither taken up nor even imagined by those within the "narrow confines" of the dominant dialects of English. Moreover, the charged, preaching African American voice, usurping the most eloquent idioms of the English language, is marked by what Johnson calls intoning or "a matter of crescendo and diminuendo in the intensity – a rising and falling between plain speaking and wild chanting . . . [in which] a startling effect is gained by breaking off suddenly at the highest point of intensity and dropping into the monotone of ordinary speech" (10). As recognized by Pearl Williams-Jones, this is a performance allied in many ways to that of the singing voice: "In seeking to communicate the gospel message, there is little difference between the gospel singer and the gospel preacher in the approach to his subject. The same techniques are used by the preacher and the singer – the singer perhaps being considered the lyrical extension of the rhythmically rhetorical style of the preacher" (381). This is not merely to say that the dynamic intricacies of intoning reveal the fact that the African American speaking voice resembles and is imbued with the singing voice but, rather, to acknowledge the extent to which African Americans approach and assume the speaking voice – and in this instance the "word" of Western Christianity – through an incipient preoccupation with what might be imagined as the *alterity* of the singing voice: "Inherent [to both peformances] . . . is the concept of black rhetoric, folk expressions, bodily movement, charismatic energy, cadence, tonal range and timbre" (381). Summarily stated, because the *singing voice* invariably revises the *signing voice*, it marks a point of exorbitant originality for African American cultures and expressivities.

The *singing voice*, by its peculiar indirection, stands as a primary means of undermining and revising the unacceptable cultural imperatives of dominant *signing voices* in New World landscapes. This alterity of the singing voice finds partial exposition in Jacques Derrida's critique of the "transcendence" and "idealization" ascribed to voice and speech in Husserl's phenomenology. Derrida rehearses, in order to show that signs would be superfluous to Husserl's philosophical project, the idealized and intuitional self-presence of what Husserl calls "expression" (meaningfulness). "Expression" is understood as independent of and *presenting* what Husserl terms its worldly "indication." According to Derrida, the self-presence implied by this transcendent coincidence of "expression" and "indication" would require neither sign nor signification. For self-presence operates "without having, at least apparently, to pass through the world" (1973, 75).[4] Thus, for Husserl, the essential *meaning* of speech and the voice mistakenly lies entirely outside the materiality of the sound that produces them or of any other worldly element. Derrida counters Husserl's mistaken reasoning by reiterating that speech and the voice, in order to be speech and the voice, must in fact always "pass through the world." In a word, Derrida gainsays Husserl's underprivileging of the *sound* of speech and the voice – precisely the action of the African American singing voice. In this way, Derrida's claims serve curiously to illuminate the physiological dynamics openly exposed by the African American singing voice as well as its disruptive force as a sociohistorical presence in the Enlightenment West.

Still, Derrida's correction of Husserl falls substantially short of the corrective supplied by cultures of the singing voice. African American singing voices not only point out but emphatically charge with significance the underprivileged sound, or means, by which voicing "pass[es]" through the world." Unlike Husserl's speech and Derrida's antinomian silence, the African American singing voice emphasizes – rather than merely glances at – the spatial, material, dative, or enunciative action of voice. Singing voices undo voice as speech per se. By highlighting the enunciative or vocative aspect and moment of voice, singing voices mark the *absence* that allows iteration and repetition. They imprint above all the pure sonorous audibility of voice, and not a seemingly absolute proximity to fixed meaning and identity. Singing voices iterate or repeat nothing per se, because speech is declined insofar as they do not singularly intend to effect, or direct, the meaningful word but first of all to affect, display, or deploy – even displace – the meaningful word. Consider again Frederick Douglass's retrospective understanding of enslaved African Americans singing "unmeaning jargon . . . which, nevertheless, [is] full of meaning to themselves" (31). Singing voices emphasize the *infinitude* of "unmeaning" that presupposes and inaugurates signification. Like the French social philosopher Georges Bataille's *sovereignty*, which is posited as original and negative to Hegelian lordship,[5] singing is the peculiar moment original and negative to speech. It is an obverse correlate of the sign[6] and of lordship. Because they are primarily voice as sound and material, singing voices occlude voice as a transcendental value prior to form, or as an idealized iterability approximating spacelessness in time.

In summary: The sign is iteration; iteration is closure; closure is power; and the singing voice, for the diasporic African, undoes all three in a landscape in which iteration, closure, and power belie her or his presence.[7] Having a "different" appeal to the ear, the singing voice removes the priority of signification by dis-quieting, or as stated earlier, disturbing the *presence* of signification. The *presence* of signification is supplanted by the *absence* of signification for, in lieu of meaningfulness, the singing voice displays the meaninglessness, the apparently "unmeaning" sound, that enables *the* voice and *the* idealized sign to occur. To invoke Bataille again, one might say, singing is the unrestricted expenditure of speech; it paralyzes and discharges speech and, as Derrida writes of the supplement of the origin, it "substitute[s] [itself] for another signifier, for another type of signifier that maintains . . . [an authorizing] relationship with the deficient presence [i.e., the supplement], one more highly valued by virtue of the play of difference" (1973, 89). This more highly valued but deficient presence in the New World is the self-proclaimed, self-evident value of "white" skin, a highly valued but deficient presence because its value is maintained only through an inexorable mediation of the Other through *signs* of lordship. Hence, the *singing voice* represents the enabling, antinomian third moment of a dialectic seeking to refuse it.

Singing voices mark counterpresences, countercultures, and counterliteracies so that, as opposed to the signing voice, they compose the primary legacy of African diasporic populations.[8] Singing (even its spelling ludically disturbs "sign/signing") remains, one might say, a peculiarly African American possession in New World landscapes. In the same way they constitute acoustic disturbances, singing voices announce a crisis in New World economies of voice – New World economies of the sign, rationality, racial genius, as well as psychic and social agency. In their disturbance of the already scripted significance of *signing voices* and of literacy, singing voices reopen the very issue of making *sense* in the New World. What one comprehends when one attends to the history, exigencies, and performitivity of the African American signing voice is the interconnectedness of two conditions that necessarily challenge privileged order: first, the *mindful* existence of groups outside the bounds of a dominant sign system (and its attendant political and social configurations); second, alternative resources for measuring and calculating human value. The issue of counterliteracies is, at bottom, one of social obedience, as Robert Pattison points out through his insight into contemporary concerns about functional illiteracy: "The presence in the midst of our society of a large group of people who because of a lack of basic skills cannot respond to written information imperils the existing order of society just as certainly as if the same group consciously chose to disobey or ignore this information. The final result is the same: a failure of social obedience" (Pattison 179). In other words, among the most significant functions of literacy are mediating, disseminating, and enforcing the prescriptives of sanctioned civic identity and practice. Consequently, the act of giving preeminence to social meaning that lies elsewhere amounts to initiating a challenge to sanctioned identity and practice.

That the African American singing voice redacts an alternative cultural logic in this way and, in doing so, an imperative cultural contestation is made clear, for example, by reactions of the U.S. cultural establishment to so many forms of African American musical expressivity, such as coon-music, ragtime, the blues, rhythm and blues, nascent rock and roll, and, at present, rap.[9] Particularly informative is the reaction to the overwhelming influence and popularity of nascent jazz in the 1920s. Defined by the music historian Frank Tirro as "the music that came into being through the African-American experience in the southern part of the United States during the late nineteenth century and . . . at the turn of the century" (99), early jazz happens to be the African American musical form coinciding with the appearance of the major technological innovations responsible for inaugurating, defining, and fixing mass media popular culture. A partial list of these innovations includes the development of the phonograph in 1887, the advent of primitive radio technology also in 1887 with significant developments in 1906 and 1912, the arrival of patented movie-viewing technology in 1891, the first mass production of short moving pictures in 1894, the first "story picture" in 1903 (*The Great Train Robbery*), the first two-dollar movie in 1915 (*The Birth of a Nation*), modern radio broadcasting and programming in 1920, experimental frequency-modulated (FM) transmissions in 1934, and the construction of the first television transmitting station in 1935.[10] Summarily stated, jazz emerges coincidentally with mass mediated cultural forms and technologies that begin to set the agenda for a singular recreational and social imagination uniting U.S. populations and geographies. Keeping in mind that the overwhelming power of twentieth-century popular culture lies in its "public-ity," one immediately sees that whatever it chooses *to make public* becomes a matter of important social concern. Twentieth-century mass culture forges public identities that tie all those under its sway to the marketplace and the easily recognizable and accessible commodities of the marketplace at the most intimate and minute levels of desire. Accordingly, the African American singing voice – made available for mass consumption in startlingly authentic form by these advances – introduces disturbing social, verbal, and bodily performances into the most intimate and minute domains of civic and personal identity formation. At the cultural moment of its emergence, jazz is understood – whether by those of the dominant culture embracing or reviling it – as a "specific symbol of rebellion and of what was new about the decade" (Ogren 6). It is attacked, therefore, "as 'noise,' and compared . . . to a plague or disease threatening to destroy the civilized world. Most criticisms clustered around moral, aesthetic, or professional values challenged by jazz" (153).

These virulent reactions to disseminated African American cultural forms take aim at the exemplary *transformative* power they hold for modern culture at large. Revealing as much, the social historian Lewis Erenberg summarizes as follows one important dimension of the reaction against the culture of jazz and the cabarets to which it gave life:

> Of all the caberet's activities, the public character of dancing aroused the bitterest and most prolonged attacks. To reformers, the close physical contact and body expression connoted loss of self-control. The lifting of legs, the jerking of shoulders represented an unreserved demeanor on the part of youth and womanhood in general. The fact that respectable women danced forms originating among inferiors, sensual blacks and Latins, moved critics to envision the enshrinement of undisguised sexuality and lower-class behavior. . . . Here was uncontrolled inundation by inferior peoples and the abandonment of civilized restraint. (81)

As does the African American singing voice in general, jazz production and reception play provocatively upon the materiality of the body, emphasizing a meaningful experience of the body and a relationship of identity to the body not easily co-opted by the approved imperatives of script.

Indeed, at stake in many ways is the peculiar configuration of individual sovereignty characterized earlier as crucial to the concept of modern Western subjectivity. For jazz – and the African American singing voice in general – reserves in the public or civic domain a configuration of the body fundamentally alien to its pronounced configuration as property open to contractual exchange in a capitalist marketplace. The capacity of the body to labor (as either voice or kinetic force) is made violently self-referential, insofar as its capacity to labor is not exchanged or transferred anywhere outside the ludic extemporaneous jazz performance.[11] Just as the attendant African American performance of dance openly redirects one's capacity to work, the singing voice redirects one's capacity to speak. In a landscape in which African American presence is initially premised on ruthlessly exacted labor, dance seems a singularly important activity in which immanently resistant communality is expressed and achieved insofar as the capacity of the body to work is taken and dispersed "uselessly." Similarly, the singing voice redirects one's capacity to make sense where mediums of sense are most often monopolized to alienating ends. Dance, as it ludically redirects the

capacity of the body to work, exchanges the alien "value" inherent
in the status of chattel (or outsider) for the "value" of a resistant
self that finds no self-recognition in officially sanctioned "work."
Dance, this is to say, can be understood as one means of establishing
the *rule* of the self in circumstances that provide very little opportunity to do so. Like the singing voice, it can be considered a sub-
versive African American sign for the most intimate control of one's
body, self, community, and expressivity. In dance, the capacity to
work is recreated in a novel, subtly meaningful and satisfying form.
In a landscape in which not only legal and legislative systems but
also mediums of sense operate to disbar African Americans, it provides an imperative model for recognizing African American appropriations of sound. As the singing voice proves the indirection of
speaking and of *serious* sensibility, dance proves the indirection of
work. This is not to say that *in the first place* the intent of dance is to
initiate challenges to capitalist ideological tenets of work and the
body, but it is to say emphatically that dance as it is valued in African
American communities inevitably reveals the necessary *contrivance* of
those tenets. The characteristics of African American dance, like
those of the African American singing voice, place one clearly outside a set of primarily self-proprietory and possessive contractual relations:

> The basic characteristics of African dance, with its gliding,
> dragging, shuffling steps, its flexed, fluid bodily position as op-
> posed to the stiffly erect position of European dancers, its im-
> itations of such animals as the buzzard and the eagle, its
> emphasis upon flexibility and improvisation, its concentration
> upon movement outward from the pelvic region which whites
> found so lewd, its tendency to eschew bodily contact, and its
> propulsive, swinging rhythm, were perpetuated for centuries in
> the dances of American slaves and ultimately affected all Amer-
> ican dance profoundly. (Levine 16)

In short, the body that jazz *de-scribes* in public and civic spaces belies,
rather than underscores, the morality and rationality of individuality
and individual contractual possession conceived in terms of aliena-
ble labor.

Nonetheless, it is important to recognize that individuality, like
its analogue the signature, is a premium ignored only at great civic
peril. Of necessity, the "capitalist form of political relations [initially
configured], rapidly and abruptly, in the last years of the seventeeth

century and the two decades following" (Pocock 69) always recuperates individuality and its implied individual as paramount points of cathexis. To neglect or defy this legacy of individuality and the individual, as do the African American singing voice and its analogues, is to court strict repudiation by the post-Enlightenment mind even as it contemplates aesthetics. This is unmistakably the case with T. W. Adorno in the very famous 1938 essay "On the Fetish-Character in Music and the Regression of Listening," in which he deprecates popular music. Repeatedly lamenting that "[t]he liquidation of the individual is the real signature of the new musical situation" (276), Adorno perceives jazz and its influences as dehumanizing since they are the foremost forms of the new musical situation. In his view, the problem is that jazz and "the whole jazz business" (278) bring virulently to music the alienating processes and effects of capitalist commodification, creating conditions whereby "[i]mpulse, subjectivity, and profanation, the old adversaries of materialistic alienation, now succumb to it" (273). That is, "[i]n capitalist times, the traditional anti-mythological ferments of music conspire against freedom" (278). The commercial and cultural success of jazz forcefully signals the moment when "the age-old sacral function of music as the locus for the taming of impulses" (297) is supplanted by empty transactions in which "[t]he feelings which go to the exchange value [of an object] create the appearance of immediacy at the same time as the absence of a relation to the object belies it" (279). In other words, people marvel at their ability to acquire the latest and most sought after objects and experiences, rather than establishing mindful relations to the objects and experiences themselves. Forfeiting individuality, they discover in music only a posture or relation that constitutes them as a mass of compulsive consumers. The individual, even in what should be a liberating relation to music, is subordinated to and hopelessly lost in the circulation of commodities and capital. Masses of people thus

> call themselves jitterbugs, as if they simultaneously wanted to affirm and mock their loss of individuality, their transformation into beetles whirring around in fascination. Their only excuse is that the term jitterbugs, like all those in the unreal edifice of films and jazz, is hammered into them by the entrepreneurs to make them think that they are on the inside. Their ecstacy is without content. That it happens, that the music is listened to, this replaces the the content itself. The ecstacy takes pos-

session of its object by its own compulsive character. It is stylized like the ecstasies savages go into in beating the war drums.
It has convulsive aspects reminiscent of St. Vitus' dance or the
reflexes of mutilated animals. (292)

In this central passage, which invokes the disqualifying Western
shorthand of primitivism and animality, Adorno's language and de-
nunciation become almost hysterical. Nevertheless, these are not the
most salient matters to be noticed. More importantly, one needs to
register the way in which the central term of Adorno's analysis betrays the objectives of the analysis. The result is that Adorno widely
misplaces his critique. Overlooking its intimate connection to the
sociopsychic relations he hopes to resist, Adorno posits that remaining faithful above all to the prized matter of "individuality" moves
one along a line of greater – *not lesser* – resistance to sterile relations
in which "the fetish character of the commodity" necessarily pre-
dominates and "the quantum of possible enjoyment has dis-
appeared" (278). Adorno decries the fact that "the listener is
converted along [her or] his least line of resistance, into the acqui-
escent purchaser" (273). Certainly, Adorno is correct in discerning
what he bemoans as "the theological caprices of commodities"
(280) in the characteristic social interactions of modern society, but
he is just as certainly mistaken in believing that the line of *least*
resistance to this type of interaction is somehow intrinsic to the ki-
netics of jazz performance and reception. On the contrary, in very
large part, the line of least resistance inheres in the very concept of
individuality he wields as a standard and refuses to relinquish. More
than to the particularities of jazz, the social dynamics he decries are
tied to notions of individuality that presume that "a man's energy
and skill are his own, yet are regarded not as integral parts of his
personality, but as possessions, the use and disposal of which he is
free to hand over to others for a price" (MacPherson 48). In sum,
Adorno unaccountably inverts the relation between jazz culture and
the constitutive forces of market relations that commodify and dis-
seminate jazz (and many other commodities) to populations already
conscripted as avid and practiced consumers and capitalist subjects.
Unaccountably, Adorno conflates the evils of capitalist existence *foremost* with jazz culture. One should eschew his misstep, however, and
recognize that a "[p]ossessive market *society* . . . implies that where
labour has become a market commodity, market relations so shape
or permeate all social relations that it may properly be called a mar-

ket society, not merely a market economy" (48; emphasis in original). The culprit is much more the notion of individuality that Adorno prizes and that is ideologically indispensable to possessive market societies than the jazz to which he takes violent exception. By no reasonable account can Adorno justifiably center his critique of the dehumanizing fetishism of market society in "the stubborn counting of beats" (280) he associates with jazz. This is not to say that the commodities offered to the public by the music industry (jazz or otherwise) do not contribute to and perpetuate the social relations of capitalism; it is only to state, as a corrective, that they neither initiate nor form the prime locus of these relations, as Adorno would seem to have it.

Put differently, Adorno demands from what he perceives as troublesome jazz culture the feat of wholly repudiating or standing outside the unsatisfactory dynamics of capitalist social configurations. He oddly burdens jazz culture with the task that neither the most "traditionally" learned, the most politically astute, nor the most militant of modern efforts has yet accomplished. What is more, Adorno completely misses the antagonistically transformative relations that jazz and the African American communities from which it arises have to Western market societies – that, upon examination, prove the actual objects of his denunciations. It is entirely correct to claim that jazz, its cultural analogues, and the communities from which they arise have by no means rebutted or annihilated the social relations of market societies, but it is equally imperative to acknowledge that they have managed unmistakably to infuse their recognizable characters into these market societies, when precisely such an eventuality has been vehemently resisted from the first. To repeat an important point, in the same way it provides an important means of disrupting the symbolic appropriation of speech from which African Americans are excluded, so the singing voice provides a primary means by which African Americans may exchange expended, "valueless" selves in the "New World" for productive, recognized selves. African American cultural influences remain, for example, at the center of the social upheavals that occasion "[t]he shift from entertainment in a private, formal setting to a more informal, public arena mark[ing] a movement away from Victorian gentility" (Erenberg xiii). To its dismay, and to this day, the United States finds itself in many ways an "africanized" nation. Ralph Ellison makes this point powerfully and succinctly in "The World and the Jug": "[W]hatever the efficiency of segregation as a socio-political arrangement, it has been far from absolute on the level of *culture*. Southern whites cannot walk, talk, sing, conceive of laws or justice, think of sex, love, the family or freedom without responding to the presence of Negroes" (116; emphasis in original). One can very easily imagine – by turning on the radio or television, or simply noticing the dress of suburban youth – that this situation is far from regional. For these reasons, Adorno could not be more mistaken in his observations than when he opens his famous essay by stating that popular music as represented by jazz "seems to complement the reduction of people to silence, the dying out of speech as expression, the inability to communicate at all. It inhabits the pockets of silence that develop between people molded by anxiety, work and undemanding docility" (271). Completely to the contrary, the African American singing voice and musical production provide, if anything, as the foregoing argument of this chapter attempts to outline, a fundamental means for African American populations to extricate themselves from harshly imposed and dehumanizing silences. Insofar as they provide alternative management of information, the somatics and logic of the African American singing voice both open up and resettle the question of "value" as it is formulated within the circumstances of the "New World."

In his essay, Adorno clearly – and, in the end, illogically – recapitulates this question of value in its most alienating form. This form is a routine dismissal or vilification of African American prescience, agency, and self-performance, a vilification stated unaccountably, in this instance, in terms of the crippling sociopsychological consequences of capitalist subjectivity. However, as routinely as such management of the question of value articulates propositions to annul the evidence and the potency of African American cultural presence, the project betrays itself. Such efforts only yield, at best, a peculiar vision of African American communities as paradoxical *present absences* proving, nonetheless, nodal points of "New World" self-consciousness.

The historian Nell Irvin Painter, in the process of making keen and helpful criticisms of the work of a fellow historian, Michael O'Malley, states the whole matter in an extremely provocative way. The exhange between Painter and O'Malley appears in the April 1994 issue of *American Historical Review*, in which O'Malley aims to examine "the tension between the ideal of freedom in self-making and the comfort of fixed identity as it appeared in debates about money, value, citizenship, and race between 1830 and 1900" (371).

Painter's most pointed criticisms of this article, "Specie and Species: Race and the Money Question in Nineteenth-Century America," concern O'Malley's overlooking the fact that "[t]he racial side of the equation of race and money is less figurative than the monetary." Painter argues that O'Malley inadequately explores the ways in which enslaved African American bodies concomitantly serve as the debased physical engines of the economy as well as abstracted signs of worth circulating within the economy. That is, O'Malley neglects the fact that "[b]efore 1865, the vast majority of African Americans were, literally, property, and . . . served simultaneously as an embodied currency and a labor force."[12] Thus, for enslaved African Americans the issue O'Malley explores only as metaphor is not metaphorical at all: "Enslaved persons, along with real estate, were property subject to exchange, and, as such, they undergirded the economies of eighteenth-century New York City as well as that of nineteenth-century southern states" (398).

The peculiar issue of the alienating question of value is raised here in starkly materialist and illuminating terms by Painter. That is, it is paradoxically the very valuelessness assigned to African American bodies that enables them to stand as the ground on which speculations of and concerning value are made. Because African Americans are positioned outside the value of the fully human, they become instruments and signs by which great value is produced and measured. In sum, the valuelessness of African Americans is always proclaimed *unreasonably* in the *name* of value. In the same way that this paradox patently defines the material terms of the U.S. slaveholding regime as pointed out by Painter, so too it characterizes the social theorizing of Adorno and innumerable others, whether in learned or popular traditions. Both materially and immaterially, as it turns out, African Americans and their self-performances prove crucial sites at which valuelessness and value conflate. Upon examination, it becomes vivid that a subtle and slyly empowering mark of this conflation for African Americans is the singing voice. Disrupting and intervening in the seemingly closed economy of value, the singing voice and its agents highlight and play upon the convergence, contingency, and compromised boundaries of value and valuelessness.

3

(FURTHER) FIGURES OF VIOLENCE: THE STREET IN THE U.S. LANDSCAPE

The enduring paradox of the concomitantly valueless and valuable status of African Americans in the dominant cultural imagination of the United States is well presented in the opening pages of *The Wages of Whiteness* by the historian David R. Roediger, who describes the efficacy and ubiquity of African American communities as *present absences*. Even as African Americans are taken as exemplary signs of the absence of a variety of human attributes and social proprieties (not to mention being enforced as physically absent from certain sociopolitical spheres), African American communities remain centrally present to and for the identity that dismisses them. The acknowledgment of such supplementarity is, of course, by now a commonplace of poststructuralist understanding – however, a commonplace inadequately pursued in relation to the dynamics of race (a matter taken up in Chapter V). Thus, what Roediger's statements manage to do is to render unmistakable the connections between economies of race and the academic commonplace of the deconstructive supplement. The second paragraph of *The Wages of Whiteness* reads as follows:

> Even in an all-white town, race was never absent. I learned absolutely no lore of my German ancestry and no more than a few meaningless snatches of Irish songs, but missed little of racist folklore. Kids came to know the exigencies of chance by chanting "Eeny, meany, miney, mo / Catch a nigger by the toe" to decide teams and first batters in sport. We learned that life – and fights – were not always fair: "Last one in is a nigger

94

baby." We learned to save, for to buy ostentatiously or too quickly was to be "nigger rich." We learned not to buy clothes that were a bright "nigger green." Sexuality and blackness were of course thoroughly confused. (3)

Roediger's recollections demonstrate ways in which "blackness" proves central to the self-formation of U.S. subjects.

This centrality, however, is the centrality of expenditure and remains, from the vantage of African Americans, an insistent feature of cultural violence directed at us at even the most minute and seemingly insignificant levels of U.S. civic life. The question arises, then, of what it means to have a strict assault of one's identity be a routine feature of self-formation in U.S. culture – a fixing and negating of one's identity often having the corollaries of poverty and physical violence. What are the particulars of negotiating social and civic relations in a society in which one remains part of a constantly expended present absence? An expenditure both physical and symbolic? The story of Ann Petry's *The Street* provides one complex and compelling answer. *The Street* is a narrative in which the dynamics of this kind of insistent, yet often surreptitious, cultural violence is ultimately rendered graphic and immediate. By exposing as false the apparently radical separation between the African American ghettos of New York, or any American city, and the stately wealth of Connecticut, or any all-American suburb, the novel exposes as false the seemingly radical disparity between those understood as valuable and those taken as valueless. It exposes, in other words, the forgery of radical difference between locations of blackness and whiteness in the U.S. landscape, both physical locations and the symbolic ones suggested by Roediger.

Petry's reissued novel[1] reiterates that the initiatives of the dominant cultural formation in the United States, initiatives urgently in need of revision, extend insidiously beyond the institutionalizing of material poverty and physical violence in African American communities. These initiatives reside in even the most minute features of sociosymbolic self-naming and self-recognition, which can be just as accurately called misnaming and misrecognition. Arriving at this understanding is the upshot of the difficult education of Lutie Johnson, the protagonist of Petry's novel. The story of Lutie's education is one in which the ultimate instability and insubstantiality of these sociosymbolic acts and placements become apparent. To this end, *The Street* recounts a story in which the mastering and masterful *sign-*

ing voice in the U.S. landscape, the voice disseminating the dominant sociosymbolic narrative, finds itself challenged by the sly alterity of the *singing* voice, a voice assuming (as already suggested) much more than mere "traditional" speech. *The Street*, then, addresses twentieth-century urban attempts to "redefine black identity" (Roberts 141) – attempts that in the characteristic mode of the operations of value depend on the ostensible strictness of boundaries and the ostensibly uncompromised discretion of the entities they separate.

In important aspects, the strict separations involved in Lutie Johnson's predicament concern ratios of time and space that, as it turns out, are closely related to the possession of or disenfranchisement from voice and the "sign." The configuration of value in relation to racial blackness and whiteness is one that, like all formations of value, attempts to forge radical difference – an attempt, the novel pursues, to reiterate "radical" difference between blackness and whiteness in terms of a "radical" difference of space and time. *The Street* suggests ways in which cultural forces forge for Lutie and her community existences marked ideally by the condition of "timelessness in space," while those most privileged in the culture are seemingly afforded the condition of "spacelessness in time." The philosophically and materially powerful mechanism of time is monopolized by a dominant community, like voice and the "sign," as precisely the mark of their radical difference, privilege, value. Indeed, the sociologist of science Helga Nowotny recognizes the powerful political and social contexts and efficacy of time. Considering the many cultural deployments and managements of time in her study *Time: The Modern and Postmodern Experience* she observes:

> [It] becomes clear that time represents a central dimension of power which manifests itself in the systems of time that dictate priorities and speed, beginning and end, content and form of the activities to be performed in time. . . . Today systems of time are chiefly fixed by the market and the state. The market fixes the time via the work to be done and the exchange relations between time and money. The state imposes its system of time via the legal system and thus structures the lives of its citizens. . . . The law dictates biographical status from when until when somebody is a child, a youth, or an adult; which times are earmarked for military service or are given off for the birth and education of children, when the withdrawal from working

life and going into retirement becomes obligatory. On the market, time is subject to the more universal medium of money with regard to the material and social range of its effects (105–6)

In other words, insofar as Lutie faces a difficult education poised around a struggle for voice in the U.S. landscape, she faces as well the exigencies of a social condition deeply defined by structures of time (and its apparent antithesis space). She faces an education as to the coimplications of the sign, voice, time, presence, and transcendence.

Still, although the narrative architecture of the novel is very intricate, the plot itself is not overly complex. The narrative begins with Lutie's quest to find an apartment for herself and her son, Bub. Putting aside her disappointment in the building on 116th Street that she finally settles for, Lutie is certain she will be able to better her lot eventually, and her imagination releases her much of the time from the depression and oppression of her surroundings. Much of the action of this early section of the novel is psychological; the narrative point of view shifts from character to character, all of whom share psychological spaces as tense and desperate as Lutie's. Finally seeking more than imaginary relief from the pressures facing her, Lutie enters the corner bar and casually sings along with the blues song playing on the jukebox. Boots Smith, a band leader, overhears and offers her the opportunity to sing with his band. After her first performance and as her sense of success and a promising future grows, Lutie's prospects turn severely for the worse. When she returns home late in the night from her performance, the building superintendent attempts to rape her and she is rescued by Mrs. Hedges, another tenant. Seeking revenge for his thwarted desires, the superintendent tricks Lutie's son into mail fraud and Bub is eventually arrested. Very quickly, Lutie's circumstances, environment, and community seemingly conspire against and overwhelm her. She turns to Smith for the cash to retain a lawyer for Bub, and, in the moments when she faces him in his apartment waiting for him to decide her fate, Lutie sees herself as a beleaguered pawn manipulated by others as well as an overwhelming set of circumstances. These circumstances, she begins to understand, are premised foremost by the social realities of race, gender, and class in the United States. In her sudden rage she bludgeons Smith and thus, it seems, ensures her exclusion from the mythical life of the orderly suburbs that she had long desired to enter. Lutie flees her former life and home, leaving behind even her incarcerated son.

Opening and closing with images of garbage that metonymically represent 116th Street and its community, *The Street* exposes, and Lutie Johnson comes to recognize, the restricted economy in which "refuse" is caught in the U.S. landscape. Discrete relationships between value and the Other, or between authority and the Other, do not exist. Where radical division is proclaimed, vigilant jurisprudence in fact operates. While U.S. capitalist society and its cultural apparatus reflect keenly their productions – prosperity, security, civil order – they at the same time, unaccountably and implacably, reflect their expenditures and residuals – the Third World, the African American, poverty, violence. *The Street* opens as follows:

> There was a cold November wind blowing through 116th Street . . . [which] found every scrap of paper along the street – theater throwaways, announcements of dances and lodge meetings, the heavy waxed paper that loaves of bread had been wrapped in, the thinner waxed paper that enclosed sandwiches, old envelopes, newspapers. (Petry 1)

As these initial images of refuse soon attest, the system of exchange in which 116th Street exists is an economy regulated by its tree-lined, suburban antithesis, which Lutie desperately longs to enter. Stirred by the November wind, "the bits of paper . . . danc[e] high in the air, so that a barrage of papers swirl[s] into the faces of the people on the street" (2). However, once the narrative switches to scenes of Connecticut, similar bits of paper take on a very different significance. The reader learns that Henry Chandler, by whom Lutie was once employed as a housekeeper, "manufacture[s] paper towels and paper napkins and paper handkerchiefs . . . [because] 'Even when times are hard, thank God, people have got to blow their noses and wipe their hands and faces and wipe their mouths. Not quite so many as before, but enough so that I [Chandler] don't have to worry'" (29). Connecticut, then, creates and profits by the expenditure and refuse of the street. The street remains the haunting, impoverished, and converse silence of the U.S. assurance: "Richest damn country in the world" (43). It remains the unbearable silence that increasingly overwhelms Lutie once she returns to New York after leaving her job as a housekeeper in Connecticut. *The Street* is the story of Lutie Johnson's growing apprehension and articulation of the workings of a restricted economy in the U.S. landscape, an economy whose operations are camouflaged by a discourse of radical difference. The narrative details Lutie's increased accounting of a hostile economy of presence, an economy in which she and the community of "the street" are reserved as enabling absences, as requisite silences that make audible the productions of signing voices.

The marked similarity between Lutie's arrival in Connecticut and her arrival several years later on 116th Street in Harlem shows the indiscretion of the system in which she is held and that she comes eventually to understand. When she steps for the first time from the train in Lyme, Connecticut, and is received by Mrs. Chandler, her employer, Lutie discovers a white woman not much older than she, who offhandedly "point[s] out the places as they r[ide] along" (36). Mrs. Chandler, wearing real pearl earrings and leather moccasins that catch the sunlight, names Connecticut for her newly arrived housekeeper, gesturing easily at the Connecticut River and other sights. Metaphorically, Mrs. Chandler completes this act of naming by turning her car into a "smaller road where there were big gates and a sign that said 'private road' " (36). Mrs. Chandler during this episode, rather than Lutie, commands and controls the "sign." That is, in a dialectic of presence and absence, speech and silence, Lutie is conflated with silence.

Identically, when Lutie arrives, several years later, notwithstanding radically different surroundings, on 116th Street in Harlem, searching for an apartment, she is faced again with the projection, rather than the project, of the sign. She is not the one empowered to perform the act of naming, but the one who must still submit to the act of naming, the one who must puzzle out the sign placed offhandedly before her. Rather than being privileged with enunciation, Lutie is faced with the task of silent interpretation:

Each time she thought she had the sign in focus, the wind pushed it away from her so that she wasn't certain whether it said three rooms or two rooms. If it was three, why, she would go in and ask to see it, but if it said two – why, there wasn't any point. . . . The wind held it still for an instant in front of her and then swooped it away until it was standing at an impossible angle on the rod that suspended it from the building. Three rooms, steam heat, parquet floors, respectable tenants. . . . Parquet floors here meant that the wood was so old and so discolored no amount of varnish or shellac would conceal the scars and the old scraped places, the years of dragging furniture across the floors, the hammer blows of time and children and drunks and dirty, slovenly women. (2–3)

In the same way that the signs offhandedly proffered by Mrs. Chandler stand as signs of proprietorship without rather than within the street, so, too, the sign "stand[ing] at an impossible angle on the rod that suspend[s] it from the building" is a sign of proprietorship from without rather than within the street. For this sign, which "stand[s] at an impossible angle," is owned, like the building from which it is suspended – as the reader learns later – by Junto, a white entrepreneur who profits hugely from the refuse, or expenditure, that is the street.

Junto is a self-made entrepreneur who, years earlier, began to amass his wealth by recycling garbage collected from along the curbs and in cans set out on the street. Entering into several partnerships, he eventually accumulates a fortune that includes apartment houses, at least one bar, one nightclub, one dance band, and at least one house of prostitution. By means of a virtually invisible proprietorship, he recirculates the expended street as a resource of the restricted economy that is responsible for the wealth of Connecticut:

> No matter what it cost them, people had to come to places like the [bar owned by] Junto. . . . They had to replace the haunting silences of rented rooms and little apartments with the murmur of voices, the sound of laughter; they had to empty two or three small glasses of liquid gold so they could believe in themselves again. (147)

Indeed, Junto is invoked, ultimately, as the embodiment of the "awful silence" (420) indigenous to the street, the unbearable, "creeping silence that could be heard under the blaring radios, under the drunken quarrels in the hall bedrooms" (144) of his apartment houses.

Like everyone else who lives in the street, Lutie can never entirely elude these "deepening pools of an ominous silence" (433) that ensure and symbolize the exclusion of all those who live in the street from the profit of U.S. *presence*. Nevertheless, at the moment when she begins most completely to comprehend the significance of the street, the obscenity inscribed upon it, and the unbearable silence characterizing it, she also sees the apparition of Junto materialize before her in her apartment:

Before it [the silence] had been formless, shapeless, a fluid
moving mass – something disembodied that she couldn't see,
could only sense. Now, as she stared at the couch, the thing
took on form, substance. She could see what it was.

It was Junto. Gray hair, gray skin, short body, thick shoul-
ders. He was sitting on the studio couch. The blue-glass coffee
table was right in front of him. His feet were resting, squarely,
firmly, on the congoleum rug. (418)

Junto lounges comfortably, sitting "squarely, firmly" in Lutie's tiny
apartment, because he inhabits the apartment no less than Lutie.
Thus, the American who does not live in the street is, nonetheless,
the proprietor of the sign both within and without the street.
Junto materializes as the principle of U.S. presence that takes the
street – its absence – as the principal, capital, or means of its presence:

What white Americans have never fully understood – but what
the Negro can never forget – is that white society is deeply
implicated in the ghetto. White institutions created it, white
institutions maintain it, and white society condones it. (*The Kerner Report*, 2)

Because the dominant U.S. presence operates even in the places
of its absence, Lutie struggles to escape a hostile economy that im-
molates her at virtually every turn. U.S. self-proclamation and the
converse silence of the street – Connecticut versus Harlem – exist
in a relation of which the most telling characteristic is the contra-
dictory positions Connecticut and the street bear to the future. In
the street, the future, unbearable and unmanageable like the sign,
overwhelms and cages one. But in Connecticut the future remains
manageable and tractable to the point where it predictably and immediately yields material benefits, reassuringly offering "[t]he belief
that anybody could be rich if he wanted to and worked hard enough
and figured it out carefully enough" (43).

In the street the future is terrifying not because it stands as an
infinite, vacuous unknown but, rather, because it stands as an endless expanse of the emptiness, or absence, already known. When one
looks into the future one cannot

see anything at all but 116th Street and a job that pa[ys] barely
enough for food and rent and a handful of clothes. Year after
year like that . . . the thought of day after day of work and night

after night caged in that apartment that no amount of scrubbing would ever get really clean. (147)

One views the ceaseless possibility of hunger and vulnerability, and
the seemingly endless postponement of desire. One sees the absence
of anything except the absence already present. The future in the
street is so thoroughly dispossessed that the thought of it cannot
usually be borne.

In Connecticut, by contrast, the future is so thoroughly possessed
that it seems already present in the present. The thought of the
future is always borne. The future is responsible, in part, for the
wealth of the Chandlers and their friends. It is also expressly responsible, in part, for the fluctuations of their moods, since the
Chandlers and their friends live in a world

> where the price of something called Tell and Tell and Ameri-
> can Nickel and United States Steel had a direct effect on emo-
> tions. When the price went up everybody's spirits soared; if it
> went down they were plunged in gloom. (43)

The future in Connecticut, rather than despairingly absent, is so
palpably present that it is meticulously scrutinized and wagered
upon. Indeed, the historian J.G.A Pocock, in his careful reconsideration of the revolution in notions of "property," "personality,"
and "civic order" in the eighteenth century, provides a succinct and
vivid characterization of the temporal world in which the Chandlers
and their Connecticut constituency exist:

> Government stock is a promise to repay at a future date;
> from the inception and development of the National Debt, it
> is known that this date will in reality never be reached, but
> the tokens of repayment are exchangeable at a market price
> in the present. The price they command is determined by
> the present state of public confidence in the stability of gov-
> ernment, and in its capacity to make repayment in the theo-
> retical future. Government is therefore maintained by the
> investor's imagination concerning a moment which will never
> exist in reality. The ability of merchant and landowner to
> raise the loans and mortages they need is similarly depend-
> ent upon the inverstor's imagination. Property – the material
> foundation of both personality and government – has ceased
> to be real and has become not merely mobile but imaginary.
> (112)

The crucial focus of this peculiar mobility and imagination is the closely guarded future, and, in this way, whereas the street seemingly possesses no future, Connecticut possesses and covets a direct relationship to the future. Accordingly, the chronological sequence of *The Street* is exceedingly intricate. Action taking place in Connecticut is generally rendered by the "and then, and then, and then" rhythm expected of narratives and characteristic of the successive influence of the future, whereas action that takes place in the street virtually forgoes the future-laden, expected "and then, and then." *The Street* is excessively populated with flashbacks and unexpected changes in narrative perspective that reconstitute and reconceive actions already narrated, interweave and juxtapose multiple rehearsals of past events, and distractingly postpone the currency of the future. Rather than the future's succeeding the present moment in the street, the present moment appears to succeed the present moment oppressively. What might be called a conventional chronology – in which the present moment seeks and acquires its fortune or future – deteriorates as the narrative progresses. This deterioration occurs in correspondence with the upshot of Lutie's difficult education, which is an acknowledgment that the influence of the future does not exist in the street.

Only with foreboding irony is the opening episode of the book – in which Lutie takes an apartment for herself and her son, Bub, on 116th Street – rendered by what might be termed a *fortunate* chronology, this is to say, a chronology realizing "that which is to befall [it] in the future" (*OED*). Fortunate chronology is the type of chronology ultimately monopolized by Connecticut, and the misleading *fortunate* chronology of the opening scene of the novel arises from the fact that Lutie arrives on 116th Street still "absorbed [by] some of the same spirit" (43) that she witnessed absorbing the Chandlers and their friends in the Connecticut countryside. She does not yet understand that the future as it exists in Connecticut cannot, by design, exist in the street. In this way, the *fortunate* chronology of the novel's initial episode almost immediately begins to dissipate.

At the beginning of the novel's second chapter, Lutie, on her way home from downtown Manhattan, recalls the Connecticut landscape. An advertisement of an immaculate kitchen posted in a crowded uptown subway train draws Lutie at length and in peculiar detail (some thirty pages) into a recollection of her tenure as a maid in Connecticut with the Chandlers and of the loss of her husband consequent to that stay. Yet she longingly conflates with her own future the immaculate rooms of an expansive Connecticut suburb, a longing and a set of images that ironically move the narrative at length into the past. Equally, Lutie's reverie is paradoxical because she in fact overlooks (even as she recalls it) the actual past in Connecticut – a past in which the expansive seduction of a Connecticut suburb, rather than engendering a wonderful future, precipitated the collapse of her family and her home life.

Complementing this thematic irony, the prolonged recollection of Connecticut arrogates the fortunate chronology that opens the novel. The fortunate chronology surreptitiously removes, or displaces, itself as a feature of the present moment in the subway car below the street. The fortunate recollection of Connecticut degenerates and disrupts the fortunate presence (or present-ation) of Lutie in the subway car below the street. By returning to a recollected past in Connecticut, the future-laden "and then, and then, and then" characterizing Lutie's presence (or present-ation) suspends and, therefore, annuls its characterization of that presence, a fortunate presence that seems uncontested at the opening of the novel.

Certainly, analepsis, prolepsis, and syllepsis, various suspensions of fortunate chronology, occur in every narrative that attends to recollections and, thus, recapitulates past events or undertakes any of a series of other achronological moves. However, *The Street* so thoroughly explores this suspension and, hence, abeyance of a fortunate chronology that the annulment of a *promising* time or chronology becomes a chief, rather than an incidental principle of the narrative. The teasingly meted out pace of *The Street* becomes unexpectedly and profoundly mired in this annulment. Moreover, the future-laden "and then, and then, and then" of the initial fortunate chronology is frustrated further by the minutely measured pace of the four hundred and thirty-six pages of the book. Another way of stating this observation is that less seems to "happen" in the street than in Connecticut.

Once she leaves the subway, Lutie makes her way to the crowded counter of the butcher shop and then to the overflowing sidewalks in front of Junto's apartment house, where she discovers and scolds Bub for shining shoes to earn change, a pastime she sees as initiating him into a lifetime of menial labor that holds "no future." As she climbs the stairs to her apartment with Bub in tow, she recalls – deferring the present moment again – the time she first saw the gaudy, disappointing colors of her freshly repainted apartment. After dinner, she tempers her anger and frustration, by allowing Bub

an evening at the movies and herself an outing to Junto's bar down
the street. The restive Lutie leaves her apartment for a night of
skittish adventure and relief, and, at this point, the reader suspects
the narrative will begin to proceed in earnest. Yet, surprisingly, the
narrative has already proceeded in earnest, which is to say, the deferred, minutely drawn present moment *never* yields in the course
of the narrative to the fortunate chronology most characteristic of
a recollected Connecticut. Flagrantly preempting a fortunate progression, the narrative perspective changes abruptly from that of
Lutie to that of Jones, the volatile and lecherous superintendent of
the building, who inhabits the oppressive stasis of the present moment with a longing intensity that is a lurid male complement of
Lutie's absorption with the myths of Connecticut.

From the newly admitted perspective of Jones, the narrative regresses to the episode of Bub as a shoeshine boy and – at length –
regresses further to a scene of Jones helping Bub to build his shoeshine box. With equal attenuation, the narrative then turns to
Jones's past, then to his tense relationship with Mrs. Hedges, a prominent tenant of the building and silent cohort of Junto. It turns next
to Jones's relationship with Min, the woman with whom he currently
lives. Tracing the fit of lust and fantasy animating Jones, the analep-
tic narrative even returns to the opening – dissemblingly fortunate
– episode of Lutie's renting her apartment. The narrative also recapitulates the seemingly unimportant moment when Lutie first sees
the gaudy colors of her freshly painted apartment, an event previously recollected by her thirty-two pages earlier:

> In the apartment she looked at the rooms, and at first she
> didn't say anything until after she had looked in the bathroom,
> and then she said, "What awful colors!" He couldn't help look-
> ing disappointed, but then she added with surprise in her
> voice, "Why, the windows have been washed. That's wonder-
> ful." And he had begun to feel better. (101)

With unexpected rehearsal of the past succeeding unexpected rehearsal of the past, the hapless chronology surprises the reader in
much the same way as the clash of "green in the living room, yellow
in the kitchen, deep rose color in the bedroom, and dark blue in
the bathroom" (100) first shocks Lutie.

But still more preemptive and unexpected is the immediate leap
in point of view to that of Min, the sheepish woman who has lived
with Jones in the oppressive atmosphere of his apartment for two

years, rapturous at having eluded the menace of rent. Admitting the perspective of Min, the narrative further reconstitutes and reconceives from a new vantage moments that have already been narrated. Thus, not only does the present moment distractingly return and succeed itself, but the multiplicity of narrative perspectives crisscrossing each other intensifies the stasis of the present. In turn, the narrative embraces the perspectives of Lutie's son, Bub; of the enigmatic and seemingly ubiquitous Mrs. Hedges; of Boots Collins, the band leader who insinuates himself into Lutie's life; and even of a petrified white teacher employed at Bub's elementary school, Mrs. Rinner. Each reappearance of already narrated events from a new vantage reveals increasingly that the horror of the present moment, in addition to its stagnancy, lies in the fact that it is unexpectedly and with equal intensity multiply populated. In its close and staggering overpopulation, the present moment, which is the only time allowed to exist in the street, becomes spatial, which is to say, the press of present moment upon reconstituted present moment mirrors the press of person upon person, of tiny, dingy room upon tiny, dingy room that above all characterizes the street.

In effect, time in *The Street* degenerates and compresses itself into space. The initial fortunate chronology of the narrative, deferring itself until it becomes seemingly spatial rather than temporal, records, in this way, the "grim social reality in which one faces an old age characterized by the same grinding poverty that destroys youth before it can flower and that makes work still necessary even when one is no longer capable of doing it – the only distinction between middle and old age" (Sherley Anne Williams 77). Reflecting and incorporating itself as the poverty and refuse in the street, time collapses into space – for time in repletion, the future, does not exist. Time exists in the street as the impossible *lack* of space.

Introduced and emblematized on the second page by Junto's sign, which stands "at an impossible angle," the issue of space is the issue with which the novel begins and that most insistently determines Lutie's aspirations and frustrations. For the protagonist's first quandary – how to escape the unacceptable atmosphere of Pop's seven rooms – is resolved by puzzling out whether Junto's sign advertises two rooms or three. Later provoked into her reverie on the subway by an advertisement of an immaculate kitchen, Lutie recalls at length the "kitchen in Connecticut... [which] changed her whole life" (56), the recollection replete with inventories of rooms with "big windows that brought the river and the surrounding woods almost into the house" (38). Opposingly, Lutie's life in the street is measured out by tiny filthy rooms she cannot escape: "Dirty, dark, filthy traps. Upstairs. Downstairs. In my lady's chamber. Click goes the trap when you pay the first month's rent. Walk right in. It's a free country. Dark little hallways. Stinking toilets" (73), Lutie recites to herself in a moment of frustration.

Insistent attention to rooms equally marks Lutie's most hopeful moments. When Boots Collins slyly offers her the opportunity to sing her way out of the street, the hope that Lutie struggles to suppress takes shape as a conviction that "[t]he first thing she would do would be to move and then she would get some decent furniture" (190). Ironically, however, the large comfortable rooms she fantasizes about in her future are, in fact, past recollected rooms of Connecticut, mere phantoms of desire. For, in the street and in the narrative, the present moment remains merely the site of an ironic intersection of past and present, a confining site for the irrepressible collapse and conflation of a past that is the future, and a future that is the past. The present merely provides a restricted space for unrestricted collapse and conflation, and the complex nature of this collapse and conflation is most fully suggested – appropriately enough – by events that mark the center of the narrative.

The night before she sings for the first time with Boots's band, Lutie returns home to find that, afraid of the dark, Bub has gone to sleep with the light on. She learns also that Jones spent most of the evening in the apartment with Bub, and she is roused, later in the night, by a nightmare of Jones howling and chained to the building. Once fully awake, she is faced with the equally grim memory of a youth stabbed to death on a Harlem sidewalk, then with a memory of a young girl taken, slashed and bleeding, into a Harlem emergency room. In the aftermath of her nightmare and these memories, Lutie sees clearly the press of the street, understanding that for people forced to live there "their bodies [are] the only source of relief from the pressure under which they live[ ]" (206). In order to return to sleep, she yields herself to a rare moment of anticipation – the anticipation of singing with Boots's band. She begins with equal anticipation in the morning to set out the clothes she will wear to sing. She discovers, however, one of her blouses smudged and wrinkled and realizes, after questioning Bub, that Jones soiled and crushed the blouse when he sent Bub out of the apartment on an errand. Immediately and unexpectedly, revulsion replaces anticipation; Lutie's hopeful rush into the future is overwhelmed by an episode first narrated one hundred pages earlier.

Once more, the past prophetically meets the future, and the future belatedly meets the past. The moment in the novel most replete with promise for the future is, therefore, equally replete with the horror of the past. A past that iterates an insistent pressure of enclosure collides with a future retaining that insistent pressure. Past and future intersect, collapse, and conflate in the space and material represented by Lutie's blouse. The blouse, soiled and crushed, symbolizes, at its disruptive – that is, simultaneously regressive and progressive – moment of discovery the unwanted past, which will continually haunt and confront Lutie. It stands as a symbol that the future does not exist in the street except, ironically, as an indefatigable past and present in which the future is already prophetically enclosed.

Whereas fortunes can be made in Connecticut by the buying and selling of futures, in the street there is literally no future to speak of, to think of, to dream of, to buy or sell. Lutie's dilemma resides in her attempt and hopes to attain the riches of time; however, within a U.S. economy of presence, time is the privilege of Connecticut, and space the quandary of the street. The intricate, suspended, abeyant chronology of *The Street* betrays again and again and again this particular relationship of time and space, a relationship for which Lutie's soiled blouse stands as a principal symbol.

Lutie Johnson's predicament, in short, is one defined by a radical and arbitrary separation of time and space. Although space and time equally compose the uncompromising paradox in which humankind exists, space connotes material, the essence of mundane reality, whereas time seems divine, a higher priority with which the material, the spatial, intersects. Despite the fact that nothing can "take place" except in the space of the world, time retains greater priority, because it proves more intractable and possesses greater inconceivability, mystery, ineffability. Nothing in the matter or the experience of humankind can possess time in the way space can be possessed. Indeed, this impulse to refuse the contingency of time and space is the very impulse Derrida slimly critiques in Husserl's phenomenology, a project that seeks to remove the space of the world and all phenomena in order to arrive at immaterial essence. With this seeming opposition in mind, it is fair to say, then, that plenary designations of time inaugurate or originate transcendence and metaphysics

– particularly the act of claiming time for oneself and one's purposes (speculative or otherwise). To be marked, on the contrary, by the plenary designation of space, as is Lutie by virtue of her race, gender, and class, amounts to being relegated to an opposing and subaltern meanness.

This is to say that contemplations of issues of the highest order are necessarily implicated in dynamics of social power and, moreover, in some way reflect meditations on time. At bottom, the particulars of social and civic organization are at stake in cultural instantiations of time, as Lutie's predicament demonstrates. Issues of time are privileged elements of issues of the highest order or, in other words, what is understood as the transcendent and metaphysical; these matters, like all canonized cultural forms, prove one of various "means by which culture validates [social] power" (Lauter 23). Because all issues of the highest order press invariably on the more mundane terms of existence, conceptions and regulations of time directly constitute a "politics of time." The anthropologist Johannes Fabian argues as much in *Time and the Other*, his revolutionary study of the "disciplinary" practices of anthropology that sets out to demonstrate that "[t]ime, much like language or money, is a carrier of significance, a form through which we define the content of relations between the Self and the Other" (ix).

Fabian, in his examination of discursive practices defining the field of anthropology, explores the ways in which the placing (or displacing) of Others in a temporal scheme remains a crucial element in processes of politically subordinating and socially managing Others. The peculiar work of the anthropologist, Fabian contends, participates centrally in these processes, as suggested by the central contradiction of the discipline: "The Other's empirical presence [in the ethnographical phase of work] turns into his [or her] theoretical absence [in the final product of anthropological knowledge], a conjuring trick which is worked with the help of an array of devices that have the common intent and function to keep the Other outside the Time of anthropology" (xi). Anthropology, as a disciplinary structure, yields a prime example of the way in which time is never a neutral or natural agent in social interactions or the production of knowledge but, instead, is always implicated in the very terms of political and social struggle:

Among the historical conditions under which [anthropology] emerged and which affected its growth and differentiation

were the rise of capitalism and its colonialist–imperialist ex-
pansion into the very societies which became the target of our
inquiries. For this to occur the expansive, aggressive, and oppressive societies which we collectively and incorrectly call the
West needed Space to occupy. More profoundly and problematically, they required Time to accommodate the schemes of a
one-way history: progress, development, modernity (and their
negative mirror images: stagnation, underdevelopment, tradition). In short, *geopolitics* has its ideological foundations in
chronopolitics. (144; emphasis in original)

That is, the appropriation of time and its configurations is a signal
concern in the regulation of and interactions among differing social
classes, cultures, races, nations.

Time, then, allied with the sign and voice, is a principal register
of presence, and this coimplication of the sign, voice, time, presence, and transcendence is also powerfully rendered for the "New
World" in Judeo-Christian traditions. The Judeo-Christian God –
like the sign, voice, time, presence, and transcendence – operates
"without having, at least apparently, to pass through the world"
(Derrida 1973, 75):

> "And the earth was without form and void. . . . And God *said,*
> Let there be light: and there was light" [Genesis 1:2, 3; em-
> phasis added]. "And they heard the voice of the LORD God
> walking in the garden in the cool of day" [Genesis 3:8]. "In
> the beginning was the Word, and the Word was with God, and
> the Word was God" [John 1:1]. "And the Word was made
> flesh, and dwelt among us" [John 1: 14].

Spacelessness in time, God, the Word, is plenary speech and plenary
presence. In this way, at the same time one claims the prerogative
of considering what lies superordinate to the common materiality
of the world, one claims for oneself an approximation of the most
powerful instantiation of voice and presence. In the deposition or
designation of the transcendent, one claims pure time and approximates notions of God and notions of the "civic" power of God.

Opposingly, timelessness in space is the antithesis of God *and of
the voice.* Timelessness in space marks pure materiality and, far from
providing access to the reality of God and transcendence, is the
reality of the unanimated, or dead body. (It is important to maintain
a distinction between the dead body, which is understood here as

obdurate materiality, and death. Death is any conceptualization that attempts to make sense of the dead body.) In this way, timelessness in space is the nethermost condition of obdurate materiality – a plenary absence of the voice.

The godliness or transcendence of the voice (always presupposing this antithesis of spacelessness in time and timelessness in space) dictates in many ways the cultural violences of value examined here.[2] A seizure of the apparent transcendence of the voice,[3] its fixity and its sign, appropriates – in addition to configurations of mere presence and absence – the prerogative to determine configurations of spacelessness in time and timelessness in space; in the United States those who bear white skin are understood in relation to spacelessness in time, significance, animation, the divine, whereas those who do not are understood in relation to timelessness in space, bestiality, culpability, obdurate materiality. However, this radical separation of time and space is precisely the relation into which the singing voice intercedes in the United States. Notwithstanding the nature of its performance, the singing voice, by virtue of its qualified resemblance to a dominant idealization of not "having, at least apparently, to pass through the world," disturbs any radical separation of time and space, any separation aiming at plenary designations of presence and absence. As suggested by the analysis of the previous chapter, it provides in both historical and philosophical senses an Other vocal presence disturbing dominant configurations of presence and value.

The singing voice represents, most patently in its ritualization during the contemporary popular concert, the Godhead of "the voice," one might say, in the act of assuming an impossible presence and time *in* space. The singing voice, thus, represents the transcendence of "the voice" incarnating itself with gross spatiality. It performs an Other, or profane, hagiology.[4] Recall, or imagine for a moment, the dimensions of such venues as McNichols Arena in Denver, Reunion Arena in Dallas, the Joe Louis Arena in Detroit, the Spectrum in Philadelphia, Madison Square Garden in New York, the Forum in Los Angeles, or even Meadowlands Stadium in New Jersey, filled with uproarious audiences. The singing voice, in such popular settings, plays itself out in rare material dimensions. The time of the popular concert is overwhelmed by its dimensions. In a manner of speaking, the gargantuan dimensions of the performance echo the *significant* spatiality of voice that the singing voice, in fact, dis-covers. Furthermore, not only is the space of the performance privileged during the popular concert, but, to a hyperbolic degree, the space, or body, of a *particular voice singing* is privileged. Recall that within these popular concert venues thousands upon thousands of bodies gather to witness *the body* from which *a voice* (not "the voice") emanates and to witness that particular body in the act of deploying, immediately, the materiality of voicing.

In many ways, during the popular concert, transcendence is refigured in deference to the spatial, or material – an underprivileged Other moment of *significance*. A celebratory absence of speech (constituting the singing voice) usurps the authority and apparent spaceless fixity of speech. As a result, dominant value and authority are confounded, and the vantage from which value and authority operate is altered; an antinomian third moment of the U.S. dialectic of presencing admits a new presence and a new speech. That is, in these moments, because of the form, etiquette, interactions, and even vocal performatives of the ritual, "extensive white participation" in black cultural forms in the United States becomes abundantly clear, as well as the extent to which "white America has always had an intense interest in black culture" (Rose 5), despite its most cherished initiatives to dismiss that culture altogether. Adorno's essay, "On the Fetish-Character in Music and the Regression of Listening," considered in the previous chapter, attests to the transformative power of African American cultural forms for U.S. culture at large and also to the ambivalence with which those transformations are received.

Thus, it is not merely incidental that deliverance from "the street" and its confining life offers itself to Lutie Johnson in the form of singing. When Lutie sings absently in Junto's bar the night she sends Bub to the movies, she relieves and recasts – less immediately than the immense spectacle of the popular concert, needless to say – the absenting silence endlessly plaguing the street. Lutie's voice reinvests and reanimates the experiences of the street, for voice at these moments belies routine relations to signs. Playing on the spatial, material, dative, or enunciative action of voice, Lutie iterates nothing per se and, in doing so, undoes speech; she discloses significance and import at sites where routine *signs* of speech attribute none. As she sings in the corner bar, recasting signs and iterations that more usually mark the street,

[h]er voice had a thin thread of sadness running through it that made the song important, that made it tell a story that

wasn't *in the words* – a story of despair, of loneliness, of frustration. It was a story that all of them knew by heart and had
always known because they had learned it soon after they were
born and would go on adding to it until the day they died.
(Petry 148; emphasis added)

In telling a story "that [is]n't in the words," the seductive import
of Lutie's voice arises from an insignificance imposed on it, its as-
sertiveness from supplication, its presence from a designated absence. This absent entry into presence is the very transaction Lutie
hopes literally to *capitalize* on, when offered the opportunity to sing
with Boots Smith and his band. She knows that, by singing successfully, she might escape the quandary in which the issue of time
becomes an impossible issue of space; she might be able to reap
immediately the promise and profit of music and of ludic ritual,
which prompt the "same people who had made themselves small
[downtown] on the train . . . suddenly gr[ow] so large they could
hardly get up the stairs to the street together" (57). The singing
voice expends the old and affords a new dispensation. It is fully
capable, Lutie understands, of exposing, entering, and altering the
dominant economy.

Never merely beguiled by the sign of value, the singing voice
overwhelmingly interrogates such a sign and turns its critical exposure not merely to a new vantage, but to new ad-vantages. Since, as
Barbara Herrnstein Smith reminds us, value is always a sign of
good(s), and the matter that might inhabit the sign of value infinitely
variable, the economics of value remain, at bottom, those vicissitudes
by which a particular inhabitant of the sign of value attains and
retains its status as positivity, gain, benefit, *goods* in a particular situation:

> [I]t appears that "good" operates within the discourse of value
> as does money in a cash economy: *good* is the universal value-
> form of value and its standard "measure"; it is that "in terms
> of which" all terms of value must be expressed for their com-
> mensurability to be calculated. (Herrnstein Smith, *Contingencies
> of Value* 146)

With this observation in mind, it is fair to say the singing voice revises the matter inhabiting the station of *good(s)* that is invariably the
measure and sign of value. In its interrogation of *signs of value*, the
singing voice does not simply displace a valuable sign of the signing

voice; it recuperates and recirculates that performative displacement, so as to obtain or usurp the status of good(s) and a position of value. It confounds transcendence – hyperbolic value – in order to admit an Otherness, or profanity, that reenacts and, in so doing, displaces already *significant* value.

Controverting signs established by the *signing voice,* the *singing voice* rehearses an alternative rendition of space and time than that imposed upon the street, an original rendition admitting the future. The performance of the singing voice, vocal movement and removement, interrogatively eschews the strict "forms" required by the privileged per-form-ance and in-form-ation of the signing voice. Eschewing normative form and in-form-ation, singing discourse more closely reflects a plenary spirit of time, since form – which it evacuates – is most indispensable to obdurate materiality. The singing voice approximates more closely than speech the unfixed fluency of spacelessness in time. It more exactly represents a veritable introduction of the future. What is more, whereas the signing voice that usually dominates the singing voice falsifies the presence of obdurate materiality in its configuration of transcendence, the singing voice acknowledges and displays the inexorable contingencies of a space always within spacelessness in time. The dynamics of the singing voice demonstrates, in effect, that "[t]ime not only transpires 'in' space, but space 'indwells' time" (Taylor 50). This disturbance by the singing voice of the radical antithesis of spacelessness in time and timelessness in space recreates African Americans as in-voiced, rather than onerously em-bodied. The cultural productions of African Americans, thus, become original and troubling agents of value and significance. By means of these cultural forms, African Americans create, in their absent situations, "noise and tumult [that is] horrible"[5] and, ultimately, valuable in their ability not to be disregarded.

The tractable, *significant* future of Connecticut and its returns are precipitated, then, only by a "literal" forging and disguising of space and time, a falsification that presents itself as pristine and authentic. Within *The Street* the abrupt, unexplained suicide of Jonathon Chandler signifies and exposes the falseness of the signs and voicings of Connecticut in a manner complementary to the performance and dis-coveries of Lutie's singing voice. Chandler shoots himself in the living room of his brother and sister-in-law during one of the two Christmas holidays Lutie spends in Connecticut. Arriving only the night before Christmas, he reaches quickly into a drawer the next morning, retrieving a revolver that he momentarily fingers as "Mrs. Chandler . . . hold[s] out a package to Lutie" (Petry 47). Lutie then sees Jonathon "h[o]ld [the gun] under his ear and pull[ ] the trigger" (47). Immediately, amidst the spacious rooms of Connecticut obdurate materiality appears – furthermore, obdurate materiality unassignable to a radical distance of the street.

The violent and disruptive death puts an end to the celebration around the Christmas tree, but, with greater finality, a reciprocal end is put to the disruptive death. Phone calls are made and the sign under which Jonathon Chandler dies is revised as "an accident with a gun" (49). With similar abruptness and finality, "[t]here [appear] three cars in the garage instead of two. And Mrs. Chandler [hires] a personal maid and there [i]s talk of getting a bigger house" (49–50). This is to say, the dominant, lucrative, "authentic" future in the U.S. landscape does not acknowledge but, rather, refuses its past. This violent past is unearthed by the circumstances, performances, and disturbances of the singing voice, in much the same way it is beguiled by a *signing* performance in which it is forged into the palpable future. The singing voice exposes and imperils, then – to play on the occasion of Jonathon Chandler's death – a god that does not rise in fact, but only nominally, from the dead.

Put differently, since space and time in the U.S. landscape are already signified, and since African Americans (and a violent past) are generally dispossessed by these configurations, the singing voice discovers an Other acknowledgment of space and time or, to turn the phrase meaningfully, an acknowledgment of an Other space and time. Of course, this Other acknowledgment proves always insufficient and compromised, as do the dominant configurations themselves. Nevertheless, in *The Street* the disruptive possibilities of this transaction of the singing voice are largely foreclosed, because Lutie does not easily relinquish the sign, which the singing voice overwhelmingly interrogates. Her protracted acceptance of the forged, ruling fictions of Connecticut forecasts her ultimate defeat by the dominant circulation of value and the sign in the U.S. landscape. That defeat is forecast because she concomitantly holds on to the very matter she would overthrow. Lutie pursues, despite her firsthand experience, not merely the financial security of the Chandlers and Connecticut, but the stylized fiction of U.S. "home and family." She continues to believe in a fraudulent, pristine ideal and disregards the fact that she witnesses the fictions of Connecticut written deceptively and disagreeably before her. She ironically pursues an idealization of the violence (and significations) that oppresses her.

She attempts to overlook the indiscretion of the "American dream." But, ultimately, acknowledging this indiscretion is the upshot of her difficult education. U.S. idealization, whether symbolized by "Benjamin Franklin" (64) or a white picket fence, is aptly phrased the "American dream," for, as Freud argues repeatedly and at length in *The Interpretation of Dreams*, dreams are always "centered elsewhere[,] [their] content . . . arranged about elements which do not constitute the central point of the dream-thoughts" (196). As understood by Freud, the dream is the fantastic product of a wish fulfillment that displaces and condenses the materials of a latent content into materials of a manifest content. In her uncritical pursuit of the "American dream," Lutie overlooks any underlying connection between the dream and the refuse that lies around it, and from which it is formed. One might add – cautiously and with some reservations – so does Freud, when he writes at the conclusion of his general analysis in *The Interpretation of Dreams*, "All that is ethically offensive in our dream-life and the life of phantasy for the most part disappears [outside the realm of material reality]" (470). That the signifying, authorizing activities of the dream exhaust themselves entirely within the realm of the dream is precisely the vision Lutie must and does discard by the conclusion of *The Street*.

In other words, part of the vision Lutie relinquishes by the end of the narrative is an uncritical acceptance of the powerful and numerous signs marking out the normative dream of U.S. life. Insofar as the singing voice substitutes control of the sign for a controverting performance of the sign, Lutie's ambition to sing is thwarted by her resolute and unambiguous attention to the sign. This resolute attention is finally as ironic as the anticipatory rush into the future that collapses with the discovery of her soiled blouse. Indeed, forecasting Lutie's impending and ultimate defeat to the sign, a defeat that reinscribes a history of defeats to the sign, the events of her return home following her first night singing in a nightclub reaffirm the startling juxtapositions made plain by her discovery of the soiled blouse. These events begin to dispel for the reader the conviction that "she and Bub were leaving streets like this" (230).

When Lutie enters the darkened foyer of her apartment building, a trembling and deluded Jones attempts to rape her and, as profoundly as her voice earlier filled the room where men and women lingeringly remembered it "as though still joined together by the memory of the music and the dancing" (226), her voice fails her at this time. Moreover, when she recovers her voice and finally screams, the "pair of powerful hands" (236) that rescue her – a portent as ominous as Jones's attack – turns out to be those of Mrs. Hedges, Junto's silent cohort. As it was before, Lutie's anticipatory rush into the future is again foreclosed: by the violent attack of Jones, then by the equally unexpected rescue at the hands of the immense Mrs. Hedges, who seems to incarnate – in her corporeality and close connections to Junto – the indiscrete agency of U.S. presence in the places of its absence. In these moments of struggle, it becomes clear that Lutie is thoroughly possessed (and dispossessed) by the dialectic of the street and Connecticut, an authorizing binarism she wishes both to escape and to attain even as it negates her aspirations.

As a consequence of the struggle, the apparent insuperability of the sign in the U.S. landscape asserts itself more immediately than ever. The thwarted Jones conceives a plot to ensnare Lutie's son in criminal mischief, since, delirious and angry, he seeks revenge. He devises a plan and the next day convinces Bub that by stealing letters from neighborhood mailboxes he will be able to help the police catch criminals. Jones seduces Bub with tales of elaborate espionage and with the promise of payment for his work. He engages the authorities and the law of the authorities against Lutie and Bub by ensnaring them in a flagrant transgression of the operations of the U.S. postmaster general, a term highly suggestive in the context of the street, which might, consequently, be understood as the "Post-Master General," broad principles regulating the circulation of signs in U.S. culture. This is to say, Jones, in effect, brings down on Lutie and her son the wrath of an unindividuated, overdetermined postbellum master that no longer imposes exacting terms of existence on African American communities by means of legislated physical enslavement but, instead, by more immaterial and interpellative violence. The "Post-Master General" – to borrow the distinctions of Louis Althusser – is a phantasmatic but potent agent of an ideological state apparatus, which operates by more subtle means than the patent violence of the repressive state apparatus. The force of the "Post-Master General" and ideology itself lies in their determination of "the imaginary relation of . . . individuals to the real relations in which they live" (Althusser 80). In short, through the circulation of signs, the unindividuated, overdetermined "Post-Master General" forges the U.S. social and civic imagination.

The postmaster general, in the U.S. landscape, remains the official and ubiquitous exchequer of the sign, of letters and packages and labels, just as an equally ubiquitous but less palpable Post-Master General remains arbiter of more insidious signs, that is to say, of other letters and packages and labels – of the configurations, finally, of absence and presence, spacelessness in time and timelessness in space. Unlike the openly coercive antebellum master, the Post-Master General cannot rely indiscriminately on the gun, the whip, the knife but must primarily rely upon a subtler violence of signification – a violence inherent, for example, in the *significance* of U.S. law and whatever happens to operate under the sign of U.S. law.[6]

The Post-Master General, is responsible for the *present* economy of the sign as it stands. Jones, in short, releases on Lutie and Bub the "literal" force of official circulations of the sign in the U.S. landscape. To be sure, Jones enlists the imagination and confidence of Lutie's son by seemingly making real the mythic narratives of surveillance, police, and spies that play elegantly and seductively across the movie screens of the neighborhood. Bub's downfall mirrors Lutie's, for, in the same way Lutie is ironically beguiled by the mythic fictions of Connecticut that exclude her by design, Bub is beguiled by mythic intrigues of policing and espionage activities that in the street where he lives are aimed precisely at excluding him from the very prosperity and civil order that require patrolling and maintenance. As it turns out, the separate idealizations to which they subject themselves are not so separate and, ironically, their blind idealizations are both myths of surveillance. The privileging of Connecticut as well as the operations of the general economy of signs are nothing if not based on a specular or scopic regime, as is suggested by the image of the ubiquitous Junto, surveying matters through an enormous mirror in the neighborhood bar that he owns. Junto, one remembers, is the figure who links the poverty of the street with the accumulative privilege represented by Connecticut, the figure who profits by the expenditure of the street in deference to the accumulative privilege to which it stands in stark contrast:

Whenever [Lutie] had been in here, [Junto] had been sitting at that same table, his hand cupped behind his ear as though

he were listening to the sound of the cash register; sitting there
alone watching everything – the customers, the bartenders, the
waiters. For the barest fraction of a second, his eyes met hers
in the mirror and then he looked away. (146)

Jones focuses on Lutie and Bub the specular gaze of the Post-
Master General, which, although ubiquitous, is discernible only
"[f]or the barest fraction of a second." Under the force of such
surveillance, Lutie's aspirations to attain the privileges of time are
dashed, as assuredly as they are by her discovery of the soiled blouse,
and as assuredly as her buoyancy is dispelled by the scuffle in the
foyer with Jones and Hedges. Finally, time is refigured for her in
terms of an ultimate *absence* of the voice. Rather than an open and
in-voiced future at the end of the narrative, Lutie is faced with the
dead body of Boots Collins, the leader of the band with which she
sings. Like Mrs. Hedges, Collins is an operative of Junto. He is, above
all else, the musical instrument of Junto. It is Collins who offers
Lutie the opportunity to sing, an opportunity that ostensibly would
in-voice her but that is, in fact, a snare to entrap her as "whore."
This is a sign that is highly consequential for Lutie and her dilemma.
   As elaborated by scholars of black feminist thought such as Hazel
Carby, Patricia Hill Collins, and Deborah Gray White, "whore" is a
long-standing sign under which black female bodies are read in the
U.S. imagination. African American women, as these scholars doc-
ument, have been and continue to be socially encoded as jezebels,
which is to say, women "governed almost entirely by [their] libido[s]" (White 29). This social encoding provides "a powerful ra-
tionale for the widespread sexual assaults" (Collins 77) made on
African American women, but, what is more, such assumptions even
play routine and significant roles in the U.S. judicial process.
"Again, attitudes of jurors seem to reflect," writes the legal scholar
Kimberlé Crenshaw, "a common belief that black women are different from white women and that sexual aggression directed toward
them is less objectionable" (413). This encoding of black female
bodies is a potent sign circulated within the general economy and
defines in part the specific *absence* of African American women from
the social condition of U.S. presence. Accordingly, it is a sign that
plagues Lutie again and again in *The Street.*
   This signification positions African American women in a peculiar
social, civic space well formulated early in Billie Holiday's *Lady Sings
the Blues.* Holiday writes of her grandmother, "And she used to tell

me how it felt to be a slave, to be owned body and soul by a white man who was the father of her children" (8). African American female bodies are positioned by this social and legal arrangement as the site of an outrageous conflation of two "normatively" disparate economies – one libidinal, one pecuniary. Black female bodies are constructed as the site of outrageous and conflicted identity, an outlandish site at which (impossibly) identified terms converge: Erotic life and libidinal activity are interwoven with pecuniary property and financial exchange. Forming a site of singular and patent perversion at which both social mores and civil symbolic exchange are ineluctably corrupted, the cultural space specified for/by black female bodies directly contradicts the powerful yet specious cultural logic presuming the "normal" upshot of male sexual discharge is "natural" relations of affection and kinship markedly distinct from and indifferent to relations of market exchange. Put differently – despite the force of all that is "normal" and "natural" – uncanny black female bodies prove the means by which male sexual discharge is unaccountably (yet fortuitously) linked to capital accumulation and its attendant structures of impersonality. These bodies are constituted as unique sites at which the apparent disparity between legitimate market exchange and the advertised sanctity of family are irredeemably disrupted.

In point of fact, however, conceptual and legal proscriptions against the conflation of the market and the familial (which ought to subsume the erotic entirely in strictly controlled ways) are never wholly unqualified. Gayle Rubin, for example, points out that when one considers matters closely one recognizes that "[s]ex law incorporates a very strong prohibition against mixing sex and money" with one crucial exception, which is "via marriage" (19). The seeming opposition between the familial and the market is ultimately spurious. Thus, to position black female bodies historically and legally as the exclusive site at which these proscriptions do not obtain, rather than acknowledging this point of fact, amounts to incorporating by law and custom black female bodies as the paramount site at which sexuality is routinely and perversely commodified in monetary terms and money routinely (and with equal perversion) accounted in sexual terms. African American female bodies are thus established as what might be understood as the ur-site of "prostitution," a site of both social and natural pollution. As it is with the body/person who is a slave, the body/person who is a prostitute is in some ways indistinguishable from the structures of the market.

This identity is inscribed for the slave in terms of one's relation to one's labor and for the prostitute in terms of what is imagined as one's most intimate relation to one's body.

To put the matter in terms explored in the previous chapter, the figures of the prostitute and the slave represent distinct varieties of contagion on the implied "free will" of the possessive individual in a market society. The slave, by force of law and patent coercion, is ostensibly divested of free will; however, the opposite is seemingly true for the prostitute, for the terms of self-propriety as defined by possessive individualism are abrogated in the figure of the prostitute precisely because they are exercised with a disquieting exorbitance. That is, free will and person-ality are vanquished by a hyperbolic rendition of themselves. This exorbitance arises from disregard of the fact that, as much as it demands an interpellative allegiance to the market, the central proviso of possessive individualism demands an equally significant measure of resistance. The tenet that one's "energy and skill are [one's] own, yet [are] regarded not as integral parts of [one's] personality, but as possessions, the use and disposal of which [one] is free to hand over to others for a price" (Macpherson 48) implies that certain aspects of one's energy and skill – "integral parts of [one's] personality" – must remain outside and inimitable to the market. Otherwise, one conducts oneself, in commodifying those integral parts, which include erotic life, as though one were simply coterminous with the market. In this way, self-propriety problematically exceeds an affinity with the market and becomes unqualified identity with the market. In other words, one conflates, rather than counterposes, the terms of personality and impersonality.

It is the imposition of this condition by the U.S. slave regime that Holiday's grandmother relates. Her recollections demonstrate graphically the way in which African American women's lives are powerfully scripted so that the most intimate relations they bear to their bodies are fixed as the ground of an ironic exile from the material and psychic goods of personality – an ironic exile, because such relations are usually taken as the point of individual separation from the market and its structures of impersonality, rather than the determining point of identification with them. Scripted concomitantly in terms of slave and prostitute, the black female body seems the uncanny synthesis of a legislated disbarment from possessive individualism and a perverse and freely exercised exorbitance of possessive individualism. The racialized and gendered status of African American women yields a willful willlessness, or alternately a "will-less 'free will,' " that marks them by nature – which, as it turns out, is always social circulation – as "whore."

Although in not nearly as brutal terms as those articulated by Holiday's grandmother, Lutie acknowledges early in *The Street* this powerful sign under which she is seemingly always read:

> Here she was highly respectable, married, mother of a small boy, and, in spite of all that, knowing all that, these people took one look at her and immediately got that now-I-wonder look. Apparently it was an automatic reaction of white people – if a girl was colored and fairly young, why, it stood to reason she had to be a prostitute. If not that – at least sleeping with her would be just a simple matter, for all one had to do was make the request. In fact, white men wouldn't even have to do the asking because the girl would ask them on sight. (Petry 45)

The notion that access to Lutie's genitalia is almost as uncomplicated a matter as the purchasing of groceries or a newspaper or any other number of routine transactions is shared by most of the characters Lutie encounters: the Chandlers and their friends, Jones, Boots, Junto, Mrs. Hedges, and Mr. Crosse, who auditions singers.

It is the oppressive power of the sign – "whore" – as it is inscribed on the bodies of African American women that, after much deferral, Lutie confronts at the climax of the novel, a confrontation that ultimately writes her out of the phantasmatic U.S. polity she wishes fervently to claim. In brief, Lutie's act of scripting herself *without* this sign, in her most violent effort to resist its imagined legitimacy, turns out to be the very act that forever scripts her outside the bounds of the all-American suburb. Although not absolute, the oppressive powers of the sign are far-reaching, for Lutie's paramount moments of resistance to it secure the dissolution of her most cherished aspirations. Its far-reaching power is signaled not only by the dashing of Lutie's aspirations, but also by the fact that the climactic struggle is triggered by Jones's bid for revenge, an intrigue that openly pits Lutie against the U.S. "Post-Master General" and its management of an official restricted general economy of signs in the U.S. landscape. The overriding irony of this ultimate confrontation is that its outcome merely reiterates Lutie's absence from the exclusionary terms of *presence* of the restricted general economy, an absence already secured at the beginning of the narrative despite her inability to recognize it.

Nonetheless, equally important to this climactic turn of events is the fact that they occur in the apartment of Boots Collins. Lutie knows no better than to secure a lawyer she cannot afford and, in fact, does not need in order to obtain the release of Bub, who is incarcerated. She turns to Boots to borrow the two hundred dollar fee quoted by a lawyer who experiences the same sense of good fortune he would "picking two hundred bucks up in the street" (392). Thus, if it is Boots who introduces the opportunity to employ the revisionary allowance of the singing voice in the narrative, a revisionary allowance circumventing much of the effect of the restricted general economy of *signs* in the U.S. landscape, then, equally, it is Boots who is instrumental in foreclosing that revisionary allowance for Lutie. Boots is the one who initially offers her the opportunity to sing, an opportunity that would ostensibly in-voice her but that turns out, in fact, to be another attempt to signify her as "whore." Differently stated, Boots ensures that the *singing* voice, despite itself, performs with unambiguous attention to the sign for he is, above all else, the musical instrument of Junto, the means by which the unrestricted expenditures of the singing voice are revised so they are managed in accordance with the restricted circulation of the general economy of signs.

In this way, the climactic events seemingly belie the fact that the law of the Post-Master General sustains a restrictive system of expenditure into which the unrestricted expenditure of the singing voice intercedes and, accordingly, disturbs. The seeming invulnerability of the dominant symbolic economy is apparently confirmed by the far-reaching extent of its operations; it appears to extend even into the ludic alterity symbolized by African American music, a recess intended precisely to elude or revise it. It seemingly operates as ubiquitous, unequivocal, and stable, allowing no Other option than submission to the prescribed circulation of its general signs – to signs of a *certain* absence that it self-interestedly designates.[7]

In a phrase, when Lutie murders Boots and her in-voiced future is summarily supplanted with "a speechless mass of flesh" (428) that is his dead body, her own absence in the U.S. landscape is summarily confirmed. The dead body of Boots pointedly signifies the *unfortunate* end of the narrative. For once again, the future – that is, time – collapses unaccountably, and this time with overwhelming finality, into space – obdurate materiality. The obdurate materiality of "the speechless mass of flesh" signifies the final lapse and relapse of the narrative. The death of Boots becomes, as it were, the unfortunate

rehearsal of the earlier death of Jonathon Chandler. Or, in the idiom of space, the death of Jonathon Chandler is dis-placed unfor-
tunately onto Boots Collins at the conclusion of *The Street*. The point
here is to underscore that, although Lutie is faced with another
(which turns out to be an-Other) dead body, at this point in the
narrative the crisis occurs in an absence of the "literal" powers of
general significance. Whereas the abrupt and disruptive death of
Jonathon Chandler is revised to sustain the carefully managed significance attributed to the world of the Chandlers, no revisionary
apparatus obtains at the climactic events of the novel besides Lutie's
desperate and passionate assertion of her own significance.

Insofar as Lutie's desperate violence confirms the limits of the
dominant symbolic economy, it confirms Other options than submission to the prescribed circulation of general signs. These pen-
ultimate moments of the narrative thus mark not only "the
resignation Lutie has sought to avoid" (Griffin 118) but, moreover,
moments of dearly purchased integrity. What is more, outside the
voicings and dissembling revisions of Connecticut, the dead body of
Collins, the upshot of Lutie's violent self-assertion, brings the Post-
Master General indisputably to the surface of *The Street*. This is to
say, Lutie's murder of Boots responds to and remarks greater, more
significant violence. Lutie exposes, by means of her murderous performance and its complex ironies, intricate, seductive relations of
violence that maintain, as though unenforced, the reified configurations of the general U.S. economy of presence. Presence, value,
and authority, despite appearances to the contrary, remain presence, value, and authority only insofar as they overmaster, expend,
and occlude a "cultural vestibularity" (Spillers "Mama's Baby" 69)
that is "literally" disfigured. Lutie's violence reiterates, then, in unsettling, undisguised form the widespread but continually revised
and therefore more subtle forms of violence pervading the narrative.

Another way of understanding this observation is to recognize
that until this conclusion, which most fully and ironically resumes
the fortunate chronology of the opening sequence of the narrative,[8]
the street has seemed merely the disordered space of the press of
person upon person, of tiny, dingy room upon tiny, dingy room.
However, with the intervention of agents of the postmaster general,
initiated by Jones, Lutie finally comes face to face with Junto, who
seems "as though he were a piece of that dirty street itself, tangible,
close at hand, within reach" (Petry 422). Junto exerts a powerful

influence on the circumstances of and occurrences in the street although seemingly never present himself. He is the very incarnation of the Post-Master General in *The Street*; he is responsible for the operation and circulation of the signs determining Lutie's condition in the U.S. landscape: He owns the sign that hangs in front of her apartment building. He operates the bar in which she seeks momentary relief. He operates the sign "music" that seduces her into a keen anticipation of an absent future, and he attempts to impose the sign "whore" that she resists fervently and that initiates the closing violence of the narrative. He maintains the seemingly impregnable economy that places Lutie in "some previously prepared classification" (41) and circulates her as though she were a package.

The climax of *The Street* is duplicitous, then: One cannot ignore the fact that the climatic violence occurs in the seemingly "unmasked" form of intraracial violence, nor the fact that the consequences of the violence are dire. The violence sustains the incarcerated space of Bub; exterminates the fluent black male musician; and silences the black woman singer. It effects, in short, a profound intraracial unvoicing and spatial containment. Still, at the same time, the violence proves a quizzical redaction and revelation of the dense, complex, and convoluted antecedents precipitating it. Unvoicing and spatial containment betray far-reaching, but virtually imperceptible overdeterminations. One is prompted to think, for a moment, in terms of Richard Wright's Bigger Thomas, an absent presence in *The Street* of a different sort. For Petry's novel, like *Native Son*, contains pivotal violence that lays bare

> a vast dense ideology of [white] racial superiority that would justify any act of violence taken . . . to defend white dominance; and further, to condition [African Americans] to hope for little and to receive that little without rebelling. (Wright xii)

The Street ends, so to speak, where Richard Wright's *Native Son* begins. The complex and revealing act of violence that draws Lutie Johnson out of the long narrative of Petry's novel is closely akin to the violence that introduces Bigger Thomas into the long narrative of Wright's. The separate acts of violence "react to and answer the call of the dominant civilization whose glitter c[omes] . . . through the newspapers, magazines, radios, movies, and the imposing sight and sound of daily American life" (xiii), a daily life that

> contain[s] no spiritual sustenance, ha[s] created no culture
> which c[an] hold [African American] allegiance and faith,
> ha[s] sensitized . . . and left [African Americans] stranded . . .
> free agent[s] to roam the streets of [U.S.] cities, a hot and
> whirling vortex of undisciplined and unchannelized impulses.
> (xix)

In short, the duplicity of the climatic violence in *The Street*, concomitantly an act of defiance and surest mark of defeat, calls profoundly into question the very essence and the very boundaries of the murder that takes place.

For these reasons, the ubiquity of the enforced general economy is only virtual. Only the music co-opted by and transacted in the name of Junto, the co-optation and transaction symbolized by the figure of Collins, falls within the comprehension of an enforced general economy. Ludic improvisations that take place within the interstices of a generalized, U.S. musical performance effect an *absence* not designated, but self-determined. Such interstitial improvisations effect an Other absence that would be more accurately unaccounted as presence within an enforced, general economy.

Such an improvisational performance – a radically Other presencing and enfranchisement – occurs, ironically, at the moment when Collins, under instructions from Junto, informs Lutie that she will not be paid for singing with the band. At an intermission, most of the band members leave the stage, but

> [t]he pianist and one of the trumpeters stayed in the bandstand. The trumpeter was experimenting with a tune that had been playing in his head for days. The pianist turned sideways on the piano bench listening to him.
> "Ever hear it before?" he asked finally.
> "Nope," replied the pianist.
> "Just wanted to make sure. Sometimes tunes play tricks in your head and turn out to be somep'n you heard a long while ago and all the time you think its one you made up."
> The pianist groped for appropriate chords as the man with the trumpet played the tune over softly. Together they produced a faint melody, barely a shred, a tatter of music that drifted through the big ballroom. Conversation and the clink of glasses and roars of laughter almost drowned it out, but it persisted – a slight, ghostly sound running through the room.
> (302–3)

This original music emerges from the interstices of the nightly commercial performance and is counterpoised to the moments Junto attempts through Boots to assert his influence over Lutie. Curiously, in the moments immediately preceding the murder of Collins, the act that proves in one sense her ultimate act of defiance but in another her final act of defeat, Lutie unaccountably recalls these floating, insinuating shards of music, the "fragment of a melody" (422) performed by the two musicians reluctant to leave the bandstand during the intermission.

Just as the improvisational and unaccountable musical creativity of the two intent musicians ruptures at its margins the restricted economy presiding over the sign "music," so too Lutie's act of striking and killing Boots ruptures (also at its limits) the economy that oppresses her. Rather than acquiesce to the certain absence ascribed to her Lutie attains an Other, self-declarative absence, nonetheless, included by exclusion within that economy. She effects a faint, original, violent reply to an economy determining her as a pure, impossible absence – that is, an absence entirely without presence.

Just as summarily as Lutie's aspirations are foreclosed at the climactic moments of the narrative, the peculiar insistence of the improvised music of the pianist and one of the trumpeters in Boots's band metaphorically endorses her presence. Settling itself nigglingly in Lutie's mind at the moments of the violent crisis, the "faint melody, barely a shred, a tatter of music" (303) marks another interstice. The apparently acute and ultimate collapse of time overshadows, but does not entirely occlude, insistent returns of melody – a metonym of the singing voice – and it is precisely this inability to occlude entirely an Other presence that reveals the usually unremarked general operations of violence. In other words, Petry's narration of Lutie's murder of Boots aims at reiterating the widespread and significant violences sustaining the economy of signs and presence superintended by the Post-Master General, even though the exposure, like the improvised music, is perceptible only "[f]or the barest fraction of a second."

Only from the vantage of the overmastered and occluded "vestibularity" can presence, value, and authority (denying their existence as dialectics and denying their ineluctable violence) be fully significant. This vantage is the vantage of Lutie and of others in the street, and it is inscribed at peculiar and fastidious length in Petry's novel. This vantage reveals the duplicity and significance of Connecticut and it is the perspective of the singing voice, the ritual magic of the Other that not only garners attention for the Other, but, furthermore, proclaims the attention of the Other. It is the urgent perspective of an inside that is designated outside.

The enforcement of such an extreme perspective upon Lutie and others in the street amounts to their being inscrutably violated. Disinherited from time and reified in space, they are presented with "death," for to remove people from the voice, from signification, from time, and seemingly to immure them in obscurity and obdurate materiality are to figure and enforce their death – a death by no means natural. Rather, this death is the upshot of perpetual "murder."[9] Lutie's murder of Boots is illuminating in precisely this way. Its patent violence betrays the in-form-ation and sign-ificance of greater, commanding violence. One discovers, in reading this *information* and *significance*, value, the arcane nexus of violence and authority. Similarly, one discovers the beguiling refusals of value to signify its own dialectics, which is to say, the attempts of value to confine its perceiver within it and apparently to confine itself within itself.

Value (and its correlate authority) is a presentation that remains inexorably, to borrow the words of James A. Snead, "not one of nature, but one of force" (75). Equally to the point are the words of U.S. television's inane yet triumphant fictional master spy Maxwell Smart, whose assignment is to battle and vanquish Kaos, and who, despite himself, always does. In the immediate aftermath of one of his post-1960s escapades, Smart consoles Agent 99, both his partner in surveillance and his wife, with the following brief soliloquy: "What are you talking about '99'? We have to kill, maim, and destroy! We stand for everything that's good, fine, and decent in the world!"[10] Value, that is to say, inevitably remembers itself by dismembering the Other. The counterproject of *The Street* and its singing voice is, on the Other hand, to re-member the Other by dismembering value.

PART TWO

REASONINGS AND
REASONABLENESSES

4

DE-MARKING LIMITS: READING NEW
CRITICAL BLA(N)CKNESS

It may seem a radical shift in focus to turn from considerations of the alterity symbolized by African American musical production to the scope and kinds of attention underwriting the literary academy. The shift seems not so radical, however, when one reflects that, "as the NCTE [National Council of Teachers of English] survey accurately shows, by the end of the 1950s, one could study American literature and read no work by a black writer, few works by women except Dickinson and perhaps Marianne Moore or Katherine Anne Porter, and no work about the lives and experiences of working-class people" (Lauter 27). In other words, the established circulation of *signs of value* investing itself in racial and other forms of exclusion obtains equally at the site of the academy. Exclusionary arrangements of "knowledge" superintended by the academy – the paramount site of literacy and the life of the mind as they are popularly understood – reiterate hostile configurations of value challenged by the alterity of the singing voice and interrogated at length in Ann Petry's *The Street*. The seemingly unbridgeable disparity between the performance of an honorific critical appraisal on a limited selection of objects and the ludic, excessive performance of the singing voice reiterates the forgery of radical difference already outlined. Upon closer examination, one recognizes the fashioning and refashioning of relationships across boundaries and borders, as one does at all sites of value.

The issue is not so much disparity as diacritical opposition – in this instance, diacritical opposition poised around the matter of "mental and moral cultivation" (Viswanathan 5) or, more starkly

131

put, poised around the Western "logic of cultural literacy – i.e., the transparent relationship of writing to thought" (Judy 42). The academic literary enterprise, the disparity would have it, patently engages all the powers of literacy and the life of the mind, whereas the activity of the singing voice does not. The two performances are understood to specify the terms of cognition and of the ludic as well as – not coincidentally – whiteness and blackness, thereby conflating distinctions between literacy and illiteracy and black and white. These four terms, in effect, form a spurious homology, so that, as much as literacy represents a privileged state of mind, it also connotes the redundancy of the material body and, ultimately, the alleged, overwhelming corporeality of blackness. The apparent disparity between the two performances, which amounts in the end to the notion that only one is an accountable sign of value in the highest terms of post-Enlightenment Western culture, masks the violence determining that very configuration, masks (like all signs of value) "a site for anxiety about corruption, about containment, about penetration" (xx). What the diacritical configuration reveals is an operation of violence and "its relation to that which has to be protected so that the [hegemonic] group might know itself *against a particular social, political, and historical threatening reality*" (xx; emphasis in original).

This conflation of notions of blackness and whiteness with notions of literacy as visible sign for the life of the mind is, as already suggested, a highly consequential one. It remains an instrumental measure in long-standing "New World" attempts to manage "the question of race [which is] really the question of who one believes to be human, ultimately where one draws the line between those to whom we extend our deep species of loyalty and those, *across the divide*, whom we enslave, experiment upon, or decide to exterminate" (Lauter 276; emphasis added). Insofar as the academy is another cultural site at which this conflation obtains, it is also another cultural site deeply interested in the management of the question of race and the *divide* race entails. Although the activities of the singing voice and of the academy are both cultural performances, only one is officially charged with the task of "the affirmation of an ideal self and an ideal political state" (Viswanathan 20). Only one "function[s] as the guarantor of [established] civil society through its regulating of the collocation of the discourses of political power and knowledge" (Judy 12). The academy (and the life of the mind it represents) involves itself profoundly in the disposition of citizens

and persons, and its seeming irrelevance to the performance of the
singing voice plays an important role in its disposition of social subjects.

In effecting these dispositions, the academy rehearses the way in
which dominant forms of value and their *insignificant* violences –
beyond marginalizing the Other – render obscure the perspective
of the Other. Value both specifies a relation defined above all by
diacritical marks and occludes that relation in order to figure itself
in the singular, discrete terms of a boundary signaling above all the
self-evidence of the valued form itself. Operations of value depend
on emphases placed on the centrality of a fetishized boundary, the
advantages and disadvantages accruing on either side of it, as well
as the transgressions of the boundary necessary to maintaining its
efficacy (all of which it is the task of an Other investigation of value
to expose). Although with a different type of guile than at less discursively self-conscious sites, these same dynamics operate at the site
of the literary academy since, in keeping with virtually all situations
of the U.S. cultural imaginary, what remain occluded, as documented by the NCTE surveys referred to by Paul Lauter, are experiences and communities represented by performances of the
singing voice.

To imagine the shift in scrutiny from the performances of singing
voices to the signing practices of the literary academy as radical or
tenuous immediately grants, then, one of the fundamental presuppositions of the U.S. literary academy, which codifies, by the mid-
twentieth century, its enduring institutional configuration as well as
– not coincidentally – protocols securing that "no work by a black
writer" stands as the object of its honorific critical appraisal or professionalized and specialized processes of reading and dissemination. The relations of whiteness and blackness as they are defined
by the dynamics of the valued and devalued in the broader U.S.
cultural logic are also cathected at the site of the academy.

The dynamics of the valued and the devalued shared with the
broader culture recapitulate themselves not only in *practice* that can
be gauged in terms of racial (and other) exclusions but, moreover,
in the *theory* of the literary academy. For, neatly enough, the scope
and kinds of attentions underwritten by highly consequential New
Critical programs in the academy rehearse very closely the guileful
dynamics of anatomized value. Like the performance of value itself,
these protocols rely preeminently on the centrality of a fetishized
boundary signaling, above all, the self-evidence of the bounded val-

ued form. The variety of critical programs joined under the title New Criticism hold in common the penchant to specify the literary text as an "autonomous" object in and of itself, having a peculiarly independent existence from industrial, prosaic, disturbingly "democratic," modern society. The literary text, the valued form under the stewardship of New Criticism, provides a quintessential object for eliciting "anxiety about corruption, about containment, about penetration."

New Criticism develops protocols presupposing that

> [o]n the one hand, poetry [i]s separated from morality, religion, science, psychology, sociology, and history while being unified internally by complex aesthetic and dramatic equilibriums and harmonies; on the other hand, poetry [i]s "a simulacrum of reality," an "imitation," based on "experience" [*WWU* 194], which offer[s] "knowledge of a whole object" and "the full body of the experience" [*EFD* 105]. (Leitch 32)[1]

The enabling designation of an outside (the extraliterary) and an inside (the literary) so important to New Critical protocols receives perhaps its most forceful and renowned articulation in the essays "The Intentional Fallacy" and "The Affective Fallacy" by W. K. Wimsatt and Monroe Beardsley.[2] Boldly asserting the hypostasized, autonomous state of the poem, the final statement of "The Affective Fallacy" posits that "though cultures have changed and will change, poems remain and explain" (39). Literary objects are bounded and made discrete, given separate ontological status, by New Critical declarations, which ultimately accrue into disciplinary developments that are anything but fleeting.

Rather than local or transient, New Critical premises emerge as fundamental presuppositions for the twentieth-century literary academy. It is no exaggeration to claim that "[t]he success of the New Criticism in 'institutionalizing' its methods and values is the major story of modern criticism" (Cain 120). New Critical programs espouse in the early decades of the twentieth century the version of U.S. formalist poetics that by the middle of the century is institutionalized as the set of theoretical assumptions remaining to the present the most potent and ingrained of the various competing developments in professional literary critical discourse. Although New Criticism is only one of many competing elements of the discipline in the early decades of the twentieth century when the literary academy is struggling for institutional configuration, the influence and persistence of New Criticism so overwhelm those of any of its competitors that it cannot be overlooked as the crucible out of which the literary academy definitively emerges. This disciplinary history is made clear, for example, by Gerald Graff in *Professing Literature*, as well as vigorously acknowledged by Peter Rabinowitz in *Before Reading*.[3] William E. Cain expresses the matter as follows: "New Critical beliefs and practices, though no longer in fashion, are also no longer in dispute, because they have been widely accepted as the foundation for criticism. . . . The New Criticism is so woven into the fabric of critical discourse that its assumptions are not recognized as assumptions at all" (112). The figural, conceptual, and cultural constraints of New Critical formalism persist in the academy, but no longer as the varied theoretical phenomena of previous decades. New Critical assumptions remain so potent and pervasive as to appear a natural, and therefore usually unscrutinized, part of what it is that the literary academy imagines that it does. "New Criticism is not so much in decline or dead as it has won eternal life as the [intuitive] core or essence of criticism" (Cain 106).

The importance of close reading to literary scholarly activity is certainly one element of this intuitive core, as is reliance on the primacy and symbolics of fetishized boundaries – boundaries that reproduce to a significant extent the ones examined and censured in Ann Petry's *The Street*. This is to say, *The Street* exposes, by virtue of both the terms of its narrative and its fortunes in the literary academy, the fact that borders are carefully contrived, carefully managed, and profitable enterprises whether they happen to separate all-American suburbs from African American communities or the literary from the extraliterary (or, indeed, the literary from African American communities and all-American suburbs from African American literature). The economies of racial, sexual, and class difference portrayed in the novel, as much as they define basic aspects of "the street," equally define institutionalized critical discourses overdetermining the fate of such texts in the academy. Insofar as the intentions and the attentions of Petry's novel – reissued in 1985 – controvert established conceptions of boundaries, they underscore in doing so a central issue of post-1960s literary critical debates, which is the interest of the literary academy in divides first fully theorized, fetishized, and institutionalized by New Criticism. It is important to note that 1986 is the midpoint of the first decade in which post-1960s challenges to the disciplinary status quo put into question with unprecedented far-reaching force institutional imperatives maintaining the putatively autonomous ontology of literary texts. In this way, insofar as the semiosis and the aesthetics as well as the disciplinary situation of the *The Street* possess relentlessly "social" faces, the boundary that would mark the "radical" separation of the literary and the extraliterary is severely compromised and made ambiguous. The novel's complex and taxing portrayal of reified racial and sexual economies – circulations of blackness to the advantage of whiteness and of femaleness to the advantage of maleness – insistently exposes for its reader both the problematics and profitability of illusory boundaries. *The Street* – as one might claim of most, if not all, African American literary texts and concerns[4] – abrogates the certainty of such boundaries.

The effect of disciplinary estimations of boundaries, whether consciously or intuitively maintained, is made abundantly clear by Cheryl A. Wall's articulation of the influence of African American women's writing and the criticism it has generated on the post-1960s literary academy: "Not only has the criticism of black women's writing been transformed over the past two decades; this criticism has transformed other critical discourses as well" (15). Plainly put, whether or not institutionalized critical discourses admit their relations to keenly social forces, their late twentieth-century metamorphoses in response to the admittedly social formation of the "vivid new fact of national life" (Spillers, "Cross-Currents" 245) that is African American women's creative and critical writings belie the denial.

Making even more explicit the consequences of the transformation alluded to by Wall, Deborah E. McDowell observes in the same year (1989) that "[a] scant ten years ago, scholars in search of criticism on black women writers faced a huge vacuum that abandoned them to their solitary carrels with only their own thoughts to bounce against each other. Since that time, however . . . we have arguably a small industry" (51–2). The emergence of that small scholarly industry remains one very patent indication that textuality, the *sign* of privilege over which the academic discipline of literary studies presides, has been reconceived in some quarters within unorthodox designs and across openly and intentionally transgressed boundaries; scholarly activity focusing concerted attention on texts by and the creativities of African American women writers records the emergence of formerly unimaginable literary scholarship. Unprecedented scholarly activities represented by critical voices like those of Wall, Spillers, and McDowell plainly advertise that the conceptualization of boundaries separating the discrete literary text and the "radically" distinguishable extraliterary sphere are already components of extraliterary discourses invested in reified economies of blackness and whiteness and femaleness and maleness. Differently put, the emergence of formerly unimaginable literary scholars – by virtue of the novel application of their energies and, indeed, by their very presence – clarifies ways in which New Critical protocols and their continued, intuitive currency constitute a subset – or subtext – of U.S. social discourse long invested in expropriations of blackness and femaleness in the name of value.

As significant as it is to recognize how post-1960s developments expose ways in which influential protocols remain implicated in sublimations of whiteness routine to U.S. doxa and formations of value, it is also important to recognize the inadequacy of viewing highly controversial desublimations of "whiteness" in merely the binary terms of a new visibility for the invisible, the centering of the marginalized, or a return of the exiled. Because of the peculiar dynamics of boundaries, the more openly controverted situation of "whiteness" and its relation to literary critical protocols calls, at least, for a tripartite conceptualization. It is useful, in this way, to gauge the controversions within the post-1960s literary academy in terms of the concept "bla(n)ckness": a *blankness* informed and confirmed by an asymmetrical relation sustained with *blackness* (among other things). Forgoing the apparent polarity of whiteness and blackness, the neologism "bla(n)ckness" does not designate a set of tensions or alignments that might resolve themselves by inversion. Rather, it attempts also to account for the inevitable violence[5] enforcing the juxtaposition of the two. Bla(n)ckness invariably embodies a profound skepticism concerning boundaries and, in this particular case – to borrow a phrase from Valerie Smith "the reification of boundaries that historically have excluded the writing of black women [and others] from serious consideration within academic and literary establishments" ("Theory" 57).[6] "Bla(n)ckness is a threefold concept comprehending (1) cultural discourses enforcing exclusionary U.S. doxa, (2) *unthinkable* and alternative discursive paradigms, (3) the dissymmetry obscured within the enforced, ostensibly symmetrical binary opposition of the two.

In *Hegemony and Socialist Strategy: Towards a Radical Democratic Politics*, Ernesto Laclau and Chantal Mouffe provide a model of "articulatory practice" that is useful for beginning to conceptualize

bla(n)ckness. Laclau and Mouffe define articulation as: "the construction of nodal points which partially fix meaning[,] . . . the partial character of this fixation proceed[ing] from the openness of the
social, a result, in its turn, of the constant overflowing of every discourse by the infinitude of the field of discursivity" (113). Articulation consists, in other words, of fixing meaning in a field in which
the possibilities for fixing meaning are open and infinite. The resulting "structured totality" (of nodal points or articulated "moments") remains significant at the expense of "any difference[s]
that are not discursively articulated" (105), which is to say, at the
expense of underprivileged and occluded "elements" of the discourse.

Discourse, in brief, is the structure, or paradigm, of meaning
fixed by social practice and maintained by a particular articulatory
practice, and, in the light of this model of articulation and discourse,
bla(n)ckness can be thought of first of all as the infinite, unfixed,
and underprivileged field of discursive elements underlying reified
articulatory practice. Bla(n)ckness made *significant* necessarily disfigures dominant discourse in order to figure one previously unarticulated – an implicated and silenced Otherness, the significance of
which is unthinkable in terms of the dominant discourse. Over and
above representing an unthinkable challenge to a dominant discourse, bla(n)ckness appropriates the privileging relationships of articulatory practice, which it, at the same time, dismisses. It matches
the violence of dominant discourse with newly meaningful violence
of its own; that is, it effects an unthinkable and alternate discursive
paradigm by reappropriating the erasure of discursive elements
(possibility) by discursive moments (realization) – the very erasure
that it calls into question: Hence, bla(n)ckness might be thought of
as the concomitant abrogation and transgression of the distinction
between traditionally significant discursive moments and traditionally unmeaning discursive elements. Although bla(n)ckness nonetheless distinguishes the two in order to reform the sign, it reveals
that the sign and "unmeaning jargon" are inevitably entangled. It
is bound not to one, but to two fields of discursive meaning yoked
in "a [reified] system [that] only exists [despite all efforts to the
contrary] as a partial limitation of a 'surplus of meaning' which
subverts [the system]" (111).

Recall the analogous performance of the singing voice, in which
an agent of the voice foregrounds the apparently unmeaning
materiality of her or his voice as much as, or even more than, tra-

ditionally meaningful iterations. During such a performance, enunciation is made to empty the enunciated. The usually silent materiality of the voice does not, as usual, defer to significance but is instead made significant itself. Speech reserves the incorporation of itself as fixing and determinative power in order – concomitantly and obversely – to incorporate itself as unfixed iterative power, in other words, infinite unfixed speech that allows an Other speech.

Bla(n)ckness, then, exposes the exorbitance, inadequacies, and failures of traditionally significant practice and traditionally significant signs or, in a phrase, marks a crisis for dominant signification. In this manner, the small scholarly industries remarked by McDowell exchange, in both theory and praxis, institutional discussions of the discrete text for discussions refunctioned by the indiscretions of race, gender, sexuality, and class. Such scholarly activities promote the insight that "like all value, literary value is not the property of an object or a subject but, rather, *the product of the dynamics of a system*" (Herrnstein Smith, *Contingencies* 15; emphasis in original) – a system as much extraliterary as literary. Remarkably, then, given the institutional history of literary study, the literary text is placed in "the street" and, just as remarkably, *The Street* and its extraliterary concerns are placed within institutional sites (sights) to which they were once contrary, adverse, and *unimaginable* (and to a considerable extent they remain so). This turn of events proves greatly disturbing to a U.S. public and system of higher education that imagine themselves confronted for the first time in their history with "overtly ideological scholarship" (D'Souza 52), even as they matter-of-factly secure, for example, that the overwhelming majority of Ph.D. accreditations (86.2 percent in 1991) are granted to caucasians.[7] Rather, what is really so disturbing are the force and clarity of the revelation that "so-called noninstrumental approaches [to literature and other matters] are themselves always already implicated in the raging battle in one's society and culture" (West 200–1).[8] In short, unprecedented scholarship in the post-1960s academy merely places adverse issues at sites (sights) where they have always been – although in a very different light:

> Culture does not stand above or apart from the many other activities and relationships that make up a society, including the socially organized forms of domination, exploitation, and power pervasive in our society and its history. Granted, cultural practices foster social solidarity and collective identity. But that

does not keep them from participating in social divisions and exclusions. Granted, culture is a state of reciprocal relationships and mutual understandings. But these achievements are not inevitable; they do not belong to culture categorically. Indeed, whether conceived as spirit, consciousness, superstructure, or the symbolic, culture is not a realm unto itself or a separate domain. (Brenkman vii)

Comprising the most fraught and hotly contested point of the post-1960s debate, the issue amounts to the acknowledgment that such a postulated restricted and restrictive space (whether ontological or institutional) is, above all, *socially* constructed and maintained.

Recognition of the powerful role of poststructuralist theories in the ascendancy of these insights is a commonplace. Poststructuralism "denotes a variety of critical practices and theoretical agendas that arose out of structuralism as both a reaction to and modification of many of its tenets," and these "theories and practices in general share an oppositional stance toward traditional intellectual categories" (Childers and Hentzi 236–7). Taking the work of Jacques Derrida as a point of definition, one can say poststructuralist theories engage with both rigor and playfulness the abundant consequences pursuant to the intellectual moment "when everything became a system where the central signified, the original or transcendental signified, is never absolutely present outside a system of differences" (Derrida, "Structure" 249). In the wake of this intellectual moment all cherished structures – the cogito, the subject, identity, the author, discourse, the text, origin – become the effects or traces of the differential play of conscripted terms of an arbitrary system. In theory, all these structures become fundamentally "undecidable," invariable sites of an aporia, and encourage even more disturbingly the recognition that an apparent binary engagement "is never the confrontation of two terms, but forms instead a hierarchy and the order of a subordination" (Derrida, *Limited* 21).

The advent of this far-reaching intellectual movement is identified most often with the imported speculations of four prominent French intellectuals: the "jouissance" of Roland Barthes, the "deconstruction" of Jacques Derrida, the "archeology and counter-memory" of Michel Foucault, the psychoanalytic theory of Jacques Lacan. However, the speculations of these Continental thinkers and the work their theories spawn are not so inherently troubling as to account for the ardor of pronouncements of crisis in and around

post-1960s literary critical activity. For example, the work of the former Yale critics Harold Bloom, Paul de Man, Geoffrey Hartman, and
J. Hillis Miller – which is often considered the initial instance of the
poststructuralist boom in the U.S. academy – attests to the modest
nature of the threat posed by imported poststructuralist thought.
The critical productions of the Yale school pose no challenge to
long-standing discursive privileges powerfully institutionalized with
New Critical protocols.[9] The routine narrowness of the work of the
Yale School vis-à-vis race, gender, sexuality, and class recapitulates
the long-received imperatives of those protocols, which is a denial
or neglect of the social embeddedness of any cultural apparatus.

Despite its vilification, it is not theory itself nor poststructuralist
theory as such, but the new communities employing the insights and
ethos of poststructuralism, the novel uses to which they are put, and
the new perceptions they are employed to underwrite that are most
responsible for the earnestness with which the post-1960s academy
is pronounced in crisis. The very salient point that the sway of theory
is by no means new is convincingly explicated by Paul de Man in
"The Resistance to Theory":

> The predominant trends in North American literary criticism,
> before the nineteen sixties, were certainly not averse to theory,
> if by theory one understands the rooting of literary exegesis
> and of critical evaluation in a system of some conceptual gen-
> erality. Even the most intuitive, empirical and theoretically low-
> key writers on literature made use of a minimal set of concepts
> (tone, organic form, allusion, tradition, historical situation,
> etc.) of at least some general import. In several other cases,
> the interest in theory was publicly asserted and practiced. A
> broad shared methodology, more or less overtly proclaimed,
> links together such influential text books of the era as *Under-*
> *standing Poetry* (Brooks and Warren), *Theory of Literature* (Wel-
> leck and Warren) and *The Fields of Light* (Reuben Brower) or
> such theoretically oriented works as *The Mirror and the Lamp*,
> *Language as Gesture* and *The Verbal Icon.* (5–6)

The theory that does not appear as "theory" is received and accepted New Critical formulations, which insist upon an intrinsically
literary domain and an adulterating extraliterary one (disparaged as
"politics" or now as "cultural studies"). Putting the matter differently, William E. Cain substantiates de Man's observations as follows
(although I believe he never fully appreciates the import of his state-

ment in terms of race and gender – despite the concluding chapter of his book):

> The truth is that the New Criticism . . . seems to be powerless [at present] only because its power is so pervasive that we are ordinarily not even aware of it. So deeply ingrained in English studies are New Critical attitudes, values, and emphases that we do not even perceive them as the legacy of a particular movement. On the contrary: we feel them to be the natural and definitive conditions of criticism in general. (105)[10]

Hence, rather than theory itself, it is the dissolution of ensconced New Critical tenets in deference to diffusions of the discrete literary text into the cultural, ideological, and social economies in which and with which it is produced, consumed, and imbued that accounts for passionate calls of alarm. The issue, in other words, is really the retheorizing of the discrete literary text in "responsive[ness] . . . to the situations and perspectives of women, blacks, children of immigrants, and other minority or non-elite social groups" (Herrnstein Smith, "Curing" 3).[11] This point cannot be overstated; it is paramount to note also that exposures of these long-standing and formerly unacknowledged power dynamics of literary value realize not *valuelessness* but, instead, controversions of value.

There are two matters to be insisted upon. First, it is not theory itself, nor poststructuralist theory as such, but their inflections in terms of race, gender, sexuality, and class that are most responsible for the cries of alarm. Second, perhaps the most startling disclosure of the post-1960s speculative projects resisted by the humanist academy is the disclosure that, in a variety of ways – bodily, chorally, deliberatively, and, when allowed, learnedly – African Americans have always been grappling with the most difficult and perplexing of intellectual matters. For, if one accepts the fundamental poststructuralist premise that "[w]hat 'presents' itself [in processes of signification] is the representation of nonpresence, what Derrida calls 'otherness,' 'difference,' [*sic*] or 'alterity' " (Allison xxxvi), then one is precariously close, it seems to me, to valorizing the highly complex contingencies of African American (and other subaltern) cultures. One is also precariously close to recognizing that the complexities of poststructuralist thought only merely begin to rehearse or comprehend, in the narrow way of "Reason" (and its intellectual undoing), the various intricate ingenious tasks of African American cultures in the New World. Restated, one is grossly mistaken if one believes "blackness is associated solely with concrete gut level experience conceived as either opposing or having no connection to abstract thinking and the production of critical theory" (hooks 23).[12] What one is forced to recognize is that, as a matter of course and survival, African American cultures invariably concern themselves with the imperative knowledge that "[t]he concept of [a New World] centered structure – although it represents coherence itself, the condition of the *epistemes* of philosophy or science – is contradictorily coherent," and, moreover, that this "coherence in contradiction expresses the force of a [white] desire" (Derrida, "Structure" 248; emphasis in original). In short, the spectre faced by the post-1960s academy is that, if understood as engaging noteworthy intellectual concerns, the jouissance of Barthes, deconstruction of Derrida, archaeology and countermemory of Foucault, and psychoanalytic intricacies of Lacan are foremost the urgencies at a variety of levels (and are foremost "indicated" – to use the terminology of Husserl) in African American cultures and existence in the landscapes of the New World.

This potentially immense disturbance of poststructuralist thought is made distinct in Mark Taylor's 1984 allegorization of the transgressive nature and focus of poststructuralist thought. In his study *Erring*, Taylor presents the condition of the "grotesque" body as an exemplar of "[t]he free activity of play [that] enacts rather than represses [the] paradoxical coincidence of presence and absence" (159). In its radical reconsiderations of such naturalized cultural concepts as self, history, writing, and the book, this paradoxical free play is a central motif of imported poststructuralist thought. Taylor's understanding of the grotesque body reads in part as follows:

> The grotesque body incarnates the liminality of the trace by disrupting every identity that is only itself and by upsetting all sense of propriety. Because the grotesque body is utterly transgressive, it is totally liminal. Such a body is not merely found along the boundary; it *is* actually a border or margin. The grotesque body is never individual, for it transgresses every isolating limit. . . . The body as grotesque is the body that eats, drinks, shits, pisses, and fucks. The boundary between the bodies is a permeable membrane; it has gaps and holes to let the inside out and the outside in. This interplay of inner and outer makes all bodily events interstitial. . . . While radical opening mortally wounds proper identity, conclusive closure marks the

end of the body. When inside is only inside and outside is only outside, when eating, drinking, pissing, shitting, and fucking stop or are stopped, vital current no longer flows and the body truly dies. (162; emphasis in original)

The profound disorder and iconoclasm of taking a philosophy allegorized in these terms as the basis for scholarly thought and investigation is quickly apparent. The grotesque body – "eat[ing], drink[ing], shit[ting], piss[ing], and fuck[ing]" – far from being taken as an endowment of or for scholarly thought, is most readily understood in the United States[13] as the lurid, negligible, and, above all, *unthinkable* African American body, female or male – or indeed as any female body (especially at its most mysterious: its moment of giving birth).[14]

In a landscape in which African American bodies are emblematic of a reviled and excluded "grotesque," how can one speak seriously and learnedly of "liminality," the "transgressive," of "boundar[ies]," or "border[s,]" and "margin[s]" without, at the same time, speaking seriously and learnedly of African Americans, the bla(n)ckness of African Americans, and the bla(n)ckness of other Others? This speculative possibility is untenable, since U.S. cultural production as well as U.S. scholarly production are distinctly marked by "the inability of white people to grab hold of and securely retain an appreciation of the realities of black existence" (Williamson 234), an existence violently and ungenerously determined by "white people." Insofar as the grotesque is necessarily the African American body, it cannot, without some measure of disturbance, be thought in the U.S. landscape and cannot, without very great disturbance, be taken as of value or significance. Such speculative possibilities are most often, as a matter of course, determined speculative impossibilities. Interest in the "never individual" life and "interstitial" nonidentity of "grotesque" black bodies never easily enters U.S. culture, or U.S. contemplative thought, of any period.

Thus, the potential iconoclasm of poststructuralist speculation is so vast it puts under suspicion – in ways that are finally deeply troubling – not only the most entrenched and revered presuppositions of literary study but also unfathomably entrenched U.S. doxa. Whether within or without the academy, U.S. doxa is based on politically efficacious sublimations of whiteness that rest uneasily on bla(n)ck speculation. No matter how open or mediated, it enacts a disqualification or pathological bracketing of dark-skinned others as the enabling maneuver of New World thought, popular and learned. Thomas Jefferson, in the late eighteenth century, for example, writes, "[i]n general, [African American] existence appears to participate more of sensation than reflection" (139). Early in the nineteenth century, G.W.F. Hegel proposes that "[w]e must lay aside all thought of reverence and morality – all that we call feeling – if we would rightly comprehend ['the African']; there is nothing harmonious with humanity to be found in ['the peculiarly African'] character" (97; emphasis in original).[15] Abraham Lincoln, in the mid-nineteenth century, writes, "I agree with Judge Douglas [that the African American] is not my equal in many respects – certainly not in color, perhaps not in moral or intellectual endowment" (53).

One might draw on a variety of figures and extend the chronology as close to the contemporary moment as one wishes and, in doing so, delineate the enduring, hostile context and problematic for African American cultures. This indispensable element of the discourses of the New World informs, for example (even if sometimes increasingly less identifiable), four very different, historically diverse, and revealing U.S. texts – three overtly "extraliterary" and one literary critical: Thomas Jefferson's *Notes on the State of Virginia*, George Fitzhugh's *Cannibals All!*, the Southern Agrarians' *I'll Take My Stand*, and "The Intentional Fallacy" by W. K. Wimsatt and Monroe Beardsley. Although such information might not always be patent, the enduring extraliterary concern with blackness is an element of all four texts. Of particular interest, to this end, are Jefferson's objection to "incorporat[ing] the blacks into the state" (138), Fitzhugh's mid-nineteenth-century accounts of the lot of enslaved African Americans, the geographical and historical metaphors initiating the single Southern Agrarian essay that openly considers the presence of African Americans, and the glib references of Wimsatt and Beardsley to the "public" status of the literary object. Other texts might be effectively substituted for these; however, what the posited resemblance of these four reveal is that institutionalized along with New Critical claims for literary objects and discourses as distinct from the vagaries of openly social concerns is the inconsistency of the position vis-à-vis the bla(n)ckness forming an inevitable concern of New World discursive and social formations.

Thomas Jefferson's 1787 *Notes on the State of Virginia* is introduced in a 1954 edition as "a book for today . . . valuable both as an introduction to Jefferson and as a commentary on problems as relevant

to our own generation as they were to his" (xi). William Peden, the
author of this introductory statement, speaks more truthfully than
he knows, because the irrationality of Jefferson's assessment of what
he imagines as grotesque African American bodies remains insistently relevant today. Jefferson enumerates "physical and moral"
objections to "incorporat[ing] the blacks into the state":

> Whether the black of the negro resides in the reticular mem-
> brane between the skin and scarf-skin, or in the scarf-skin itself;
> whether it proceeds from the colour of the blood, the colour
> of the bile, or from that of some other secretion, the difference
> is fixed in nature, and is as real as if its seat and cause were
> better known to us. . . . Is it not the foundation of a greater or
> less share of beauty in the two races? . . . Add to these, flowing
> hair, a more elegant symmetry of form, their own judgment in
> favour of the whites, declared by their preference of them, as
> uniformly as is the preference of the Oran-ootan for the black
> women over those of his own species. The circumstance of su-
> perior beauty, is thought worthy of attention in the propaga-
> tion of . . . domestic animals; why not in that of man? (138)

Whereas the grotesque body proves exemplary of the poststructuralist "coincidence of presence and absence" that Mark Taylor
wishes to present, to Jefferson's mind, that body – of which the
African American is unmistakably emblematic – proves worthy of
little, if any, speculation beyond ways to maintain its subjugation. In
this passage, the grotesque African American body is first characterized in the terms most recurrent to eighteenth-century thinkers of
science, philosophy, and belles letters, the terms of light and enlightenment. "Th[e] brightening of the life of the mind is the
theme of the age" (Noonan 1); thus, the leading preoccupation and
metaphor of the age announces the preemptory disqualification of
African Americans, "the black of the negro," even before appealing
to the auxiliary issues of "symmetry" and "beauty." Specifying,
then, the disenfranchising deformity and the plain inconsequence
of African Americans, Jefferson notes that "[i]n general, their existence appears to participate more of sensation than reflection"
(139). He fixes the admissability of African Americans into only a
world of "negligible" corporeality. Nevertheless, although his conclusion is forgone, African Americans paradoxically represent an interstitial bestiality[16] to Jefferson's mind. In point of fact, the oddly
flawed logic of Jefferson's "physical and moral" objection under-

scores the extent to which African Americans are profoundly *un-thinkable* in the U.S. landscape.

First, it is important to note how peculiar it is for a putatively rationalist thinker to define membership in a republic according to idiosyncratic determinations of who does or does not possess physical beauty, whether or not one agrees with the criteria of beauty being employed. Nevertheless, in delineating the all-important divide – or boundary – between peoples, white and black, humans within the civic order and beasts without, Jefferson invokes a correlation that troubles the very distinction he is making. Jefferson, in order to make his declaration, invokes a principle that ignores the declaration being made: "The circumstance of superior beauty, is thought worthy of attention in the propagation of our horses, dogs, and other domestic animals; why not in that of man?" An undiscriminating correlation between people and beasts is invoked in order to establish a distinction between greater men, worthy of membership within the republic, and lesser men who, because of a more inveterate bestiality, are not. Jefferson overlooks his principal principle at the rationally conclusive moment of his judgment; in order to establish a distinction among humans, he violates the very distinction between humans and animals that lies at the heart of his seemingly rationalist definitions of "the humans" populating the U.S. republic. In order to argue for gradations of (or a boundary between) greater and lesser humans, Jefferson dismisses the underpinning boundary between humans and "horses, dogs, and other domestic animals." Without involved qualification, his ostensible logic proves unaccountable.

In effect, contrary to Jefferson's convictions as well as the convictions of many others, it becomes clear that a grotesque and unexamined irrationality, rather than any coloring "resid[ing] in the reticular membrane between the skin and scarf-skin, or in the scarf-skin itself," determines African Americans as negligible, grotesque bodies. Yet, notwithstanding many others pointing out and my pointing out this violent irrationality, there has always been and continues to be formidable resistance to examining the unthinkable logic rendering African Americans unthinkable – examinations imperative to African American cultures themselves. It is the spectre of programmatic and institutional acknowledgments of African American cultures, African American consciousnesses, and, above all, the various and continuing oppressions of African American peoples that precipitates the crisis of reason evident in Jefferson's "physical and moral" objection – a crisis that, like the alarms of post-1960s literary study, oddly assumes all the ardor of a putative resistance to irrationality. If the antinomian project of poststructuralist thought also pursues a crisis of Reason, to endorse that project in all its suggestiveness amounts, in one of its dimensions, to earnestly undertaking the traditionally unthinkable speculation long dismissed in Jefferson's objection.

This unthinkable speculation, or open engagement with the seemingly relentless logic rendering the "New World" hostile to African Americans, entails reassessing with patent suspicion the "ambiguous legacy [formalized by] the Founding Fathers, who, like Thomas Jefferson, owned human beings while composing a Declaration of Independence that proclaimed the equality and liberty of all men" (Painter, "Race Relations" 126). To underscore observations already made, the point at which one recognizes signification and presence as the uncanny acts of "an endless series of reverberations" attempting a "representation of nonpresence" (Allison xxxvi), one also begins to understand the seemingly endless dilemma of African Americans in the hostile New World. One must examine disturbing inconsistencies of a form of Reason according to which "ready to make allowances for differences of condition, education, conversation, and the sphere in which slaves moved, Jefferson still subscribed [on irrational grounds] to the theory of black inferiority" (Cunningham 62).

The spectre of this examination is the spectre of bla(n)ckness and, to restate an important point, bla(n)ckness is not adequately conceptualized in terms of the mere inversion suggested by the dynamics of concepts like invisibility, marginalization, or exile. For bla(n)ckness not only remarks the inversibility of two fields distinguished by a clearly (rationally) established boundary, but interrogates as well the inadmissability of that boundary as a measure of the two fields. Because it marks a point of crossing and mixing, as much as it marks the point of the separation of the two fields, the boundary is ambiguous, ungrounded, and manipulatable. It is a highly profitable object of dominant discourses and formations – as the tortured logic of Jefferson's appeal makes apparent.

The spectre of bla(n)ckness, for these reasons, is at least threefold:

(1) Traditional discourses are radically questioned. They are exposed as grotesque and unthinkable themselves, by exposure

of the moments at which they abrogate their own premises, moments at which they transgress the very boundaries established for their self-definition and dominance.

(2) In the light of these self-riddling moments, untraditional and competing discourses are more readily apparent, for, exposed as arbitrary, dominant discourses revealed as not *uniquely* rigorous, nor coherent, nor rational, nor moral, and so on, set in relief not only their arbitrary internal principles but also the arbitrariness of their relations to Other discourses over which they are merely *dominant* and not unquestionably superior in rigor, coherence, rationality, morality, and so forth.

(3) The violence, formalized as the boundary, first setting the dominant and untraditional discourses in an oppositional relationship becomes an issue newly open to scrutiny and newly open to reevaluations of its apparent neutrality. The boundary is the register of violence marking itself otherwise; it (seemingly) fixes itself "when [open] force gives way to ideas" (Viswanathan 85) or, more plainly, when physical and social force is recast as the *force* of reason and evidence, assuming in this way an ontologically different (and neutral) status, a status in which boundaries appear as independent factors in the oppositions they set in place and maintain. One must see, on the contrary, that this independent status of the boundary depends entirely on the sanction of the dominant discourse and its stabilizing opposition. The dominant discourse slyly redoubles itself as dominant position and neutral boundary, thereby slyly casting as symmetrical (as two counterposed elements distinguished by a boundary) what is in fact unsymmetrical (two elements counterposed to one in a hostile systemic configuration).

One is led, as Laclau and Mouffe suggest in their theory of articulation, beyond misleading dichotomization and, instead, must contemplate a massive reconceptualization of what constitutes the scene of knowing, the privileged objects of interest, and the sites of both. Laclau and Mouffe elaborate their dismissal of dichotomies in the following terms:

The main consequence of a break with the discursive/extra-discursive dichotomy is the abandonment of the thought/reality opposition, and hence a major enlargement of the field of those categories which can account for social relations. Synonymy, metonomy, metaphor are not forms of thought that add a second sense to a primary, constitutive literality of social relations; instead, they are part of the primary terrain itself in which the social is constituted. (110)

To put this observation in more immediately useful terms, one can say that, looking beyond the narrowness of dichotomization, one recognizes that African Americans form an invariable part of the primary terrain in which "universal" U.S. culture is constituted. Dichotomization obscures this recognition, for beyond the opposition and inversibility of, say, whiteness and blackness, the literary and the extraliterary, one must also recognize the violent asymmetry of the pairing in the first place. It is not enough to see white and black, the literary and the extraliterary; one must also acknowledge the mutual information each holds for the other at the putative legitimization of the one and at the great expense of the Other.

Looking beyond dichotomization, then, one sees the paradox and illegitimacy of Jefferson's "boundary" and "whiteness." In his attempt to prove African Americans in some manner less than human, Jefferson makes an appeal that definitively undermines the category of human, as well as any gradations of humanity he might be concerned with. Oddly, the presence of his logic is dependent on the absence of its very (dis)enabling premise, an oddity that not coincidentally mirrors the manner in which the privileged presence of whiteness in the U.S. landscape depends on an absence understood as the grotesque and negligible African American body.

In short, bla(n)ckness exposes not only the overlooked coincidence of these ostensibly separate spheres but, furthermore, the manner in which their coincidence is dissembled. Bla(n)ckness troubles the formal connections between putatively self-evident reason and abiding concerns with the subjugation or marginalization of African Americans – as, similarly, connections between putatively nonsocial academic discourses and the same abiding concerns. Given Jefferson's open fixation with the phenotypes of African Americans, these exposures are readily made in *Notes on the State of Virginia*. Possessing a type of candor unique among the four texts considered here, only Jefferson's discussion poses the imperative matter on which Reason must be brought to bear in the terms of the "difference . . . of color[,] . . . the black . . . resid[ing] in the recticular membrane between the skin and the scarf-skin, or in the scarf-skin itself." Only Jefferson's considerations focus on naming the plain mark of the Other. This undisguised fixation, under the pressure of subsequent political, military, or moral pressures, is not reproduced by Fitzhugh, the Southern Agrarians, or the New Critics. These later cultural commentators work, on the contrary, to recast the discussion of abiding concerns with African Americans in any terms but these, that is, in any terms more apparently reasonable.

The Virginian slaveholder George Fitzhugh (1806–81) provides an important nineteenth-century example, since he "loom[s] large in the story of" the southern slaveholders' "developing class consciousness" (Genovese 119) under the rising pressure of insistent external critique. Fitzhugh, like Jefferson, unapologetically opposes "incorporat[ing] the blacks into the state" and advances the conviction to the last, which is to say, until it is overwhelmed by military opposition. Harvey Wish in a lengthy 1943 biography of Fitzhugh observes that "[i]t was inevitable for a Virginian like Fitzhugh, endowed as he was with a strong sense of loyalty to local institutions, to undertake a vigorous defense of the threatened Southern outpost of slavery" (32). Nevertheless, the terms on which Fitzhugh formulates and defends U.S. racialist convictions differ radically from those offered by Jefferson. Responsible in part is the fact that the humanist and humanitarian appeals of the antislavery movement are extraordinarily more pronounced in Fitzhugh's time, even though both writers publish after the mid-eighteenth century, when "slavery was being transformed from a problematical but readily defensible institution into a self-evidently evil and abominable one" (Haskell 107). Fitzhugh's (in)famous proslavery treatise *Cannibals All! Slaves Without Masters* appears only three years before the Civil War, an appearance well after the watershed decade of the 1830s in which the U.S. debate concerning "incorporat[ing] the blacks into the state" is dramatically refashioned.

On either side of the 1830s stand the national crises of the Missouri Compromise and the bloody controversies of the unorganized territories that lead to the Kansas–Nebraska Act. However, because of a series of rapid developments, the 1830s themselves mark a sea change in debates surrounding U.S. slave regimes and race relations. For instance, David Walker's incendiary *Appeal to the Colored Citizens of the World* appears in 1829, and, one year after its highly controversial reception, Walker is found murdered in Boston near the shop where he was a dealer in old clothes. In January 1831 William Lloyd Garrison begins to publish *The Liberator*, and in August of the same year in southwestern Virginia Nat Turner leads the bloodiest slave rebellion on U.S. soil. The New England Anti-Slavery is founded in 1831, and the American Anti-Slavery Society two years later in Philadelphia. Emancipation is narrowly defeated in the Virginia constitutional convention of December 1831, and in 1833 emancipation is effected by legal fiat in the British Caribbean. In 1836 *Slavery in the United States: A Narrative of the Life and Adventures of Charles Ball, A Black Man*, the first full-length slave narrative published under the aegis of the U.S. abolitionist movement, ushers in the age of the "classic" slave narratives (1836–65), in which "the stigma traditionally associated with slavery [is transferred] from the slave to the slaveholder" (Starling 107). The same year also inaugurates the Gag Rule controversy, an eight year battle in the House of Representatives between the North and South concerning censorship of antislavery mailings and petitions on the House floor.

In other words, the climate for public discussions of the enslavement of African Americans changes markedly from the time of Jefferson to the time of Fitzhugh. After the 1830s, for one reason or another, "[m]ost pro-slavery literature whether from northern or southern pens dwelt less on slavery than on the shape and tendencies of American society" (Tise 261). The primacy of Jefferson's revulsion at the dark skins (and other physical features) of African Americans is not reproduced in Fitzhugh's 1857 treatise. Rather than the sensational physicality of African Americans, the principal concern of Fitzhugh is the scant regard given in nineteenth-century political economies to what he understands as a figurative "whiteness." His concern is for a properly self-identical whiteness not adequately respected in antebellum social configurations. Thus, his discussion effects in large measure an erasure of blackness in order to figure and refigure sites of whiteness, and, in doing so, he provides perhaps both the most extreme and best known defense of the U.S. "peculiar institution" in the mid-nineteenth century.

The title of his treatise, *Cannibals All! Slaves Without Masters*, refers principally not to the condition and propensities of African Americans, as one might initially suspect, but, instead, to the social relations within the ostensibly nonslaveholding and emerging industrial capitalist societies of the United States and Europe. The fact that attention is shifted in this way from material bodies to the abstractions of social relations is important. Unlike Jefferson's objection to "incorporat[ing] the blacks into the state," the focus is not physical or physiological – or, more accurately stated, *is* physical and physiological only insofar as the physical and physiological are unstated but understood. The figurative "whiteness" that draws the focus in Fitzhugh's objection is properly synonymous, using his own terms, with "happi[ness]," "free[dom]," "allowance," "liberty," "right[s]," and the leisure implied by not having to "work or starve." In a perfect world, this figurative whiteness would correspond to the condition of populations understood as physically or materially "white." Accordingly, the thrust of his argument is against the misplacing of this figurative whiteness (that characterizes the South) and against the withholding of this figurative whiteness (characterizing the North). Misplaced whiteness (in the South), Fitzhugh comprehends, is the upshot of U.S. slave regimes, which render "[t]he negro slaves of the South . . . the happiest, and, in some sense, the freest people in the world" (18). On the other hand, he understands whiteness withheld as the upshot of capitalist social relations, which render the laboring whites of various populations – left entirely to his or her own means – "more of a slave than the negro, because he [or she] works longer and harder for less allowance than the slave, and has no holiday, because the cares of life with him [or her] begin its labors end. He [or she] has no liberty, and not a single right" (18–19).

These circumstances notwithstanding, it is crucial to recognize in Fitzhugh's formulations that although "whiteness" seems very much to characterize the conditions in which enslaved African Americans live (as Fitzhugh imagines them), whiteness nonetheless and decidedly emanates from elsewhere. It is a benevolence fortuitously bestowed on African Americans by the class of whites who are their masters. This benevolent act, according to Fitzhugh, is not shared by remiss northern U.S. and other capitalists in the relations they bear to the innumerable workers who (like slaves) secure and ensure their wealth. Capitalists engage in a much more widespread and villainous practice of slavery, to Fitzhugh's mind, than the slaveholders of the South, and the garish references to the consumption of flesh in the title of his book aim to expose these "uncivilized" circumstances characterizing North American and European capitalist societies. Insofar as all those who do not labor physically in their livelihoods necessarily live by means of the labor of others, they are cannibals:

> "Thou art the man!" You are a Cannibal! and if a successful
> one, pride yourself on the number of your victims quite as

much as any Fiji chieftain, who breakfasts, dines, and sups on
human flesh – and your conscience smites you, if you have
failed to succeed, quite as much as his, when he returns from
an unsuccessful foray. (16–17)

The discussion is not put in the terms of the visibly grotesque body
or of immediate, racially lower orders of existence, such as Jefferson's observation that "[i]n general, [African Americans'] existence
appears to participate more of sensation than reflection" (139).
Instead, it is phrased in terms of unrecognized threats to social order and largesse *figured* in the terms of an imagined grotesque body
and imagined racially lower orders of existence. Unlike Jefferson's
argument, Fitzhugh's fails to look primarily to the grotesque bodies
that populate U.S. territories "on the same stage with whites, and
where the facts are not apocryphal on which a judgment is to be
formed" (139).

Fitzhugh, as does Jefferson, writes of flesh, but this shared point
of their considerations most fully marks the distinctions between
their shared objection to "incorporating the blacks into the state."
The flesh in Fitzhugh's analysis is the metaphorical flesh of figurative cannibalism, not the dark flesh of African Americans standing
as the sign of a "difference fixed in nature."[17] The figurative flesh
represents, not a fixity of nature, but a structure of social relations.
The matter, as Fitzhugh puts it, does not concern at all the peculiarities of the flesh of African Americans. It concerns the complexity
and imperatives of pervasive social relations – best managed by the
whiteness disseminated and ensured by the slaveholding societies of
the U.S. South.

Slavery, in the scheme Fitzhugh proposes, is the universal condition of labor, and he undertakes his defense of the southern "institution" by comparing the southern system of slavery to what he
proposes as another more exacting, less humane capitalist system of
slavery. The pervasive, cannibalistic social relations of humankind
may be uncivilized in some forms but need not necessarily be so.
They may be civilized by carefully "institutionalizing" – and, so to
speak, "mastering" – them. Fitzhugh writes:

You, with the command over labor which your capital gives you,
are a slave owner – a master, without the obligations of a master. They who work for you, create your income, are slaves,
without the rights of slaves. Slaves without a master! Whilst you

were engaged in amassing your capital, in seeking to become
independent, you were in the White Slave Trade. (17–18)

The metaphorical flesh of the cannibalism conceived by Fitzhugh
most closely approaches incarnation as the white flesh of the down-
trodden workers within capitalist political economies. Fitzhugh examines, instead of a juxtaposition between blackness and whiteness,
as does Jefferson, a remarkable incongruity of whiteness and whiteness: The workers within a capitalist political economy are disbarred
from the "happi[ness]," "free[dom]," "allowance," "liberty,"
"right[s]," and leisure implied by not having to "work or starve."
The whiteness that characterizes and might be disbursed by ruling
classes is, ironically, withheld from those workers who most assuredly
should be its recipients so that, by means of a heinous oversight, African Americans possess a greater proximity to whiteness than the
working masses of white northerners and Europeans. Institutional
slavery needs to be expanded, not curtailed.

In the words of Eugene Genovese, Fitzhugh's reasoning demonstrates how "[t]he proslavery argument move[s] from the particular
to the general, from a concern with Afro-American labor to a concern with labor in the abstract, from a focus on racial caste to a
focus on social class" (118). The justification for U.S. slavery resides
in the exigencies of an abstract and difficult system of human relations. Indeed, whiteness, if one fully follows Fitzhugh's logic, is a
largesse ironically reserved for African Americans, and this understanding is precisely the conclusion that Fitzhugh would have his
reader reach. He writes as follows of the condition of African Americans in southern slave societies:

> The children and the aged and infirm work not at all, and yet
> have all the comforts and necessaries of life provided for them.
> They enjoy liberty, because they are oppressed neither by care
> nor labor. The women do little hard work, and are protected
> from the despotism of their husbands by their masters. The
> negro men and stout boys work, on the average, in good
> weather, not more than nine hours a day. The balance of their
> time is spent in perfect abandon. Besides, they have their Sab-
> baths and holidays. White men, with so much of license and
> liberty, would die of ennui; but negroes luxuriate in corporeal
> and mental repose. With their faces upturned to the sun, they
> can sleep at any hour; and quiet sleep is the greatest of human

enjoyments. "Blessed be the man who invented sleep." 'Tis happiness in itself – and results from contentment with the present, and confident assurance of the future. (18)

Fitzhugh proposes that those opposing southern slavery should not be concerned with destroying the site of such largesse but, rather, with extending it and its benevolent system of overseeing the labor of masses of workers. One could, in this way, attend to the serious social problems plaguing geographies marked by capitalism, problems that arise from a failure to appreciate fully the well-ordered mutual responsibilities of masters and slaves.

Fitzhugh's argument – which remains (despite much dissembling) an argument concerning the presence and disposition of African Americans – reconceptualizes open preoccupations with African Americans as meditations concerned with ensuring and bolstering the self-identity of white peoples. Fitzhugh curiously composes his endorsement of the continued enslavement of African Americans as if the differentiating darkness of African Americans were not the issue at all. The disappearance of dark-skinned Others in deference to this enlarged self and self-identity is, above all, the matter to be noticed, for it recapitulates the definitive move of value and value formation: an impeachment – discursive or otherwise – of the Other, a willful expenditure of the Other in an imposing production of the self. Dark-skinned Others disappear in the meditation in deference to an enlarged notion of what should be a properly discrete self, a putative "white" self and self-identity that must be pursued more diligently than ever. This obliqueness remains, it seems to me, a primary element of the discourses, and the "political unconscious" of dominant U.S. acknowledgments of race after the watershed decade of the 1830s critically raises the stakes of those acknowledgments. To modify a phrase of Frederic Jameson, the obliqueness represents "a fundamental dimension of [racialist] collective thinking and [racialist] collective fantasies about history and reality" (34) in the United States. Nevertheless, this issue is not so much a disappearance as a repression allowing "the synthetic activity of the subject" (Foucault, *Archaeology* 14) of U.S. history and reality.

Fitzhugh's dilemma is to write of African Americans as though they were not the center of his analysis, even though the question of the disposition of African Americans occasions his writing. This dilemma originates in part because he must temper, in response to the terms of widespread abolitionist appeals, the convictions he

shares with Jefferson, and his dilemma is shared, although for different reasons, by like-minded social critics of the twentieth century.

The historical record demonstrates that attempts to circumscribe
the opportunities and possibilities of the lives of African Americans
are not all limited to strategies of indirection. As detailed, for instance, by Stephen Jay Gould's *The Mismeasure of Man* or Donna Haraway's *Primitive Visions: Gender, Race, and Nature in the World of Modern
Science*, the physiognomy and other phenotypic traits of African
Americans (and other social outcasts) become the focus of a large
body of discourses in the later nineteenth century and into the twentieth century. However, for discourses that style themselves as less
invested in "advocacy of social policy couched as dispassionate inquiry into scientific fact" (Gould 47) and more invested, instead, in
apparently "larger philosophical and critical . . . issues that involved
. . . the social and economic conditions that sustained artistic creativity" (Conkin 37), or "the foundations of . . . culture" (49), or "a
world of value not accessible to the tools of science" (52), a version
of Fitzhugh's dilemma remains. If considerations of dispositions of
African Americans are admittedly social concerns, whereas one aims
to elaborate "a humanistic philosophy [supported] with objective
criteria, and beyond that with either ontological foundations or the
authority of a supernatural religion" (52), then, although for admittedly different reasons, one must share the obliqueness of earlier
nineteenth-century critics.

At the very least, African Americans represent a remarkable tropological (or paraleptic) site (sight), for, furthering the ends of industrial capitalism, U.S. society discovers itself, to this day and with
immense and variously sustained upheavals, unimaginably "incorporat[ing] the blacks into the state," an incorporation demanded
by the "democratic" premises and rhetoric of "free market" societies but that controverts, at the same time, the very founding principles of those societies, which is to say, principles invested in
"depriving [African and Asian] societies of the benefit of their natural resources and labor" (Rodney 14). Indeed, the encroachments
of industrial capitalism, from nostalgic southern perspectives, cannot be separated after 1865 from the unsettling prospect of increasingly uncircumscribed African American lives. One profound upshot
of industrial capitalism is an assault – however qualified – on strict
systems of racial caste.

Writing of the trope of blackness in her investigations of the interactions of "race, gender, and power in early modern England,"

Kim Hall discusses in *Things of Darkness* the emergence of sonnet cycles in relation to "the 'new world' – a world in which blackness is neither a purely aesthetic nor a moral category but the site for crucial negotiations of sexual politics and cultural and racial difference" (116). Hall pursues the ways in which

> [t]he economic expansion of England was a linguistic and, ultimately, an ideological expansion in which writers and travelers grappled with ways of making use of the foreign *materia* 'produced' by colonialism. Tropes of blackness were discovered by white English writers (both male and female) to be infinitely malleable ways of establishing a sense of the proper organization of Western European male and female in the Renaissance: notions of proper gender relations shape the terms for describing proper colonial organization. (4)

She explores interests in and interest yielded from emerging economies of blackness. Uncovering ways "blackness begins to represent the destructive potential of strangeness, disorder, and variety, particularly when intertwined with the familiar, and familiarly threatening, unruliness of gender" (28), Hall interrogates literary conversions of black(ness) to white(ness). Similar dynamics obtain, its seems to me, in the particular strand of U.S. thought marked out so far in reference to Fitzhugh. However, unlike the discursive phenomena investigated by Hall, these late modern U.S discourses are not interested so much in accommodations or conversions of blackness as perhaps effacements of blackness. Denial seems more the order than conversion.

Blackness remains the site (sight) of energetic transformations/erasures. This is so even within discourses claiming to stand at a distinct remove from the "forms [and denials] of political subordination" (Rodney 26) that define the "marketplace" and its social realities, discourses such as those of the Southern Agrarians of the early twentieth century, who are the often unacknowledged precursors of the New Critics. Southern Agrarianism and New Criticism, in addition to sharing leading members as well as virtually a decade of overlapping activity, champion largely identical ideological resistances to corporate industrialism, to its unprecedented social configurations, and, very stridently, to the wayward science underwriting both. Indeed, both Agrarianism and New Criticism share origins in the literary enterprise New Criticism would institutionally reform. As well as being members of the Southern Agrarians, John Crowe Ransom, Allen Tate, and Robert Penn Warren are important members of the Fugitives, a loose fraternity of poets and intellectuals centered in the 1920s around Vanderbilt University. All later became prominent New Critics. Although not a Fugitive, the New Critic Cleanth Brooks is associated with the Southern Agrarians as well.

Certainly, each group – the Fugitives, the Agrarians, the New Critics – proclaims an independent agenda and focuses on distinct concerns, the Fugitives on literary production, the Agrarians on social and political statement insofar as it furthers "the humanist critique of modernity" (52), the New Critics on literary criticism and theory. Nonetheless, the progression is telling. As their mutual memberships and common attentiveness to the literary enterprise underscore, the three groups are associated in consequential ways, and one of the most consequential – which is not necessarily separate from literary concerns – is their shared opposition to the unsettling results of corporate industrialism, opposition reiterating in more attenuated ways Jefferson's recoil from the unthinkable spectre of "incorporat[ing] the blacks into the state." Disclosing these relations and attentuations that finally privilege "the iconic text and its hermetic closures" (Niranjana 249) is the Southern Agrarian anthology *I'll Take My Stand,* usually neglected as New Critical testimony but, it seems to me, in fact a central document of nascent New Criticism. *I'll Take My Stand,* championing the neglected patrimony of the antebullum South, is a collection of twelve separately authored essays published by the Agrarians in 1930. Providing important historical contextualization for New Critical formations, it discloses that the idea of the discrete text remains no less an idea and finally no less a political idea. Although the anthology provides only oblique and generally overlooked details concerning codifications of "the iconic text and its hermetic closures," they are not irrelevant. In fact, it is precisely the ability of codifications of the discrete text to designate typographies of relevance and irrelevance that is under suspicion. The obliqueness of the disclosures, in other words, remains an integral part of their very disclosure. They remind one of the ways in which New Criticism remains an outgrowth of Southern Agrarianism and its defining nostalgia for a lost "proprietary society" (Conkin 176). They remind one, in a phrase, of historically interested origins and discernible ideological initiatives.

Indeed, what supplants the "propriety society" championed by the Agrarians is an industrial capitalist political economy infused with "emancipated" African American citizens. The political econ-

omy and social relations refashioned by corporate industrialism
subordinate (to the imperatives of commodity exchange in a
"free marketplace") political, economic, and social configurations
founded on "old assumptions of Anglo-Saxon superiority and innate
African inferiority" (11). The spread of an industrial society in
which African Americans become ostensibly "emancipated" citizens
challenges received economic, social, and cultural configurations of
Aryan male supremacy, an enduring nexus of concern for U.S., and
most undisguisedly, southern conservative thought not to be underestimated. In short, as the upheavals of the nineteenth century demonstrate, corporate industrialism and opposition to it are inevitably
linked to issues of race in the U.S. landscape.

Confirming as much is the most acrimonious – and therefore
most notable – exchange arising among the Agrarians in relation to
the publication of *I'll Take My Stand*. Robert Penn Warren's essay on
the otherwise silenced issue of race causes the disagreement, and
Paul K. Conkin, in his group biography of the Southern Agrarians,
rehearses the exchange and its significance as follows:

> Davidson had written [to Robert Penn Warren]: "It's Up To
> You Red, to prove that Negroes are country folks . . . 'born and
> bred in the briar-patch.' " Warren used the briar-patch imagery
> for his title . . . [however,] [h]is essay horrified Davidson, who,
> in alarm, wrote to Tate that the essay was not related to the
> main themes, treated the Negro problem in general terms,
> with "progressive" implications, and seemed infected by
> "latter-day sociology." In short, it did not adhere to Southern
> racial norms and might offend the very Southerners they
> wanted to enlist in the agrarian cause. . . . In this one case, Da-
> vidson decided to use his editorial responsibility and reject the
> essay in order to protect the larger project. (72)

The rich tropological site (sight) of blackness remains as crucial an
element in this twentieth-century discourse as those already considered from the eighteenth and nineteenth centuries. Configuring,
with deliberateness, a particular (in)significance for the presence of
African Americans in the United States is a paramount element of
the agenda forwarded by all the discourses. Moreover, a leading
concern for Fitzhugh and the Agrarians is maneuvering around or
silencing the matter insofar as it is possible. Warren stands his
ground and allows Davidson only small editorial changes:

Although still accepting of conventional social patterns, Warren, Ransom, Tate, and Fletcher did not want to identify Agrarianism with the racial issue. . . . Thus, only so long as the issue
it [race] raised remained offstage, separate from an agrarian
agenda, could the authors maintain even the fiction of ideological or programmatic unity. (73)

African Americans represent a great challenge to the codification
of Agrarian thought and mark at least one point of concern common to the literary and extraliterary imaginations of these southern
conservatives. The position of Allen Tate might itself be taken as
exemplary of this nexus of concern only revealed obliquely by *I'll
Take My Stand.* In particular, Tate's understanding of his Fugitive
association proves instructive:

In a sense, Tate argued that only new poetic techniques could
serve the cause of the South he came to admire, a South that
once embodied a deeply traditional culture. The literature of
the lost cause, of moonlight and magnolias, or of local color,
was not only false to the fact and exploitative of the South, but
was a literature produced for northern markets. The older poetic techniques, tied to Victorian sensibilities, were inadequate
for the task of rescuing the real South. Taking most of his cues
from T. S. Eliot, he thus made the technical cause of poetic
experimentation one with the largely political cause of restor-
ing a traditional, religious society. Had the Fugitives written
the sentimental, undisciplined, indulgent, moralistic poetry
craved by Mims, they would thereby have joined the progressive, New South crowd, or those who had already capitulated
to alien values. (25–6)

In short, Tate's literary and critical endeavors serve also as strategies to remain faithful to the social and political vision and order
of a virtually lost South. He, in other words

refused to separate his criticism and his agrarian advocacy. To
him, they represented complementary strategies for achieving
a single goal. Whether the emphasis on the integrity and truth-
fulness of a rooted and regional culture, or of a carefully
crafted poem, mattered little. Both challenged the pretentious
claims of abstract, reductionist science, and of a hollow industrial order based upon it. In his view, his criticism was indeed

consistent with, an outgrowth of, his Agrarianism, part and parcel of a lifelong crusade he waged against materialism. (141)

The social relations of "the common or American industrial ideal" (Ransom xx) and its political economy form, for Fugitive thought, for Agrarianism, and for New Criticism, the shared, unthinkable bla(n)ckness their programs variously and polemically reform. Having in common southern conservative oppositions to the "industrial ideal," Fugitive speculation, Southern Agrarianism, and New Criticism champion in separate ways attenuated visions of former and more manifest versions of social order based on exclusion. Even the U.S. Civil War, the climax of the U.S. republic's refashioning of itself in the mid-nineteenth century, marks at best a "basic argument over which white vision of America w[ill] prevail" (Harding 156) – a vision of more or of less manifest exclusion, but of the systemic exclusion of African Americans nonetheless. In the Fugitives, Agrarians, and New Critics, the attenuations of this line of vision are marked by deliberate silences or equally deliberate and effective contrivances of silence.

Whereas Jefferson examines unblinkingly the mark of difference distinguishing and disenfranchising African Americans, and Fitzhugh mediates his preoccupation with that difference by discussing an abstract complex of social relations, Robert Penn Warren in his controversial essay – which ultimately appears in *I'll Take My Stand* – demonstrates the manner in which African American difference is altogether transformed from a matter of the "skin" and the "scarfskin" to the even more immaterial matter of a misguided and "exorbitant act of faith" (255), a misguided "act of faith, not in the negro's capacity," for as the opening paragraphs of Warren's essay iterate and reiterate, there is no such capacity but, rather, a misguided act of faith "in the idea of industrialism" (255) and its power to draw African Americans within a proprietary civil order. Not only, then, do African Americans appear ultimately beside the point in the discussion, the crux of the matter lying elsewhere, as in Fitzhugh's writings, but the negligibility of African Americans themselves is more fully outlined in Warren's essay.

In "The Briar Patch," blackness is the tropological site of the obtuse and the obscure; images of "obscurity" map out the peculiar historiography undertaken by Warren to introduce the situation and problem of an African American presence in the United States. He presents a glib history in which African Americans are simply unthinkable or, in essence, entirely outside Reason and order. Within the first two pages of the essay, three chronologically aligned images of apparently unredeemable disorder inform Warren's imagination of African Americans. As though forced to forget all notions of world geography by recalling the traumatic event, Warren writes that once the ship that in 1619 brings twenty slaves to U.S. shores makes its historic and problematic delivery, it vanishes "into the obscurity from which she had brought those first negroes" (246). It would appear that outside being comprehended by either proximity to or the vision of Europeans, the lives and situations of "negroes" are unthinkable. Although the "obscurity" from which the *Jesus* emerges and that it quickly reenters may refer also to the perils and exigencies of oceanic passage, it without a doubt does refer to the unfathomable continent from which its cargo is taken. Beyond the obscurity of the middle passage lies the even more obscure, mysterious, and unimaginable place of origin of the twenty Africans, the Africans who follow them, as well as all their descendants, who through the vicissitudes of time come to conceive of "the jungle, though not many generations behind, [as] mysterious and deadly" (246) – the "jungle" being the only possible memory of Africa from a vantage within "New World" civilization. Indeed, as Warren's cursory history lays out, once emancipated, African Americans exist in a bewildering postbellum world, in which "the negro f[inds] himself [or herself] in a jungle as puzzling and mysterious, and as little answering to his [or her] desires, as the forgotten jungles of Africa" (247). The profound bewilderment characteristic of life within an originary "jungle," of the ocean passage that transports dark-skinned others to the United States, and of life proximate to a superior civilization and people constitutes the unabated condition and limit of African American life.

Warren's images – or equations – of African Americans with the certain "obscurity" of a 1619 sea voyage, with the distance geographies of "mysterious and deadly" jungles, and with the wayward vision of a "puzzling and mysterious" jungle that is *in reality* an implicitly superior civilization – reiterate the undeniable given of African American difference. This undeniable difference amounts to an inevitable disqualification of African Americans from Reason and its productions, whether the moral and economic orders of New World societies, their literature, or substantial forms of reflection. In Warren's formulation consequential racial difference is rendered apparently more alarming and unfathomable than the happenstance of biological coloring. It concerns resolutely, yet without reference to skin or scarf-skin, the innate inability of African Americans to be anything more than vacuous – to represent, to understand, to live in anything other than "obscurity," the dismissably "puzzling and mysterious," or senseless and impenetrable "jungles" of the mind, figurative and literal. African Americans cannot *imaginably* make sense, and one cannot imaginably make sense of them; rather, African Americans stand as ciphers of vacancy interfering with a U.S. search for plenitude, as ciphers of senselessness in striking relief to U.S. productions of sense. Indeed, as New Criticism subsequently bears out, African Americans in productions of sense and import do not bear mentioning – only deliberate silence.

The telling silence in this instance is, at least, twofold. As Warren's position suggests, African Americans represent the "obscure" abyss outside reasoned thought. The inability of African Americans to make ordered contributions to the society in which they find themselves renders them silent and negligible in relation to that order and society. Additionally, the Agrarian dispute over how to frame the discussion of African Americans in their volume suggests that this topic is the most volatile of those they engage and is diffused by a measured, deliberate, and compromising silence. There exist two silences, one arising from innate obscurity and one from deliberation.

Eugene Genovese highlights the vexed issue of race that would be effaced by Agrarian glibness (and more by the hermetic borders of the discrete New Critical text) by drawing parallels between the formulations of the nineteenth-century Virginian slaveholder George Fitzhugh and twentieth-century Southern conservative thought. Genovese implies the particularity and the peculiarities of the public to which the discrete New Critical text belongs:

> The Agrarians of *I'll Take My Stand* came closest to [Fitzhugh's] standpoint but could not take up, much less answer, his main point: If you will the world to be thus [an agrarian society that resists industrial capitalism], then you must will the social relationships that alone can make it thus. In fact, they spent most of their time in pretending that slavery had been only a trivial feature of Southern life. (242)

In belated, "humanist" opposition to wayward industrial capitalism, the discrete New Critical text amounts to a "verbal icon" of a public defined, in large part, by the prohibitive notions of citizenry informing George Fitzhugh's precedent, less abashed opposition to the social configurations of national U.S. industrialism. The generally unremarked but nonetheless clear affinity between the prescriptions of Fitzhugh and those of twentieth-century southern conservative thought discloses – despite uneasy silences – the fact that African American "bla(n)ckness" remains central to the countercultural preoccupations finding an apotheosis of sorts in *I'll Take My Stand* and a subsequent, more attenuated incarnation in New Criticism.

As prefaced by the Agrarian controversy, the uneasy silence into which New Criticism subsequently falls – in contrast to the logically imperative silence it unaccountably eludes – concerns not only "the common or American industrial ideal" but, more pointedly, the visible bla(n)ckness of reconfigurations of the U.S. public. Were New Critical programs faithful to the logic of the text they deploy, these silences would decidedly fall elsewhere. Wendy Steiner, several decades after the polemical heyday of New Criticism, provides a brief formulation of the logically imperative silence New Criticism eludes in order to proselytize its literary humanist corrective to "the poverty of the contemporary spirit" (Ransom, "Introduction" xxv). Steiner writes in what is meant as a rejoinder of sorts to numerous New Critical coinages:

> Fearful lest art lose its specificity in becoming externally referential (what would distinguish it from communicative discourse in such a case?), formalist critics stressed the absolute self-containment and uniqueness of [literary] meaning, a meaning untranslatable, unparaphrasable, and nonutilitarian. This is the essential principle for several New Critics, though most [are] unwilling to face up to its consequences. (26)

Its consequences are a profound silence. Were the literary object characterized, in point of fact, by introverted meaning (discrete, untranslatable, and self-contained), no critical comment outside the text would be legitimate. Were New Criticism to subscribe fully to its governing concepts of immanent boundaries and exclusions, or at least of uncompromisingly distinct literary and extraliterary topographies, there would be imperative critical silence. However, it is precisely because New Criticism does not fall into silence – except a powerful institutional reticence decades after its ascendancy – that numerous queries come to mind concerning the contrivance of a self-contained or discrete text, as well as the boundaries of its discretion. The abundance of critical activity New Criticism underwrites points out, in other words, that there is more to the matter than a posited dichotomy of estranged discourses.

For, as it turns out, as central to New Critical programs as the designation of an outside (the extraliterary) and an inside (the literary) is the paradoxical confidence that the *distinct* inside possesses a special capacity to reflect or reproduce the outside more effectively than the outside seems capable of rendering itself. In 1941, for example, John Crowe Ransom writes in the book from which the New Criticism movement took its name:

> Poetry intends to recover the denser and more refractory original world which we know loosely through our perceptions and memories. By this supposition it is a kind of knowledge which is radically or ontologically distinct. (*Criticism* 281)

Poetry is defined by an ontological distinction from a world of ordinary perception and, presumably, of ordinary discourse. As defined by New Critical speculation, it is notable, foremost, for its radical separation from the "real" world and ordinary discourse. However, at the same time it remains inside the boundary of literariness, it is noted for its redaction and heightening of the "real" world. Though they are rarely dwelt upon, the specifics of such a claim entail the recrossing, or transgression, of that same boundary that distinguishes the literary from the extraliterary *in the first place.* Still, New Critical conceptions of the radically separate status of the literary rarely underscored this fact that literature, within the bounds of literariness, must nevertheless exceed those bounds in order to engage at some point, at some level, the extraliterary world it apparently redacts. New Criticism, this is to say, only diffidently acknowledges that value is formed and resides in many places besides the poem – value that is nonetheless integral to the poem. Ransom, some fifty or so pages later in *The New Criticism,* briefly raises and dismisses this quandary:

> In what world of discourse does [poetry] have its existence? As a thing of sounds it exists in the words; as a thing of meanings it exists in *a world beyond the words.* The heterogeneity is rather extreme. We recall the old puzzle, the debate on whether the poem resides in the physical words said or in the interpretation that is given them. But *it exists in both at once.* (328; emphasis added)

The compelling specifics of "exist[ing] in both at once" are never fully addressed, so that New Criticism never fully acknowledges with any concerted or sophisticated scrutiny the fact that literature in its radical ontological distinction is nonetheless tied to the world. In many ways, the uncompromised observance of a boundary separating the literary from the nonliterary allows New Critics to mask the inevitability that "whenever one is supposed to speak of literature, one speaks of anything under the sun (including, of course, oneself) except literature" (de Man 29). Frank Lentricchia spells out the implications masked by the fortuitous theoretical silence as follows: "Literature is inherently nothing; or it is inherently a body of rhetorical strategies waiting to be seized. And anybody can seize them. . . . [Literature] is all writing considered as social practice, all writing viewed in its material circumstances and in its purposiveness. It is power as representation" (157).

On the contrary, in 1976 Murray Krieger, the most abiding and outspoken champion of the New Critics and their U.S. formalism, recasts Ransom's allusion to "existing in both at once":

> [Literature] ben[ds] its verbal forces toward literalizing its metaphor. [Its reader] . . . reacts . . . not in response to the arbitrary command of an outside faith, but in response to the internalizing directions through which, by deviation and transformation, the verbal construct has worked its way to presence from the open-ended flow of generic discourse. If he [or she] puts teleology into the poem as object, it is because this object seems to have wrestled with its teleology to make it its organizing principle. So he [or she] is forced to reify this experience into a privileged object because he [or she] is convinced that it has earned its way from within, with a system of internal relations that seems to have shaped itself into substance. (212–13)

Defending New Critical precepts against various "new Left" and poststructuralist threats, Krieger argues for what he terms the earned presence of the literary – in effect, a renewal of the call to perceive and specify the literary in discrete separation from the world it records. Krieger's reformulation continues to posit the notion of a boundary as though it were not always a duplicitous construct, a point of contact as much as separation. The boundary, then, and the apparent separation it underwrites remain points at which telling contradictions are silenced or, at least, left unscrutinized.

In other words, the dynamics by which the distinction between the separated terms allows, in point of fact, rather than forecloses, particular communication or congress is left unexamined and un-articulated to equally particular advantage. Whether deliberate or an oversight, this silence produces a notable ideological advantage, as made clear by much more widely circulated arguments made a decade later and aiming to fend off the same "new Left" and post-structuralist threats to which Krieger responds. Indeed, the most widely disseminated arguments for the special apolitical status of literature are no longer made in strictly New Critical terms. E. D. Hirsch, for example, argues in 1987 for the necessity of a "cultural literacy" that requires the teaching of "traditional literate culture." He attempts, furthermore, proceeding in his argument with careful politic, to discard the notion "that teaching the traditional literate culture means teaching conservative material" (21).[18] An intriguing portion of his argument reads:

> Literate culture is the most democratic culture in our land: it excludes nobody; it cuts across generations and social groups and classes. . . . Although everyone is literate in some local, re-gional, or ethnic culture, the connection between mainstream culture and the national written language justifies calling main-stream culture *the* basic culture of the nation. (21–22; emphasis in original)

The argument calls on one to see "literate culture" as paradoxically both self-enclosed and all-encompassing. It is nominally open to all yet, at the same time, curiously requires the superseding of com-peting cultural configurations.

Similarly, in his more polemic *The Closing of the American Mind,* Allan Bloom outlines a crisis of higher education in which he pres-ents

> the only serious solution . . . [as] reading certain generally rec-ognized classic texts, just reading them, letting them dictate what the questions are and the method of approaching them – not forcing them into categories we make up, not treating them as historical products, but trying to read them as their authors wished them to be read. (344)

Boundaries are both laid out and tellingly transgressed in Bloom's position. For instance, one might ask – as one of many questions – how one reads texts "as their authors wished them to be read" *without* at the same time "treating [those texts] as historical products"? That is, these privileged texts are unaccountably within and without history at the same time. However, in a move still more puzzling and inconsistent, Bloom concludes his treatise with the observation that "[j]ust as in politics the responsibility for the fate of freedom in the world has devolved upon our regime, so the fate of philosophy in the world has devolved upon our universities, *and the two are related as they have never been before*" (382; emphasis added). To Bloom's mind, the "classics" are properly treated only as self-contained entities, with a border imposed between them and the social and ideological world of history, despite the fact that their abiding power apparently rests in their ability to interact with, and perhaps even influence, historical forces and historical situations, such as present ones. In this way, even glancing consideration of the deployment of boundaries by Bloom and others who posit the distinct status of literature makes it clear that, just as unprecedented appearances of texts like *The Street* in the academy are social acts, so too are the varying rebuttals to such openly politicized appearances. Notions of the discretely literary are notions already implicated in extraliterary affairs. The crucial silences of these arguments, at best, incompletely mask the fact that boundaries deployed between the literary and the extraliterary are themselves implicated in matters beyond the "discretely" literary even as they underwrite notions of the discrete text and discrete literary activities. The strict binarism and the oppositions it sets up are specious.

Of course, this is not to say that the specifics of the literary text do not differ at all from those of other cultural artifacts, for this is certainly the case. However, these differences are of circumstance not kind. In his uncharacteristic study of literary value, *Work Time: English Departments and the Circulation of Cultural Value*, Evan Watkins exposes this state of affairs by considering the organizational and cultural site of work performed on the literary text. The premise of Watkins's study is that English departments, the organizational and cultural site of the literary text, are the locus of very particular work forces and of significant varieties of labor – with the overwhelming burden of labor falling to students enrolled in classes offered by English departments. Through this analytical lens, Watkins radically revises routine comprehension of the cultural positions, circulations, and value of the field known as the literary. His reconsideration of the primary location of literary praxis discloses that those positions, circulations, and values closely interact with a variety of other institutional, economic, and hegemonic formations of labor; in this way, one is clearly led to recognize that the differences marking the literary are by and large circumstantial rather than ontological.

Whereas cultural formations such as advertising and mass media directly "circulate[ ] not only goods and services, but cultural codes of behavior that facilitate the selling of goods and services as widely as possible" (155–6), cultural interventions made from the site of English departments are not so direct or dramatic. They are much more mediated because, as Watkins phrases it, "Total labor time in English is a matter primarily of a mobile labor force *circulated to English*. As a location of cultural production, English is organized around this circulation of a mobile labor force, rather than to facilitate the circulation of what is produced by the concrete labor of permanent faculty" (238; emphasis in original). The literary, then, does not so much direct public discourses of industrial capitalism as function in a disciplinary network aiming to "compensate for the absence of a hereditary class structure by sorting out and training those in each generation with the ability to succeed to professional service" (108) as it is imagined. What is much more important than the concrete labor and productions of a permanent faculty is the "surplus value" produced by faculty in the form of evaluations, which work to differentiate populations along the lines of an ostensible meritocracy. Watkins reveals that, although the terms of the coimplication of the literary and the extraliterary are not necessarily immediate and straightforward, they are nonetheless definite and significant.

Granted the novel and incisive analysis offered by Watkins, it is difficult to overlook the fact that the literary text – particularly as it is housed in the modern university – remains part of a complex social field in which various populations struggle over material and symbolic resources, rather than the location of uncorrupted, transcendent, enduring, metaphysical sets of knowledge. Nevertheless, despite the certainties of disciplinary institutionalization, this is precisely the specification of the literary text New Critical programs powerfully resist. To this end, the most famous invocations and expositions of the discrete text appear in the discussions of the intentional and affective fallacies undertaken by W. K. Wimsatt and Monroe Beardsley, who, conceiving the literary text as the poem, in particular, explain that

[t]he poem is not the critic's own and not the author's (it is detached from the author at birth and goes about the world beyond his power to intend about it or control it). The poem belongs to the public. It is embodied in language, the peculiar possession of the public, and it is about the human being, an object of public knowledge. (5)

Wimsatt and Beardsley make their appeals for the literary text as an objectified and independent artifact – its state of "concrete universality"[19] – by arguing for its necessarily communal domain. However, their notion of the cultural domain of the literary text is radically different from that specified by Watkins. Their characterization of the text as "the peculiar possession of the public" (re)inscribes the problematic notions of inside and outside already noted.[20] That the literary text, even in its separate aesthetic ontology and redaction of the extraliterary outside, "belongs to the public" is true only insofar as this new situation substitutes "impersonality" for "personality." The impersonality Wimsatt and Beardsley are proposing is not part of a diaphanous web of social relations. Rather, in what is ultimately a profoundly ironic move given the aims of New Critical formulae vis-à-vis the extraliterary world, the two separate the text from the personality of both its writer and its reader in order to provide it a status approaching the seemingly free-standing determination of the commodity in public domains. The status of the literary object, in other words, is given the facticity and palpability freely attributed, by empiricist habits of mind, to matter open to common circulation and exchange. The ontologically separate literary object is declared a public object as a valorizing move meant to open it to judicious, measured scrutiny, rather than to highlight its connections to social and civic influences, determinations, and participations:

The New Critics will seek, at first . . . organizational qualities of the poem rather than metaphysical, transcendental, or revelational knowledge. The critic will often seem to be a scientific-like investigator of the phenomenon the poetic object, neither an effusive impressionistic critic nor a seeker after arcane poetic mystery. (Berman 27)

Wimsatt and Beardsley's acknowledgment of the public contingencies of the discrete text records the slippage from the aesthetic to the civic. The complexity and perplexity of this arrangement, as already suggested, are self-contradictory. The public form of the literary text is engendered in terms of a boundary that is, ultimately, not the sign of diacritical separation but of the careful management of systemic circulations across the posited boundary. This sleight of hand is akin to the dissimulation Hayden White identifies in a different arena as the practice of historical realism, the discursive upshot of which is a fixing of very particular "social praxis as the criterion of plausibility" (102) by which reality is generally scripted. Given White's caution and the fact that the connection between U.S. civil order and issues of race may be underestimated or not mentioned, but never altogether overlooked, it is fair to say that inasmuch as the discrete literary text belongs to "the public" as an empirical object, it belongs, in particular, to a public that, in the words of Ralph Ellison, "with every . . . technological advance since the oceanic sailing ship . . . [claimed] a further instrument [for] the dehumanization of the Negro" (275). The public to which the literary text (and the mindfulness of textuality itself) belongs is always unnamed but understood. To pun on the title of Hayden White's book, the *extraliterary* public of the literary text provides a very particular "content of the form" for the discrete text.

To draw an analogy: Ralph Ellison, in his essay "The Shadow and the Act," contrues the appearance of the 1915 film *Birth of a Nation* and subsequent Hollywood portraits of African Americans as shadows of a previous act, an act involved in "[t]he problem, arising in a democracy that holds all men as created equal . . . [and that is] a highly moral one: democratic ideals had to be squared with anti-Negro practices. One answer was to *deny* the Negro's humanity – a pattern set long before 1915" (276; emphasis in original). One might conclude, from the undeniable genealogy connecting New Criticism to Southern Agrarianism and, in turn, to the line of U.S. social thought marking affinities between Agrarianism and the sentiments of George Fitzhugh and Thomas Jefferson, that the accession of the notion of a discrete literary text is similarly the shadow of such an act. The act throws many shadows.

The bla(n)ckness of African Americans is met in the instances of Southern Agrarianism and New Criticism by polemically formulated systems of thought: one undisguisedly social and political, and one earnestly aesthetic. Belied by scarce and measured references to the "Negro" by Agrarianism and by the autonomous "public" status of the New Critical text are contingent and deferred considerations of an African American *present absence* in the U.S. landscape. Allen Guttman, author of *The Conservative Tradition in*

America, underscores the importance of the measured silences be-
lying these contingencies:

> Conservativism has persisted in America as *an essentially literary
> phenomenon.* Pushed in disarray from the battlefield of political
> activity, conservatism has taken refuge in the citadel of ideas.
> The democratization of American society has made conserva-
> tism increasingly feeble as an institutionalized force, but the
> conservative's dream of hierarchically structured society of pre-
> scribed values and restrained liberty has continued on an im-
> portant and usually unrecognized aspect of American literature
> [and literary critical discourse]. Conservative novelists and po-
> ets, essayists, critics and philosophers have a place in our lit-
> erary history to which they could not have aspired had they
> depended on the [open] popularity of their attitudes. (11; em-
> phasis in original)

These observations are trenchant. However, Guttman is mistaken
on one point. U.S. conservativism is not, as he states, "feeble as an
institutional force." As E. D. Hirsch argues in *Cultural Literacy,* predetermined cues construct a predetermined reality, and it is the task
of institutional cultural sites to manage the currency of these cues –
cues that comprise, in Hirsch's careful phrase, "the information,
attitudes, and assumptions that literate Americans share" (127).
(U.S. conservativism is not feeble, merely more defensive and vigilant than ever before.) Indeed, it is important to understand that
the conservativism Guttman isolates remains powerfully and "meth-
odologically" institutionalized as long as literary study continues –
intuitively or deliberatively – to esteem notions of the New Critical
discrete text that belongs to a public whose particularities are meaningfully unstated.

This – emphatically! – is not to say that the discrete text inherently and innately serves the purposes of assuring an African American present absence within institutionalized literary study – with an
especial effectiveness at times when such an inclusion by exclusion
seems "to the public eye" to falter. Instead, all this is to say that, as
it is formulated and instituted within the literary academy vis-à-vis a
particular history, the discrete text has served and continues
(whether more or less insensibly) to serve as an instrument of subtle,
pointed exclusions, and it is important to recover and keep in mind
how these subtle and pointed exclusions have been and can continue to be effected *in the name of* the discrete text. Given the spe-

cifics of a particular historical moment, one begins to see that, despite the fact that in the manifestos of Agrarianism and New Criticism race is only tacitly, reluctantly, or not at all acknowledged, the advocacy of the southern thinkers who underwrite Agrarianism and subsequently New Criticism is an advocacy inextricably implicated with the issue of race. According to shared precepts of Agrarianism and New Criticism, "[n]either the creation nor the understanding of works of art is possible in an industrial age, except by some local and unlikely suspension of the industrial drive" (Ransom, "Introduction" xxv). For Agrarianism the lost "spirit of life" (Ransom, "Reconstructed" 21) of the Old South, and for New Criticism the discrete text propose themselves as such sites, sites set in patent opposition to the overwhelming influence of the "industrial street," a place increasingly fraught with the presence of "emancipated" African American citizens. Indeed, Nancy J. Weiss's *Farewell to the Party of Lincoln: Black Politics in the Age of FDR* provides a very detailed account of the increasing political and social visibility of African Americans during the 1930s, the formative decade of New Criticism and a decade it shares with Agrarian activity.

It is not for reasons so sheer, however, that, in the 1930s and the subsequent decade, the literary object takes on very select burdens, as New Criticism would have it, for issues of race in the postemancipation United States are inevitably conflated with or mediated through capitalist social relations and the empiricist, positivistic, scientistic mind-set underscoring them.

In this way, it is necessary to see that despite appeals to the public domain of the literary text the issues ultimately concerning Wimsatt and Beardsley are epistemological. These are the epistemological problems of elaborating an openly reasoned and articulated ground for the "specifically critical judgment" performed by professional readers and highly trained educators who should be understood as sharing an exclusive and professional competency. As Art Berman phrases it:

> Although the term *New Criticism* encompasses a variety of opinions rather than a homogeneous system, the belief that the poem itself contains characteristics, properties (in particular, the organization and the structure of language) that can be objectively identified by a competent critic, an ideal reader, is central. Not all persons have the capability to make sound judgments in these matters. (25; emphasis in original)

Wimsatt and Beardsley vie, in other words, to make the literary object an empirical public object in an effort to characterize it as open to concerted and rigorous methods of investigation and, therefore, on these grounds, an object of worth. Summarizing their famous theoretical specifications of critical fallacies that undermine the status of the discrete text, they write:

> The Intentional Fallacy is a confusion between the poem and its origins, a special case of what is known to philosophers as the Genetic Fallacy. It begins by trying to derive the standard of criticism from the psychological *causes* of the poem and ends in biography and relativism. The Affective Fallacy is a confusion between the poem and its *results* (what it *is* and what it *does*), a special case of epistemological skepticism, though usually advanced as if it had far stronger claims than the overall forms of skepticism. It begins by trying to derive the standard of criticism from the psychological effects of the poem and ends in impressionism and relativism. The outcome of either Fallacy, the Intentional or the Affective, is that the poem itself, as an object of specifically critical judgment, tends to disappear. (21; emphasis in original)

Inasmuch as the New Critical discrete text and the Agrarian "spirit of life" of the Old South are related in significant but generally unstated ways, they are distinct in equally significant and uncommunicated ways, for, whereas the silences of Agrarianism prove akin to the silences of fraternal agreement, the silences of New Criticism attempt to underwrite a widespread epistemological accreditation.

Put differently, as much as it struggles by means of its strategic silences with issues of compromised racial stratification in the social relations of U.S. capitalism, so too New Criticism struggles – like all nonutilitarian discourses – for a recognizably rational ground from which to speak with legitimacy. This legitimate ground, like all post-Enlightenment rationalisms, must be "experienced as independent of opinion, belief, and cultural background" (Feyerabend, *Method* 12), and the discrete text, the primary contrivance and primary trace of a now long institutionalized critical sleight of hand, stands as the emblem of a troubled but seductive literary "rationality." This rationality is troubled because, by means of it, New Criticism mimics and further naturalizes the coercive rationality of modern science and the industrialism and social relations it subtends. New Criticism, in effect, finds itself subscribing to exactly what it finds so disturbing in the society it opposes. At the same time New Critical theorizing appeals to an acute and enabling distinction between literature and science, it peculiarly undermines that appeal in order to emulate, as best it dare, scientific method and claims of scientific objectivity and, for a time, the sleight of hand of scientific objectivity and disinterestedness affords it a creditable and fortuitous methodological and epistemological position that, "[a]lthough opposed to 'referential' critical acts, which go 'beyond' the poem's context . . . proves highly selective in respect of what it considers that 'context' to be" (Hawkes 155).

Of this coercive rationality and its relation to industrial capitalism sociologist Stanley Aronowitz writes:

> Just as ideologies are often generated behind the backs of their makers but are nevertheless representations of a worldview that bears the unmistakable stamp of the dominant class, so science and technology, understood by practitioners as true reflections of the natural law and having the force of inevitability, make discoveries in accordance with imperatives of the domination of nature and capitalist rationality as if these were *the only possible choices.* Yet, the tendency of capital is to consciously determine the shape and significance of science and technology in accordance not only with the laws of the *blind* marketplace, but with the specific purposes of the employers. (83; emphasis added)

The discrete text operates similarly in a much more circumscribed arena to ensure for its practitioners that their particular set of choices appear as "the only possible choices," their "specifically critical judgment" as "the only possible choices." The discrete text provides its practitioners, as or even more brashly than Jefferson, Fitzhugh, or the Agrarians, an allowance to be universalists without apprehending or esteeming all of the universe, for the coercive rationality of science is self-evidently the emblem of all-encompassing exactitude and truth.

Literary criticism, which is either impressionistic or inconsistently philological as the New Critics come to it,[21] is rendered by them "rigorous," "empirical," "accountable," and "concrete" by what is an imitative and seemingly objective method. New Criticism recasts literature as a world unto itself, then populates it with calculable and verifiable elements of investigation: tensions, ironies, oppositions, paradoxes, harmonies, unities, resolutions, balances, and so on. New Critical programs attempt, in other words, to render orderly the formerly inchoate.[22] At the same time they oppose themselves to the empiricism of pervasive science and its permutations, they also follow its lead:

> While Romanticism may be explained, in part, as a reaction against the science of the Enlightenment, and while the New Criticism may be explained, in part, as a reaction against the dominance of scientific thought and technology in the twentieth century, why is it that the New Critics were, nevertheless, not real allies of the Romantics? This occurs because the literary critics in England and America in the first half of the twentieth century were reacting not against empirical science and methodology itself, which they (being empiricists) must respect and emulate, but against the *social consequences* of science and technology and an economy based upon them. (Berman 25; emphasis in original)

Science and its seeming accountability, although in ways that prove anathema to New Critical sensibilities,[23] manage to fix matters definitively, and the New Critical urgency is to do the same in terms of the literary enterprise. The result is that the drama of the discrete New Critical text is profoundly self-conflicted, since its self-enclosed drama in fact rehearses the much more acclaimed drama of science. The reconceived literary text amounts, in effect, to a troubled recognition of the irresistible power of an objective and disinterested production of knowledge and goods associated with science, which sustains the interrelated public domains and discourses of industrial capitalism, science, and a highly managed democracy with a kind of legitimacy New Critical programs aspire to appropriate for their own vision. New Criticism, then, paradoxically attempts "to establish the legitimacy of the status of poetry, and the poet, in a way not encompassed by the empiricist method, even though it requires an empiricist method to do so" (2).

Seemingly inviolate disinterestedness and objectivity ensure science, in its underwriting of industrial capitalism, the overwhelming efficacy to proselytize and reify the many racist, sexist, heterosexist, and classist social relations defining U.S. industrial capitalism. Agrarianism, on the contrary, through its inexact appeal to "an established order of human existence ... [and] that leisure which conditions the life of intelligence and the arts" (Ransom, "Reconstructed" 21), effects a hapless challenge to the industrial society it opposes and, more importantly, to the capacity of science, to "de-fin[e] rationality in a specific way" (Aronowitz 8). New Criticism, however, more aptly undertakes the challenge. In ironic and subtle capitulations to its nemesis that are not entirely intentional, it attempts to appropriate – and therefore defers to – the authority of a "rationality" monopolistically defined by science. One way of viewing this is to see that New Criticism undertakes the task of demonstrating that, as "[a] scientific proposition can stand alone" (Brooks 207), so in a different realm can the discrete literary text.

As it were, the great divide between New Criticism and that which it opposes is not invariably so great. If the boundary marking off the literary from the extraliterary seems the locus of separation, it proves equally the locus of crucial and careful managements and exchanges, the point at which affinities are also recognized. What is more, it points out the way in which the great schism between the shared nostalgic resolve of Agrarianism and New Criticism and the ends of the U.S. industrial order may remain in other important respects also more apparent than real. For instance, upon reflection, it is plain that the antipathy of southern conservative thought to corporate industrialism on the issue of an African American present absence is, to a significant degree, also more apparent than real. The U.S. industrial order and the southern conservativism informing Agrarianism and New Criticism both insist – the one more guilefully and the other more unapologetically – on forms of social and economic privilege mediated in terms of African American exclusions. The convulsive and *unthinkable* democratization long threatened (or promised – depending on one's point of view) by U.S. industrial capitalism and long resisted by southern conservativism remains in large measure unfulfilled and illusory. As the historian Joel Williamson writes:

> In 1850 Southern blacks were bound intimately to the industrial revolution through the institution of slavery. By 1915 they were no longer centrally involved in that process, and, as technology progressed, increasingly marginal in their participation in it. Both in slavery and afterward, blacks in America generally have been steadily and firmly excluded from enjoying an appreciable share of the benefits of industrialization. In the economic sphere, the story of race relations in the South and in America at large in the twentieth century is the story of black people struggling to reenter the industrial revolution and win

a larger portion of its abundant material rewards. (Williamson 282)

In other words, U.S. corporate industrialism, although it by no means signals an end to privilege, does signal an end to certain patent, traditional forms of privilege in order to fortify and naturalize others.[24] It very plainly signals an end to the forms of privilege openly sought by Jefferson and Fitzhugh but, nonetheless, shares with southern conservativism a fundamental and abiding concern with privilege mediated in terms of African American lack and exigency. Despite abundant discourses of democracy, as well as scientific disinterestedness and the rewards of the work ethic, U.S. capitalism unquestionably configures "America's 'democratic' government and 'free enterprise' system" – in the words of Manning Marable – "deliberately and specifically to maximize black oppression" (2).[25]

Even cursory scrutiny suggests that the opposition of Agrarianism and New Criticism to a burgeoning industrial order remains far less earnest than that undertaken by Marxists, chartists, populists, or other more fully engaged adversaries of industrial capitalism. Agrarianism and New Criticism are not at all interested in so incisive a critique of capitalist social organization as that elaborated, for example, in *Capitalism and Democracy* by the economists Samuel Bowles and Herbert Gintis:

> Capitalism is not merely a system of private property and market exchange of goods and services. It is also a wage labor system in which individuals (workers) transfer, within certain contractual and legal limits, the disposition over their activities to others (capitalists), in return for a wage. The centrality of wage labor to capitalism is frequently overlooked. It is often presumed that general considerations of exchange and private property are sufficient to establish the justice of capitalism. . . . The capitalist enterprise exists *precisely* as a system of authority within a system of markets. . . . The point . . . is simply that institutional arrangements resulting from freely contracted exchanges may subvert the very conditions of their legitimacy; that is, the equality and reciprocity of participating individuals. (71–4; emphasis in original)

In this passage, Bowles and Gintis undercut claims that industrial capitalism assures both democracy and a "free market"; the southern conservativism of Agrarianism and New Criticism does not aim at and is not at all interested in investigations of pervasive and tacit disenfranchisements naturalized by industrial capitalism. Rather, it is concerned almost singularly with the fate of more conspicuous forms of disenfranchisement. It finds fault not with the immanence of privilege within capitalist social organization, but with the particular forms of immanent privilege of capitalist social organization.

The fundamental discrepancy, then, between industrial capitalism and the southern conservativism of Agrarianism and New Criticism is that industrial capitalism ordains its particular arrangement of privilege under the standards of *an ostensibly disinterested and monopolistically rational production of knowledge and goods.* The institutionalized inequities of the U.S. industrial order are belied by a romance of scientific disinterestedness and myths of preeminent

> [d]emocratic institutions . . . [that serve as] mere ornaments in the social life of the advanced capitalist nations: proudly displayed to visitors, and admired by all, but used sparingly. . . . Representative government, civil liberties, [the abolition of chattel slavery,] and due process have, at best, curbed the more glaring excesses of these realms of unaccountable power while often obscuring and strengthening underlying forms of privilege and domination. (5–6)

The point is that in the same way Agrarianism, according to Eugene Genovese, "want[s] capitalists without capitalism" (242), one can say New Criticism seeks scientists without science. Southern conservativism, latterly incarnated as New Criticism, recognizes and attempts to reconcile itself, at least intuitively, to the powerful authority of ostensibly objective and disinterested productions of knowledge and goods guaranteed by the "inviolate" science undergirding democratic institutions. In effect, only varying degrees of willingness to obscure their respective "forms of privilege and domination" distinguish southern conservativism and "the common or American industrial ideal" – and, ultimately, more than any conspicuous antipathy.

Differently put, the inconspicuous affinities the intricate relationship between New Criticism and the industrial society it attempts to repudiate comprises prove much more revealing than their conspicuous antagonisms. New Criticism possesses not only a social vision it shares with Agrarianism, but a self-conflicted relationship to the science and industrial capitalism it opposes. The "spirit of life" of the Old South remains the rallying cry of an openly partisan Agrarian attempt to reclaim a lost patrimony, while the discrete text, in its shared antipathy to the industrial street, stands as a (re) transfiguration of that patrimony and as a symbol of a rigorous, objective disciplinary investigation. New Critical investigations of the discrete text claim to be, in the disinterested manner of science, "autonomous from the concerns of power and ideology" (Aronowitz 6) and, in making this claim, seek the accession and prerogatives accruing from pursuits characterized by such autonomy. Initiated under the rubric of the discrete text, the New Critical pursuit of rigor, which frees the literary text to be more than "merely a bouquet of intrinsically beautiful items" (Brooks 94), amounts to the pursuit of an intellectual respectability able to authorize a very particular, though attenuated, vision of U.S. privilege. Of course, contrary to appearance, the great discursive and conceptual powers monopolized by science are overwhelmingly invested in interested productions of knowledge and goods, and it is these strategies New Criticism attempts to assume under cover of the discrete text.

In sum, the principal legacy of the institutionalization of literary study in the U.S. academy exalts the literary text in order to deny it as an object and index of power, except the object and index of a potent, "playful illusion, of make-believe, of counterfeiting" possessing a marvelous "present body it shadows forth" (Krieger 213). The text is offered and received as an exceptional register of "human genius turn[ing] what is outside man and resistant to his order into symbolic terms susceptible of human manipulation and human meaning" (xiii). Yet, it is precisely on the grounds of this belief and exactly on this point of literary critical pragmatics that the disorders of the unprecedented small industries of the post-1960s academy query, "Human"? "Outside"? "Man"? "His"? "Symbolic" of what? "Manipulation" for whom? By whom? "Meaning" in what situation? According to what contingencies? The presumptions of an exceptional and discrete understanding of the text are construed as intensely problematic, and at stake in this examination is not merely a particular canon of primary texts as most often thought but, moreover, a canon of primary responses to texts. This reified canon of critical responses maintains a relation between the primary text and the "world" that minimizes the "worldliness" – to use the well-known term of Edward Said – of the text.[26] Scrutiny of these intuitive theoretical constraints threatens disciplinary arrangements resistant to ever acknowledging institutionalized textual study as part of "a system of forces institutionalized by the reigning culture at some human cost to its various components" (53), and, in this way, the

designation "crisis" arises within the post-1960s academy as an epithet marking continued resistance to "articulating those voices
dominated, displaced, or silenced by the textuality of texts" (53) as
textuality and texts are traditionally configured within the academy
and within U.S. culture generally.

The object-ivity of the discrete text creates borders within which
conflict is muted and, more importantly, is carefully prescribed, for
the institutional order established by New Criticism with the contrivance of the discrete text is based, as the New Critical lexicon repeatedly reveals, upon resolution and harmonization. It is this
peculiar prescription and management of conflict that are at stake
in post-1960s reevaluations of entrenched theories and literary pragmatics. The untoward prospects of these reconsiderations are that:

> the analysis of the literary text, not as a self-identical *object*, but
> as an element in a highly conflictual, ambivalent power strug-
> gle, would have consequences for the organization and prac-
> tice of the discipline of literary studies, as it is institutionally
> established, of which not the least disruptive would be the re-
> definition of its "borders," its relation to other disciplines and
> above all, to other [and I will add "Other"] modes of thought,
> whether these have been disciplined already or not. (Weber
> 49; emphasis in original)

The transfer of theoretical energies from upholding to challenging
received discretions amounts to greatly increasing the possibilities
(and bringing to light various impossibilities) about which the text
may and may not speak. Accordingly, the intensity of post-1960s
critical debate reflects attempts to fix again of what and of whom
the institutional literary text may and may not, self-evidently, speak.
The troubling dissolution of received tenets re-places the text in the
world, providing an allowance not only to understand the text in
terms of a neglected "worldliness" but, furthermore, in the terms
of an even more unsettling and virtually unrecuperable Other-
"worldliness" (to pun on Said's expression). At issue is the controversion of a "cultural investment placed in the notion of Reading
itself. The character of this cultural investment requires not, of
course, that reading be taken very seriously, but on the contrary,
that it be taken for granted" (xvi).[27] The academic debate concerns
a redefinition of the relation the text bears to the world beyond it,
a world the text reflects, recalls, comments upon.

PART THREE

SCOPIC AND PHONIC ECONOMIES

5

SIGNS OF OTHERNESS: CIRCULATIONS OF A PURLOINED LETTER UNDERSTOOD OTHERWISE

In the post-1960s academy what comes to be known as poststructuralist theory radically redefines textuality and liberates critical discourse from the world of the formerly insular text, for, as theory would have it, "*there is nothing outside of the text*" (Derrida, *Of Grammatology* 158; emphasis in original). In other words, because "our very relation to 'reality' already functions like a text" (Johnson, "Introduction" xiv), textuality is taken to be a structure or condition far exceeding a limited set of hyperrealized linguistic events. The preeminent lines of New Critical reasoning and reasonableness are after the 1960s both greatly assailed and, for the most part, eclipsed by the unruly and amorphous entity known as poststructuralist theory. New Critical programs exert their primary influence on the post-1960s academy as the intuitive center of critical practice or, most openly, in the terms of nostalgia and loss. "Theory in the United States institution of the profession of English," writes Gayatri Spivak, a paramount player in the ascendancy of deconstruction and poststructuralism in the United States, "is often shorthand for the general critique of humanism undertaken in France in the wake of the Second World War and then, in a double-take, further radicalized in the mid-sixties in the work of the so-called poststructuralists" ("Making" 788). Much more than formal exegesis, theory pursues

an analysis that focuses on the grounds of [any] system's possibility. The critique reads backwards from what seems natural, obvious, self-evident, or universal, in order to show that these things have their history, their reasons for being the way they

are, their effects on what follows them, and that the starting
point is not a (natural) given but a (cultural) construct, usually
blind to itself. ("Introduction" xv)

To simplify fifty or so years of literary critical history greatly, the
governing trend of the academy shifts from the certainties of New
Critical exegesis to the skepticisms of deconstructive hermeneutics.
And accompanying the shift, institutionalized canons, practices, per-
sonnel, as well as the discursive privileges specifying them, also begin
to be called into question. In a poststructuralist academy, uneasy
queries arise from those never entirely given voice by classic, or
institutional, discourses and values. Toni Morrison, for example, gesturing at U.S. literature broadly, writes: "The spectacularly interest-
ing question is 'What intellectual feats had to be performed by the
author or his critic to erase me from a society seething with my
presence, and what effect has that performance had on the [literary]
work?' " (11–12). In short, given the nature of poststructuralist attentions, one can be led to make what formerly would have seemed
the most wayward critical inquiries. One has the critical apparatus
to recognize openly that structures and value inhabit the world in
myriad ways and, to the extent that this might not appear to be so,
there are powerful psychic, discursive, social, and physical impositions at work. Poststructuralism enables one to undertake disciplinary scrutiny and analysis of these dynamics much more easily than
the critical orthodoxy that precedes it.
    It is equally, if not more, important to understand, however, that
in the wake of these developments value nonetheless retains many,
if not most, of its habituated disciplinary configurations, for even
though poststructuralist strategies "may serve very different masters" than those the discipline is traditionally comfortable with, "the
ideological appropriation of deconstruction [and other poststructuralist strategies] will most often manifest itself [only] in the reification of what properly function as hermeneutical strategies"(Rowe
68), and – as one might say equally of New Critical notions of the
discrete text – hermeneutical strategies are neither oppressive nor
liberating *in and of themselves*. It is the service to which they are put,
the "polity" in whose service they finally operate, that is the remarkable matter. Therefore, notwithstanding that poststructuralist
strategies take up highly influential positions in the discourses of
the post-1960s academy, this circumstance in itself is not a register
of any substantive change in relation to constituencies long disen-

franchised both within and without the academy. In the words of Barbara Christian, the majority of theorists "in their attempt to change the orientation of Western scholarship . . . as usual, concentrated on themselves and were not in the slightest interested in the worlds they had ignored or controlled" ("Race" 56).

One canonized theoretical exchange that bears out Christian's suspicions of the fundamental orientation of an ostensibly revolutionary poststructuralist academy is the exchange progressing from Jacques Lacan's psychoanalytic reading of Poe's "The Purloined Letter," to Jacques Derrida's interrogation of Lacan's reading, to Barbara Johnson's reflexive analysis of herself reading Derrida reading Lacan reading Poe. With incursions into the thematics of repetition and lack, skeptical engagements with the "real," with placements and displacements, adequations and readequations, frames of reference, and antinomian concerns with decentering, this discussion and others like it seem to announce a dramatic reorientation of scholarly concerns. However, as Christian points out, antinomian theoretical projects – and, I will add, even and especially as they are redacted in this celebrated exchange – represent an actual retreat from the Other. Nell Irvin Painter shares many of Christian's concerns; however, whereas Christian is more than ready to dismiss poststructuralist theorizing altogether, Painter articulates its general retreat from the Other and the complications of this retreat very differently, reading it in terms of race and its paramount historical situation in the U.S. landscape:

> For all the usefulness of poststructuralists, however, they cannot fully elucidate American culture, which was conceived in slavery and fathered by slaveholders. I sometimes suspect that the silence of European poststructuralists is part of what draws Americans to their thought, for Europeans' networks of theory, by denying conceptual space to race and slavery, wordlessly abolish the need to theorize on Americans' major historical embarrassments. ("Thinking" 403)

Decentered and decentering, unwilling to accept the unproblematic centrality of the center, the unproblematic value of value, U.S. antinomian speculative projects open themselves, it would seem, to acknowledging the disjunctive appearances of an Other and to demonstrating that these disjunctive appearances are integral to the well-being of ostensibly stable symbolic, cultural, and political economies placed under scrutiny; yet canonized poststructuralist theorizing most often eludes or falls far short of providing scholarly elaborations accounting for:

> damage more or less systematically inflicted on cultures produced as minorities by the dominant culture. The destruction involved is manifold bearing down on variant modes of social formation, dismantling previous functional economic systems, deracinating whole populations at best, decimating them at worst. (JanMohamed and Lloyd 7)[1]

This is to say, despite appearances – and as Barbara Christian warns sometimes too heedlessly, and Nell Painter more thoughtfully – influential poststructuralist speculations are as inclined as any other New World discourse to effect retreats from blackness and the value of blackness. The celebrated critical exchange concerning Poe's "The Purloined Letter" is ultimately exemplary of such a theoretical retreat. With some skepticism concerning the "polity" that their projects serve, one can remark in the discussions of Lacan, Derrida, and Johnson an overlooked opening for the entry of black and bla(n)ck issues into institutionalized discourses in which such issues tend to remain surprisingly unapparent and unexamined, "in spite of what we are led to believe by the abolition of slavery, the 'success' of the Civil Rights movement, and the admission of a handful of minorities and women to the academy" (JanMohamed and Lloyd 6).

In exemplary poststructuralist fashion, the discussion of "The Purloined Letter" turns on examining moments of disjuncture; it looks foremost to the moments and sites of *untoward* irruptiveness in what seems plainly a stable system of exchange. It pursues the insight that meaning or significance (or value, in the paramount terms of this study) fixes its place most remarkably only at the point of its own dissolution. On closer examination, however, the debate best demonstrates the manner in which such decentering speculation virtually returns to the center it puts in question, for Lacan, Derrida, and Johnson ultimately pursue identity rather than difference; their readings are premised on examinations of what are characterized as scenes of precise repetition, although the scenes in question by no means precisely repeat each other. Hence, their collective interrogation forecloses much that it should not, in terms of both the greater implications of their critical orientations as well as Poe's narrative.

Poe's story recounts the intrigue surrounding two similarly or-

chestrated thefts of a highly prized letter apparently containing evidence of an earlier transgression. This letter, the content of which
always remains an enigma to the reader, is stolen by a governmental
minister from the royal boudoir of an "illustrious personage" who
is severely compromised by the loss of the letter. The second theft
of the purloined letter from the apartment of the minister who has
stolen it cancels the threat of the initial theft.

In his psychoanalytic reading of the story, Jacques Lacan examines the manner in which this purloined letter "always arrives at its
destination" (53). That is, he examines the way in which the original theft is counteracted by its repetition or duplication, a turn of
events by means of which each character who successively possesses
the letter – the "illustrious personage," the minister, and Dupin
(the agent hired to steal the letter back) – attains the same position
in the triad of the "real," the "imaginary," and the "symbolic" as
the former possessor of the letter.

Jacques Derrida, in his subsequent analysis of the story, takes issue
with Lacan for too readily fixing the meaning of the letter – the
undesignated signifier – as a lack that comes to characterize each
person who successively possesses it. Lacan's error arises, Derrida
explains, because he takes into account only the content and not
the narration of the story. Derrida objects that Lacan too easily fixes
nonexistent truth in its place.

Barbara Johnson reads Derrida's engagement with Lacan as a repetition of the chain of repetitions begun within the doubling and
redoubling intrigue of Poe's story. In other words, like the characters in the story, each commentator unwittingly reenacts the crime
he would undo. Derrida's reading of Lacan, like Dupin's theft,
which reenacts the theft of the minister, which in some degree reenacts the earlier undisclosed transgression documented by the letter,
amounts to "a precise repetition of the act of robbery he is undoing."[2] All reenact the unbecoming reenactment of a reenactment.
Dupin and the minister, and Lacan and Derrida do not only retrace
but, in fact, become the trace of the transgression they would expose. The system in which all these agents – both fictional characters
and critical commentators – intervene is one that engulfs and comes
to define them all. Johnson, finally, includes herself in the series of
repetitions.

Thus, in the same way that "The Purloined Letter" is ostensibly
the tale of exemplary deductive reasoning that turns out, in fact, to
be a tale of revenge and of the mysterious, undisclosed past of Du-

pin, each critical commentary examines and becomes involved with a frame of reference distorted by a decentering systemic play. Since each of the fictional and critical agents is fated, as Johnson would have it, to repeat the transgression he or she would expose and correct, or expose and explain, this decentering systemic play amounts to the *true* frame of reference. Each agent involves herself or himself in the repetition of an inevitable drift from a designated center. The three critical discussions – amounting to the retracing of traces traced – make repetition a premium: in particular, what seems to be repetition without lack or, equally, repetition without difference or, in Johnson's phrase, "precise repetition." This characterization mistakenly depends, however, on the presumption that the second scene of robbery in which the letter is recovered amounts to an exact duplication of the first.[3]

In this vein, Lacan announces that although the minister seems to forget the letter, once he has procured it, the letter forgets the minister "so little that it transforms him more and more, in the image of her who offered it to his capture, so that he now will surrender it, following her example, to a similar capture" ("Seminar" 47). Derrida observes, " 'The drama' of the purloined letter begins at the moment – which is not a moment – when the letter *is retained* [se garder]" ("Purveyor" 195). As already noted, Barbara Johnson esteems "a precise repetition of the act of robbery" ("Frame" 219). Yet, the two scenes of robbery are not nearly as identical as reported. Crucial to the narrative is the fact that, unlike the minister's initial theft of the letter from the "the illustrious personage," Dupin's subsequent theft is accomplished when the minister is *not looking.*

In the scene of the initial robbery, "the illustrious personage," who possesses the letter, is interrupted as she reads it by "the other exalted personage from whom especially it was her wish to conceal it" (Poe 8). In this way, she is forced by circumstances to leave the letter lying in the open in order make it seem innocuous, and when the minister in question enters her boudoir and, as it were, reads the situation, he places beside the all-important letter one of his own somewhat resembling it. As he leaves, he knowingly takes the wrong letter, the letter belonging to the illustrious personage, who is observing and horrified. In the scene of the recovery of the letter, there is subterfuge, as in the first scene, but it does not take place under the gaze, and therefore within the knowledge, of the minister. In order to resolve the case and collect a reward of fifty thousand francs from the frustrated, ineffectual prefect of the police who is secretly assigned the case, Dupin visits the minister, complaining of weak eyes and wearing green tinted glasses so that he might scrutinize the minister's apartment without arousing suspicion. Once Dupin recognizes the letter, which is once again lying out in the open in order to disguise its importance, he engages the minister in lengthy conversation. Dupin deliberately leaves his snuff-box in the minister's apartments and returns in the morning to claim it. In the morning, when the minister is distracted at the window by commotion in the street, Dupin steals again the already stolen letter and replaces it, as in the first scene, with a facsimile. The minister is entirely unaware of the transaction – entirely unaware of his compromised position.

In short, what is neither accounted for nor recounted in the Lacanian, Derridean, and Johnsonian analyses of the relation between the scenes is their divergent scopic economies. Neither Lacan, Derrida, nor Johnson notes that in the first scene the principal agents see each other in their confrontation; in the second only one of the two principals sees and fully understands the moment and situation of confrontation. The visual economy of the second scene is very severely qualified, so much so in fact that the second theft is made possible only by the imposing distraction of *sound*, the issue of an entirely Other economy too slightly accounted both in Dupin's narration of his triumph and in the critical responses to his narrative. Indeed, it is an all-important oversight to miss that the primacy of the visual in the climactic scene is displaced by the phonic:

"The next morning I called for the snuff-box. . . . [A] loud report, as if of a pistol, was heard immediately beneath the windows of the hotel, and was succeeded by a series of fearful screams, and the shoutings of a mob. D—— rushed to a casement, threw it open, and looked out. In the meantime, I stepped to the card-rack, took the letter, put it in my pocket, and replaced it by a *fac-simile* (so far as regards externals); imitating the D—— cipher, very readily, by means of a seal formed of bread.

"The disturbance in the street had been occasioned by the frantic behavior of a man with a musket. He had fired it among a crowd of women and children. It proved, however, to have been without ball, and the fellow was suffered to go his way as a lunatic or a drunkard. When he had gone, D—— came from

the window. . . . Soon afterwards I bade him farewell. The pre-
tended lunatic was a man in my own pay." (Poe 22–3)

Unaccountably, the three commentators neglect this marginal
but important rupture that provides the motive force for resolving
the circulations of the coveted letter. Whereas the machinations of
the narrative seem to turn on what is and is not shown, they actually
turn on what is *heard*; whereas the visual is the overtly and highly
privileged economy of sense and significance, the story's visual commerce is ultimately interrupted and, in point of fact, sustained by
the phonic event in the street. Here, accordingly, is the inaugural
lack of the story, which must be considered in any terms but those
of "exact repetition." That is, the repetition in the scenes of robbery
taken as the focus of the Lacanian, Derridean, and Johnsonian analyses proves to be much less than precise, because the second scene
of robbery opens, in fact, onto a further scene, an unacknowledged
remainder that alternative readings might seize as the crucial determining lack in both Dupin's narration and its famous commentaries.
In this way, it seems to me that if "The Purloined Letter" can be
understood as the story of a lack and reparations of that lack that
inadvertently turn out to be repetitions of the inaugural lack, then
the primal scene of the narrative is neither the scene of the initial
nor of the repeated robbery. It proves, instead, in opposition to the
readings of Lacan, Derrida, and Johnson, the scene of lunatic commotion, disruption, and disturbance in the street allowing the privileged significance of the earlier scenes – their recognized value –
to take its place in the narrative and commentaries. This is to say
that, in more ways than one, what is lacking is what is heard: In the
same way that the noise in the street stands outside the privileged
visual economy, any account of the integrity of the noise and events
in the street and to the privileged narration and rendition of events
also remains outside what is principally considered by Dupin or the
critical commentators on the story. Following the lead of Dupin,
Lacan, Derrida, and Johnson give little to no account of the indispensable utility of what goes on in the street, and, as a consequence,
what is perhaps most lacking is that which remains beyond a series
of repetitions misleadingly understood as identical.

In the decentering poststructuralist investigations of Lacan, Derrida, and Johnson, what is lacking, or that which is undesignated
and furthest from the center, remains finally unacknowledged and
uninvestigated. To think of the two scenes of robbery as joined in

a relation of exact repetition is not only to occlude the third scene, upon which the two unexpectedly open and by which they are held in place, albeit a place of circulation, but it is, moreover, to foreclose far too quickly the disjunctive and disruptive exemplarity of "The Purloined Letter." Making this foreclosure, the critical strategies of the three commentators deny repetition much of its unstated pre-rogative – its effective determinations of originality and represen-tation, as well as its implication in "the force by which the signifier occupies its place" (Said 220) in any circumstance. All three over-look the matter that repetition – to borrow another phrase from Edward Said – "is always part of some larger ensemble of relation-ships headed and moved by authority and power" (169), authority and power ultimately seized in this instance by Dupin. Yet, in con-trast to the celebrated readings of Lacan, Derrida, and Johnson, one might still engage the theoretical and political nuances of what such a seizure and the neglect of such a seizure represent both in the narrative and in terms of poststructuralist critical strategies. For "The Purloined Letter" provides readers ample opportunity to en-gage the ways in which the systemic play it elaborates is not only distorting, but profitable and empowering as well.

However, its bears emphasizing that Lacan, Derrida, and Johnson do not err in perceiving a crucial series of repetitions in the story. Rather, they make their missteps in misperceiving the dynamics and authorizing importance of these repetitions: Lacan minimizes the agent of repetition, Derrida overestimates the uncertainty of the system of repetition, and Johnson conceives of repetition in terms of a closed and inward-looking frame of reference. In more fully elaborating the antinomian exemplarity of "The Purloined Letter," each of these positions warrants some consideration.

In speaking of the priority of the chain of the signifier in his elaborate seminar, Lacan's calculus neutralizes, it seems to me, the (un)certainty of agency. His interests lie elsewhere: "What interests us today is the manner in which the subjects relay each other in their displacement during the intersubjective repetition" ("Semi-nar" 32). He is concerned, that is, with "[t]hus three moments, *structuring three glances,* borne by three subjects, incarnated each time by different characters" (32; emphasis added). What Lacan over-looks, however, is that he must account for not only the efficacy of intersubjectivity in the story, but also the efficacy of subjectivity itself, since the system of intersubjectivity he outlines operates only inas-much as it is realized by the eccentric participation of three self-proprietary agents – Dupin, as it turns out, being the principal agent. There are two chains of signifiers to be considered – one (intersubjective) represented by the inexact repetition of the act of theft and its "structuring glances" and another one (subjective) that determines the particular but veiled psychological life and actions of the main characters. It is, of course, the individual animations of these characters that drive the plot and raise central questions. What is the indiscretion of the "illustrious personage" disclosed by the text of the letter? What are the motivations behind the theft of the overconfident minister? What are Dupin's past dealings with the minister for which recovering the letter serves as revenge?

The signifying or significant chain of relations to be assessed is not simply represented by the nodal points of a triangular intersubjectivity – or in Derrida's subsequent rendition of the narrative, a squaring of that triangulation. It is not simply that in repeating and resolving the crime Dupin ends up, in Lacan's estimation, at the allegedly feminized and irrational positions occupied first by the distressed queen and then by the careless and overconfident minister, but, furthermore, that in the name of a discrete game of espionage Dupin determines and profits by the actions of unspecified Others without that circle. Just as the circulating letter is not the only absence essential to the narrative, so too it is important to recognize that (albeit in relation to the intersubjective dynamic identified by Lacan) it is the particular, individual agency of Dupin that determines the narration of the events as well as the silences of the narration.

In short, Lacan neglects that the system and structure of circulation he identifies do not circulate by their own patent volition. He fails – to use Lacan briefly to redress Lacan – to "distinguish[ ] the function of the subject of certainty from the search for the truth" (*Four* 39), and, in this case, the subject of certainty is the intersubjective triad at which he fixes the search for the truth of "The Purloined Letter." He too easily conflates the two and, as a result, is content to believe that the intersubjective triad virtually exhausts the complexities of the narrative. On the contrary, in his corrective to Lacan's analysis, Derrida points out that there is finally no *truth*. But even this rejoinder, it seems to me, is insufficient in itself, because it neglects that, regardless of the insubstantiality of truth, there will always be the play or performance of some formation acting as truth nonetheless. Truth will always appear fixed, as Lacan's analysis too quickly confirms, whereas, on the other hand, Derrida's rejoinder overlooks the fact that various configurations managing to pass as truth are never to be entirely dismissed, for, by attaining that position, they exert ample sway. Derrida neglects the inevitable, suspect performance of truth as well as the fact that what will most closely reveal the always suspect performance is that which appears most errant, least accessible, least known, or unobserved in relation to that play of truth. By committing this oversight, he recapitulates Lacan's misstep of neglecting that the point at which truth is – always profitably – held in its place is perhaps the least accountable, least observed, yet most revealing site of that truth. In terms of the narrative, both he and Lacan fail to recognize that "certain absences are so stressed, so ornate, so planned, [that] they call attention to themselves; arrest us with intentionality and purpose" (Morrison 11).

Barbara Johnson is correct in pointing out, in her assessment of Derrida's righting (and writing) of Lacan's reading the narrative, that Derrida repeats Lacan's error in the same manner Dupin duplicates the theft of the minister. Still, as mistaken as she is in believing exact repetition marks the relation between the thefts, she is also mistaken in thinking "precise repetition" marks the relation between the readings of Lacan and Derrida. Whereas Lacan seems to define a "subject" (albeit an intersubjective one) with too much facility, Derrida too steadfastly maintains that there is no " '*real subject* of the tale' " ("Purveyor" 199). Where Lacan accounts a systemic truth of which he overlooks the sleighted and enabling disjunctive moment, Derrida virtually discounts any systemic structure. He, opposingly, appraises too generally and too singularly the presence of disjuncture.

Correcting Lacan, Derrida enlarges the scope of Lacan's too circumscribed focus limited to the scenes of theft. He takes exception at the manner in which Lacan isolates "only the content of this story, what is justifiably called its history, what is recounted in the account, the internal and narrated face of the narration[,] [n]ot the narration itself. . . . The displacement of the signifier, therefore, is analyzed as a signified, as the recounted object of a short story" (179). Lacan isolates inappropriately, according to Derrida, a "lack [that] permits the scene of the signifier to be reconstructed into a signified (a process always inevitable in the logic of the sign), permit[ing] writing to be reconstructed into the written, the text into discourse, and more precisely into an 'intersubjective' dialogue" (180). Lacan substitutes a formal structure, a series of events, for a

dynamic process, the narration of these series of events, and Derrida
aims to disturb Lacan's resultant triangular specification of the economies of desire and representation in the narrative. He squares Lacan's triad by examining the unaccounted situation of the narrator
of the story, who, importantly, both narrates and is narrated within
the tale. He aims to account for the narrative's inaugural "scene of
writing" by placing the function of the narrator within the structure
of intersubjectivity informing the story, thus revising it to include
four, not three, positions. He claims, "In missing the position of the
narrator, his engagement in the content of what he seems to recount, one omits everything in the scene of writing that overflows
the two triangles [set up by the two scenes of theft]" (198). Derrida
aims, then, to revise Lacan's mistaken conversion of the signifier
into a signified, so that the signifier might be seen as endlessly deferred, deterred, and detoured from attaining the stable value of a
signified:

> By determining the place of the lack, the topos of that which
> is lacking from its place, and in constituting it as *a fixed center,*
> Lacan is indeed proposing, at the same time as a truth-
> discourse, a discourse on the truth of the purloined letter as
> the truth of "The Purloined Letter." (185; emphasis added)

Whereas Lacan anchors his truth too easily, Derrida disseminates
nonexistent truth with virtually no qualification. He neglects that,
despite its endless deferral, nonexistent truth nevertheless acts as
though it were existent. While he too *unimaginably* imagines its play,
this nonexistent truth, or spurious signified, in fact signifies fact and
passes through the world. Derrida's corrective to Lacan works to
demonstrate that "[w]hat is neither true nor false is reality" (197),
but it in no way acknowledges that reality presents and represents
itself as true nonetheless and with very particular psychic, discursive,
and material consequences. For reasons, then, diametrically opposed to those of Lacan, Derrida makes no observance of the climactic and enabling disjuncture in the privileged economies of
desire and representation – no observance of the eruption of the
phonic within the scopic.

In effect, both Lacan and Derrida turn their attentions very
plainly to the center(s) of the narrative, despite the very decentering
intentions of their critical stances. Lacan isolates the two primary
scenes of the narrative, the thefts, and Derrida reproves Lacan, in
turn, for not properly comprehending a third scene, which is the

episode of the narration or writing of the scenes of theft included in the narrative in the first place. He chides Lacan for failing to describe more completely the *appearance* of the tale and, in doing so, employs the metaphor of the border: "On this border [the inaugural 'scene of writing'], which is negligible for the hermeneut interested in the center of the picture and in what is within the representation, one could already read that all of this was an affair of writing, an affair of writing adrift, in a place of writing open without end to its grafting onto other writings" (198–9). In the posture of looking to an informing marginality, Derrida more insistently than Lacan looks toward the fidelity of the whole: the composite of the border and the center. Rather than making the scope of his investigation truly marginal and remarking the lucrative and clandestine disjuncture fixed in the recesses of the narrative, Derrida, even more than Lacan, recounts and accounts for the most comprehensive spaces of the narrative.[4] Neither truly acknowledges the eccentricities of "a fixed center," because, in addition to designating the marginal or lack in the narrative too easily, neither seizes the opportunity to remark, beyond the presence of the lack, its essential and instrumental *utility*. They do not consider that the utility of the lack or Other – the ends for which and by whom it proves instrumental – is as important to remark as its curious present absence. This is precisely an allowance not afforded those antinomian thinkers newly conspicuous in the academy who are linked to embattled constituencies of race, gender, sexuality, and class.

Equally, Barbara Johnson makes no observances of the narrative spaces unacknowledged by Lacan and Derrida in "The Frame of Reference: Poe, Lacan, Derrida," her contribution to the exchange. "[P]lay[ing] on the spatial and the criminal senses of the word *frame*" (231; emphasis in original), she seeks to demonstrate the manner in which the frame of any analytical frame of reference always proves to be its own content. Interested in revealing that "[t]he subversion of any possibility of a position of analytical mastery occurs in many ways" (214), she fully overlooks that, in equally numerous ways, this fictive mastery manages to sustain and impose itself nevertheless. Whereas Lacan and Derrida are interested in appearances, Johnson proves interested in alignments. In brief: Lacan too precipitously fixes a place for truth; Derrida with related precipitousness precludes any point of fixation; and Johnson, with her privileging of "precise repetition," both releases and holds truth in place. She releases truth, in accordance with the priority that Derrida grants dissemination, only to have it return to its place, in accordance with the fixity Lacan ascribes to it, and so on, in fidelity to a deconstructive notion of *undecidability*. She writes:

> When Derrida says that a letter can miss its destination and be disseminated, he reads "destination" as a place that preexists the letter's movement. But if, as Lacan shows, the letter's destination is not its literal addressee, nor even whoever possesses it, but whoever is possessed by it, then the very disagreement over the meaning of "reaching the destination" is an *illustration* of the nonobjective nature of that "destination." (248; emphasis in original)

Dissemination, in Johnson's elaboration, seems more a *charge*, a certainty and a duty too easily counted on, than a principle of errant and uncertain eccentricity or *discharge*.

Indeed, explicitly proposing an identification between the analyses of Lacan and Derrida under the rubric of undecidability, Johnson writes at the conclusion of her essay:

> The "undeterminable" [i.e., Derrida?] is not opposed to the determinable [i.e., Lacan?]; "dissemination" is not opposed to repetition. If we could be sure of the difference between the determinable and the undeterminable, the undeterminable would be comprehended within the determinable. What is undecidable is whether a thing is decidable or not. (250)

In this scheme, the Lacanian and Derridean analyses apparently cancel each other out or, just as well, one seems to confirm the other. One analysis alternately and indefinitely repeats the other. Moreover, since Johnson finally implicates herself and her own analysis in this process, one might say further that all three analyses arrive at the same destination. Indeed, within Johnson's scheme, the minister and Dupin (from the primary narrative) and Lacan, Derrida, and eventually Johnson herself all are caught in "an act of untying the knot in the structure [that binds them] by the repetition of the act of tying it" (245). Each new arrival, one can safely say, constitutes a peculiar return.

Not surprisingly, then, when Johnson returns to the narrative, she returns to it only insofar as she recites (re-sites, re-sights) the textual citings of the redoubled and redoubling Lacan and Derrida. Nevertheless, the scene with which she most fully implicates herself, it seems to me, is one not mentioned by Lacan or Derrida. It is the anecdotal scene of a schoolyard game of marbles recounted by Dupin, who presents it as emblematic of the ingenious process of deduction leading to his success in retrieving the misappropriated letter. It concerns a game in which one particular player wins all the marbles of his schoolmates in the challenge of guessing whether the number of marbles held in the hand of his opponent is either even or odd. When asked, the schoolboy ascribes his success to "fashion[ing] the expression of [his] face, as accurately as possible, in accordance with the expression of his [opponent], and then wait[ing] to see what thoughts or sentiments arise in [his] mind or heart, as if to match or correspond with the expression."[5] This is the manner, one might say, in which Johnson aligns the hermeneutic confrontation between Lacan and Derrida as well as, in turn, her own engagements with Lacan and Derrida. But the undecidable identification proposed by Johnson proves even more noteworthy and more plenary than the form of identification described in the anecdote, because in her scheme identification seems to occur on all sides of the engagement. As a result, the engagement is stalemated, and one finds oneself left with precise, mirroring repetitions reverberating into undecidability.

It becomes clear, in light of this formulation of undecidability and her attendant theoretical specification of frames of reference, why Johnson pursues and elaborates notions of precise repetition drawing in the principal fictional characters as well as all critical commentators. Her theorization of frames of reference reads as follows:

It would seem that the theoretical frame of reference which governs recognition is a constitutive element in the blindness of any interpretative insight. That frame of reference allows the analyst to frame the author of the text he is reading for practices whose locus is simultaneously beyond the letter of the text and *behind* the vision of its reader. The reader is framed by his [or her] own frame, but he [or she] is not even in possession of his [or her] own guilt, since it is that which prevents his [or her] vision from coinciding with itself. Just as the author of a criminal frame transfers guilt from himself [or herself] to another by leaving *signs* that he [or she] hopes will be read as insufficiently erased traces or referents left by the other, the author of any critique is himself [or herself] framed by his [or her] own frame of the other, no matter how guilty or innocent the other may be. (240; emphasis added)

Johnson's understanding of the frame of reference is, in effect, an understanding of repetition. The frame remains, Johnson posits, a repetition of the act that initiates it. The frame is framed in its own frame, as it were. Or, alternately, the framer inadvertently frames herself or himself in her or his frame. It is imperative to recognize that, given this formulation, Johnson posits repetition without difference, repetition without lack, since, above all, each repetition redoubles the framer framed within the frame she or he frames. This formulation of repetition amounts to repetition that is plenary, wholly interior; that permutates self-sufficiently, for the transference executed is taken to be implicitly self-identical.

This discovery of repetition characterized by the permutation of an interior already framed by and anterior to itself is a notion of repetition that, ironically for an antinomian discussion, accords and accounts no space of or to the Other. This is a remarkable and paradoxical state of affairs for poststructuralist theoretical stances apparently pursuing elaborations of the decentering Other, the absent, the errant, that which lies beyond "a fixed center" or self-identity. In its redoubled and redoubling interiority, Johnson's "precise repetition" proves incapable of taking into account an exteriority outside the framed and framing frame repeatedly redoubled. In this way, the formulation of repetition is one of self-repletion, foreclosing the space of *lack* within speculative thought ironically attempting to illuminate the problematics of designating that which is the lack and the undesignated. Johnson too easily accepts the frame of her frame and too easily elides the misalignments of her alignments of the primary text and commentaries as well as commentary and commentary so that, all too clearly in her analysis, the lacking and the undesignated remain unacknowledged and uninvestigated. Her notion and employment of "precise repetition" affirm, even in a theoretical apparatus with other intentions, the inadmissability of the Other, in the same way that neither she, nor Derrida, nor Lacan acknowledges the crucial other scene upon which the two central scenes of robbery open.

In other words, because the privileged economies in the story, economies of vision and enlightenment, secure themselves only by means of the distracting incidence of wayward sound, what is heard in the story, despite its significance, is never attended to in proper detail. This oversight, I contend, is a symptom of the forestalling of some signal possibilities of the antinomian critical postures taken up, for "The Purloined Letter," rather than the story of the circu-

lating and returning of matters to their place, is the narrative and
narration of lucrative displacements too glibly unaccounted. Although it seems a narrative that turns on impressive powers of deductive reasoning and rational calculation, it turns in fact on the
exigencies of an undisclosed past and a fleetingly reported scene of
disorder in the street. What is heard, then, is a narration of overlooked, unspoken utility. As a consequence, the series of alignments between fictional characters and critical commentators are
very different than earlier understood. They concern the way in
which all slight the pivotal events in the street. The minister, rush-
ing to the casement at the moment of violent commotion, is
quickly and mistakenly satisfied as to its innocence and insignificance. Dupin, who orchestrates the distraction, only briefly claims
then dismisses it as testimony to his ingenuity. In turn, each analyst
of the story altogether overlooks the incident and the lack of its
narration as other than important to the repeated circulations of
the purloined letter.

Like the "casual observer" (Poe 6) invoked in the opening paragraph of the narrative, the agents of the critical exchange are beguiled by the "profound silence" also introduced in that paragraph
– silence ostensibly emblematic of a strict and deeply impressive
genius, isolated and inviolate deductive abilities: "For one hour at
least we had maintained a profound silence; while each, to any casual observer, might have seemed intently and exclusively occupied
with the curling eddies of smoke that oppressed the atmosphere of
the chamber. For myself, however, I was mentally discussing certain
topics which had formed matter for conversation between us at an
earlier period in the evening" (6). However, one ultimately comes
to understand that, although apparently marking self-proclaimed
reason or a strict deductive capacity, the silence overdetermines the
din finally indispensable to the narrative. Rather than the emblem
of misperceived idleness or some remarkable logical capacity, this
openly considered silence is a dour silence, counterposing and presiding over the antithetical, lucrative, and unacknowledged commotion subsequently slighted in the narration.

The most eccentric observances to be made in "The Purloined
Letter" are those secreted from innumerable "casual observer[s],"
observances of the valueless – to go by dominant accounts – but
nonetheless indispensable Other. If there is a pivotal lack in the
story, it is above all the insidious lack of the very selective, valued,
rational accounting of matters dominating the narrative. It is the

most unaccountable, unspeakable, but nonetheless meaningfully traversed spaces by means of which one can most effectively and quizzically understand dominant accounts. In the same way the disposition of such a site (sight) of planned and ornate absence is reflected in the disposition of the third and unaccounted scene in the street, analogously in the fixed values of the U.S. landscape, the terms of the space and time in which African Americans are for the most part forced to live[6] represent an exterior and unrepresented space of ec-centricity, accorded no reasonable station in the dominant narrative of U.S. value. Both are lacking in their respective frames of reference; the space of African Americans, like that of the phonic disruption, stands outside esteemed accounts of reasoning and reasonableness. For these reasons, African American and African American feminist thinkers can least afford to return, even paradoxically, like Lacan, Derrida, and Johnson, to the unquestioned centrality of "subjects" of certainty, which in the larger terms of the U.S. landscape generally prove a Euro-American subject and Euro-American specification of the narrative of the New World. Toni Morrison, for one, is strikingly perceptive in her understanding of the lack of New World forms of knowledge:

> [I]n spite of all its implicit and explicit acknowledgment, "race" is still a virtually unspeakable thing. . . . For three hundred years black Americans insisted "race" was no usefully distinguishing factor in human relationships. During those same three centuries every academic discipline, including theology, history, and natural science, insisted "race" was *the* determining factor in human development. . . . It always seemed to me that the people who invented the hierarchy of "race" when it was convenient for them ought not to be the ones to explain it away, now that it does not suit their purposes for it to exist. (3)

Briefly put, no lack is simply a lack, but is always pivotal and useful. Thus, if there is a pivotal lack in the fixations of value in the U.S. landscape, it is the violent lack of a "whitened" and, as Morrison points out, (re)fashionable accounting of matters. The pivotal lack to be investigated in the landscape of the New World is the unremarked and unspeakable lack of whiteness fixed at the site (sight) of dark-skinned Others. For those antinomian thinkers who bring projects inflected in terms of race, gender, sexuality, and class into institutionalized spaces of knowledge, recognitions of lacks, absences, eccentricities, and Others must begin with this very dark understanding.

With this in mind, one begins to understand that, like all stories of difference, the overlooked story of difference in the narrative of "The Purloined Letter" is marked by a propitious, misremembered, and unremarked turning away. Despite the details and the drift of the narration, the physical turning away of the minister at the climax of the intrigue differentiates the two scenes of theft routinely reported as identical. Moreover, this omission that is anything but incidental in Dupin's narration is duplicated by the consecutive critical turnings away from the differential turning away of the minister. The (re)production of dominant value in the U.S. landscape – the repetition of a highly *significant* narrative – operates in the same way, by turning away repeatedly from the violent site (sight) at which value is profitably fixed, the site (sight) of the Other, the site (sight) of the body of the Other subjugated, graphic, and spectacular. The unaccounted, eccentric, and decentered center of the narrative, then, is not merely the complexities of lack, but rather the turns and returns of plenary value in the relation it holds to the complexities of lack.

As does so much of the narrative, these turnings and returnings from such a site (sight) depend on the precedence of a scopic economy. As represented in its renowed exchange, the narrative seems a story in many ways best redacted, as Johnson demonstrates, by the anecdote of the schoolboy who, in a display of great deductive powers, faces down his opponents in the game of "even and odd." Regardless of the fact that the schoolboy (as far as the reader is aware) is not eventually undone by his ingenious performances like the central players in the story and its critical exchange, his engagements and success are nonetheless emblematic for the "casual observer." His "fashion[ing] the expression of [his] face, as accurately as possible in accordance with the expression of his [opponent]" (Poe 15) forms the zenith of the visual economy the narrative and its poststructuralist commentators exclusively esteem. His uncompromised position in terms of the scopic economy he manipulates is aspired to by all those participating in the circulations of the misappropriated letter. The queen, one might say, "fashions the expression of [her] face" to that of the king, in turn; the minister to that of the queen; and Dupin to that of the minister. Equally, Lacan joins in the permutations, followed by Derrida, followed by Johnson. In effect, the anecdote of the schoolboy provides the center apparently made ec-centric by the decentering, intersubjective action characterizing the narrative because, although anecdotal, it appears to provide the key to explaining the actions of the narrative taking place around it. However, like the misappropriated letter itself, this center eventually returns to its place of centrality because, with its express concern with visuality and ingenious powers of reasoning, it establishes the site (sight) to which the narrative and the apparently decentering commentaries it generates return – and to advantage. The anecdote reaffirms the scopic economy and discourse of reason privileged in the narrative.

This is to say, inasmuch as he does not face his opponent in the manner of the schoolboy but instead contrives a propitious turning away, and inasmuch as the principles governing his actions are the arcane impulses of revenge and an ultimately undisclosed past, Dupin manages nevertheless to fashion his tale in the image of the schoolboy and his deductive powers. Inasmuch as his actions are governed beyond deductive reasoning, he is able, to great advantage, to fashion his tale otherwise. Similarly, the antinomian commentaries on Dupin's self-fashioning tale confirm his advantage by more or less openly also fashioning the narrative in the image of the scopic identification delineated in the anecdote of the schoolboy.

The eclipsed story of turning away, once more fully attended to, confounds the more fashionable narrative of identity with a more unaccounted narrative of difference – difference signaled and masked as always by crucial and profitable turning away. The notion of identification, or precise repetition, that would govern "The Purloined Letter" (as well as the three critical assumptions concerning the exactness of its scenes of theft) stands, it is fair to say, as more a useful fiction than anything else, for, it seems to me, the narrative concerns above all the deployment or centering of profitable fictions. Indeed, it is the carefully centered copying of fictive lines that turns out to be one of the final acts disclosed in the intrigue. Dupin confesses: " 'Why – it did not seem altogether right to leave the interior [of the facsimile of the restolen letter] blank – that would have been insulting. . . . and [so] I just copied into the middle of the blank sheet [lines taken from a play]" (Poe 23).[7]

In fact, the narrative concludes with a series of peculiar disclosures that, although not to the "casual observer," confound the established center of Dupin's narration. These disclosures include Dupin's orchestration of the commotion in the street, the taunting inscription placed in the center of the facsimile, as well as a partial revelation of his motives – which most effectively of all reveals that the anecdote of the percipient schoolboy is the most *carefully centered fiction* of his narration of events. Immediately preceding his disclosure of the lines copied and centered in the facsimile, the reader learns briefly and incompletely that Dupin is governed as much by revenge as by reason in the intrigue, for the minister in question – whose eventual "political destruction" (23) Dupin ensures by procuring the letter "at Vienna once, did [Dupin] an evil turn, which [Dupin] told [the minister], quite good-humoredly, that [he] should remember" (23) and which Dupin now, as it turns out, has the opportunity to repay. In other words, in the closing moments of his triumphant rehearsal of solving of the mystery, Dupin reveals that his ingenious, exemplary reflections are not merely tantamount to "the production of knowledge as the collecting and disposing of evidence, or the reading and understanding of a text [or situation]" (Said 178). The play and production of reason, even though this is what one is first and most insistently led to believe, are neither singularly nor always characterized by a disinterested and penetrating rational engagement, "the central image of what counts as knowledge's perfection" (Livingston 21). The reader, instead, fleetingly discerns that what is *lacking* in the narrative – that is, the unaccounted narrative presence or, alternately, acknowledged narrative absence – are material motives of Dupin "subject not so much to rationality and scientific control as to the assertion of will" (Said 178).

Dupin's deliberations engage, as much as the intricate features of the present affair, the vagaries of a shrouded but significant past. As much as Dupin sets his thoughts upon the present intrigue, he also sets them upon *the problem of securing his own advantage in communication with the past*. Rather than representing "pure" cerebration, whatever that may be, the silence and reflections in the dark that open "The Purloined Letter" more accurately suggest operations of reason tied inevitably to a history never wholly disclosed and selectively fashioned. This undisclosed past animates in substantial measure the apparently ingenuous determinations of the present. Accordingly, it is an imperative turn of events that "The Purloined Letter" concludes with the disclosure of the carefully inscribed and centered fiction on the blank sheet, which can be taken to symbolize the crucial play and prerogative of narration in the narrative itself, even despite the fact that for the most part Dupin's image is with

great care fashioned away from whatever lunatic commotion precipitates and defines his thoughts – whether arising in the street or
from the will for revenge. In brief, the fashionable (self-)image of
Dupin, like the fashionable line of the narrative, is rendered eccentric by anomalies that, in the end, are never wholly accounted.

Because the confounding revelations closing the story introduce
developments that must be understood to Dupin's advantage, it is
inadequate to remark merely "the symbolic chain which binds and
orients" (Lacan, "Seminar" 28) the narrative – a symbolic chain
understood as the decentering action and structure of the two
scenes of theft taken as precise repetitions. It is important to note,
moreover, to whose particular advantage the action of decentering
centers itself, in whose direction the decentering turns and, as it
were, provides returns. In this way – beyond remarking eccentricities
and "the structuring function of a lack" (Lacan, *Four* 29) – a project more successfully antinomian would be to interrogate those eccentricities and that structuring function in order to turn and return
them to a concealed Other account. In doing so, one more fully
recognizes the manner in which the "reasoning" that prevails in
"The Purloined Letter" secures advantage for a particular player in
the story, as analogously the reasoning prevailing in New World
landscapes secures advantage for particular constituencies among its
multiple populations. The more antinomian project would be to
expose and (re)turn to the obverse side of that advantage.

The celebrated readings of Lacan, Derrida, and Johnson fail to
(re)turn critical attentions to the site (sight) and crisis at which
dominant speculative intentions, even antinomian poststructuralist
ones, prove insufficient. This site (sight) is one of *determination*, a
site (sight) – hermeneutical, exegetical, or material – at which advantage is fixed under the representation of value, significance, the
"reasonable." However, an alternative reading *sounds out* the site
(sight) at which advantage is fixed in the short story and requires
that the paramount yet overlooked actions occurring in the street
be taken as the site of the ineluctable appearance of an undesignated Other, a primal scene of supervised yet unremarked
bla(n)ckness. Alternative interest in the narrative demonstrates that
the point at which the disturbance plays its crucial role is a point at
which one is forced to face an alien requisite and requisite alien –
generally and profitably overlooked. The actions in the street remain inadmissible to the fashionable line of the narrative as the

result of one figuration of the events, which manages to sustain its precedence "within reason."

One should not believe that the claim here is that the undesignated but essential crowd in "The Purloined Letter" is black. The claim, rather, is that the highly significant situation of that crowd is the point of paramount "undesignation" and unaccountability in the intricate affair of the stolen letter and the two scenes of its theft. The situation of the crowd, one can say, represents the highly significant situation of the essential Other – bodies both essential and bla(n)ck. The claim is that the undesignated primal scene of this narrative can be understood in terms of the undesignated primal scene of New World societies – the Otherwise unaccounted scene of continued and attenuated violence theorized, in one context, by Hortense Spillers as "murder."[8]

Entirely missing this point of "undesignation," the Lacan–Derrida–Johnson exchange pursues an Other that is finally an-other version of the self – to accept the concept of precise repetition. The exchange neglects that the Other is always determined as both radical and radically useful. The exchange pursues a too comfortably apprehended and too familiar Other, constituted by an overinvestment in interiority and divestment of exteriority, a plenary Other that, to advantage, understands itself as lack. This is to say that the Lacanian, Derridean, and Johnsonian discussions continue to *yield* the Other as a profitable lack, rather than – and the distinction is important – *understand* the Other as a profitable lack. As elaborated in the exchange, the Other – emergent from frames of reference folded in on themselves – does not adequately accommodate models for disclosing the exploitation of racially designated Others, female-gendered racialized Others, or sexual and economic Others in New World landscapes.

Because the elaboration of the negligible notion of the Other constitutes the insistent project of all dominant discourses and economies, to delineate the notion of the Other is merely to rehearse, in spite of intentions, a hermeneutical project already in place. A more unprecedented project provides strategies for recognizing that the Other is above all a usable and utilized assignation. The construction or performance of the Other, like the commotion in the street near the conclusion of the story, realizes a supervised yet overlooked utility. The space of the Other, although it marks a point of disruption, marks moreover a harnessed and profitable disruption.

The scene of commotion in the street is the scene furthest, as it turns out, from Derrida's inaugural "scene of writing," an inaugural scene disseminating and fixing Dupin's select rehearsal of an all too fashionable (and refashionable) past. This commotion in the street suggests, on the contrary, an Other narrative rendering eccentric the one centered in the scenes of robbery: Who in the street is the "man in [Dupin's] pay" (Poe 23) starting the commotion? Does this man share equally in the fifty thousand francs gained by the recovery of the letter? Is it worth remarking that the realizing of Dupin's loyal "political presuppositions" (23) depends on "a series of fearful screams, and the shoutings of a mob" (22)? Taken as the primal scene of the narrative, the commotion in the street renders the central fiction to be read as a fiction that *unaccountably* begins with the people in the street. One can say that, although it does not return to them, the narrative turns on them because of their central utility to its resolution, a utility exemplary of the general instrumental utility of the Other. The postcolonial critic Homi Bhabha makes this observation in terms of Western speculative discourse:

> Montesquieu's Turkish Despot, Barthes's Japan, Kristeva's China, Derrida's Nambikwara Indians, Lyotard's Cashinahua "pagans" are part of this strategy of containment where the Other text is forever the exegetical horizon of difference, never the active agent of articulation. (14)

This facile "exegetical horizon of difference," in terms of the discussion of "The Purloined Letter," might be thought of as the framed and framing frame of reference theorized by Johnson – a frame intent ultimately on interiority rather than the place of an unframed exteriority of reference. Only by further Othering, then, the Otherness of antinomian poststructuralist thought and frames of reference does one arrive at spaces in which the independent discourses of Other bodies might be recited (re-sited, re-sighted). Such a reading, in terms of the narrative of the U.S. landscape, would have to account, among other matters, for the "essential" difference of those bearing African American bodies, as well as Others overlooked yet supervised at the fixed sites of U.S. value. This rereading entails a reciting (re-siting, re-sighting) of the reasonable "manner of speaking"[9] forever fashioned and refashioned in accordance with the "notion of democracy at the core of 'traditional' American literatures" (Christian, "What" 70) as well as multiple U.S. rituals; it reveals, accordingly, contrary sites (sights) remaining "in the dark" despite antinomian speculation, spaces not at all punctuated by any "mystery [that] is a little too plain" (7; emphasis in original), as is the opening darkness of "The Purloined Letter." Unlike the spaces explored by dominant poststructuralist frames of reference, they do not rehearse the already pervasive accounts of traditional "agent[s] of articulation." And, although it may not seem so at first, the matter at issue is the matter of memory. Beyond intersubjectivity, beyond inaugural "scenes of writing," beyond "in-sufficiently erased traces"[10] or framed and framing frames, repetition marks a recital (re-site-al, re-sight-al) of the past in the present sense (present tense). Hence, the difference of the Other, understood from the Other side of difference, the Other side of the frame of reference, foregrounds the "problem of how, in signifying the present, something comes to be repeated, relocated, and translated in the name of tradition, in the guise of a pastness that is not necessarily a faithful sign of historical memory but a strategy of representing authority in terms of the artifice of the archaic" (Bhabha) and the artifice of what reasonably bears repeating.

What reasonably bears repeating is symbolized by the anecdote of the prodigious schoolboy that Dupin repeats, relocates, and translates into the narrative as an account of his own actions. It is not at all "a faithful sign of historical memory but a strategy of representing [his own] authority in terms of the highly reasoned and therefore, needless to say, the valuable. Dupin narrates and, by means of being the narrating and narrated narrator, both disseminates and fixes the anecdote of the ingenious schoolboy in a "faithful" relation to his own involvement in the recovery of the letter. One must notice further, however, that, if the anecdotes of the schoolboy and of the recovery of the purloined letter prove valuable (and value always turns to advantage), the anecdote (and value) turns here to Dupin's advantage. Above and beyond any position Dupin may occupy in an intersubjective triad, above and beyond the position he may occupy in a squaring of that triad, and beyond the enclosures of any repeated and repeating frames of reference in which he may be involved, one must admit the advantageous turn of events in order to address adequately the exemplary "dis-placement-and-return" (Muller and Richardson 59) of the narrative.

However, understood from the perspective of the difference of the Other, the Other side of difference, the matter to be interrogated in "The Purloined Letter" is the redoubling of too (two?)

easily framed and too (two?) easily accounted scenes of repetition. *What bears repeating* in the narrative "in the name of [a] tradition" of exemplary reasoning turns out to be the concealed irrelevance and veiled illegitimacy of the schoolboy's prodigious success. Set within the boundaries of a schoolyard – within, as it were, the inviolate spaces of hegemonic, institutionalized knowledge, spaces plainly adverse to accounts of the fixed and neglected utility of the Other – the exploits of the schoolboy take up the position of "a central point [that] would be both the source of light illuminating everything, and a locus of convergence for everything that must be known: a perfect eye that nothing would escape and a centre towards which all gazes would be turned" (Foucault, *Discipline* 173). Ultimately, the figure of the schoolboy presides over the privileged scopic regime of the narrative. His exploits and apparent genius seemingly provide "the essence of illumination . . . [or] *lumen*" (Jay 29) for making sense of the narrative and Dupin's actions. The schoolboy is the figure in which reason and vision coincide and conflate, a convergence the privileged line of the narrative invites one to accept without interrogation and invites one to repeat in regarding the figure of Dupin. Framed analogously within the spaces of institutionalized discourses, what bears repeating in the poststructuralist commentaries on "The Purloined Letter" is the redoubling of this select perception and narration authored by Dupin, as well as their circumscribed horizon of disclosure and scrutiny.

One further anecdote underscores the point. It involves "a game of puzzles . . . played upon a map" (Poe 20),[11] and, like the tale of the schoolboy, it immediately precedes Dupin's narration of the recovery of the purloined letter. Players of this game must find on a map "any word . . . upon the motley and perplexed surface of the chart," named as a challenge. It is often hardest, Dupin explains, to find the largest words on the map, "such words as stretch, in large characters, from one end of the chart to the other" (20). Proposing that signs that are "too obtrusively and too palpably self-evident" (20) are the hardest to recognize, Dupin in confirmation proceeds to narrate his discovery of the letter lying in the open in the minister's apartment. One must note, however, that Dupin recounts only the very plain contingencies of his recovery, in effect concealing the fact that the recovery of what lies in the open involves – in and despite its plainness – matters and people remaining *in the dark*. Thus, contrary to the prefatory anecdote, Dupin's role in the affair, too plainly exposed, is finally anything but plain.

Lacan, Derrida, and Johnson in their exchange follow Dupin in a reasoned pursuit of signs "stretch[ing] in large characters, from one end of the chart to the other." They repeat and reinstate in their texts "the oscillation among models of speculation, observation, and revelation" (Jay 236) strongly bound to the notions of reason and genius presiding over the narrative and proving the narrative's finally uninterrogated center of interest and return. As a result, the matter to be remarked is not that even antinomian stories return to their center, rather, it is the lack of remarking that even antinomian stories return to their center. This lack is understandably present in Dupin's self-profiting self-narration but seems much less understandable in the self-styled antinomian attentions of the poststructuralist commentators.[12] Not all critics, however, nor more generally all inhabitants of the New World share the luxury of neglecting that authorizing lack. On the contrary, for example, the African American feminist critic Cheryl A. Wall concertedly makes such remarks when she alludes to the work of Elizabeth Bruss in her introductory essay to the collection *Changing Our Own Words*:

> According to Elizabeth Bruss, some of the same sociopolitical forces that gave visibility to the community of black women writing impelled the move to theory; these included the challenge to academic authority and to traditional humanism, the advent of a more diverse student body and the attendant curricular changes, notably the teaching of nontraditional literatures. (7)

Wall makes allusions not to the self-repeating dynamics of insular frames of reference but to the powerful disruptions and challenges to those dynamics not merely coincidental with but integral to the advent and disposition of poststructuralist theory. Wall attends to the fact that the remarking of lacks analogous to that left uninterrogated in "The Purloined Letter" and its celebrated discussions seems a paramount issue of antinomian theory. If, in this way, with numerous cries of "crisis," post-1960s critical discourse has come to celebrate the decentering chain of "precise repetitions" accounted in "The Purloined Letter" and its commentaries, one must also recognize that it has managed to preserve, for the most part, a "traditional" center to which institutionalized antinomian thought wittingly or unwittingly (re)turns. Yet, more earnestly pursuing the difference of the Other, the Other side of difference, "a situation of extreme challenge and discontent," one recognizes easily the many Other turns and returns "in which traditional [centers risk] ... losing all authority" (Bruss 18). One begins to remark, that is, many Other turns and returns remaining in the dark.

A very different text from that at the center of the considerations of Lacan, Derrida, and Johnson helps to substantiate what is at stake in the authorizing lack in question, the 1978 autobiography *A Childhood: The Biography of a Place*. The curious announcement that opens this memoir of the U.S. novelist Harry Crews reads as follows: "My first memory is of a time ten years before I was born, and the memory takes place where I have never been and involves my daddy whom I never knew" (Crews 1). Crews claims to recount as personal memory events and details that do not form a personal memory, and, what is more, he identifies in doing so the fictive and governing center of his narration: the mythical status of an absent father, who dies young while providing heroically for his family. Nevertheless, the provocation of the opening statement turns out to be more telling than he knows, for what will pass as exegesis is for the moment disclosed as hermeneutic, as "belonging to or concerning interpretation" (*OED*). The statement reflects Harry Crews's flaunting the liberty to interpret. One might say that the value – the calculus specifying and signifying the center and limits – of Crews's account is implied, for the moment, to be a fabrication. Crews, in effect, equally encourages and ignores this implication, then immediately begins to fashion a narrative of classic U.S. values, that is, classic U.S. centers, boundaries, and peripheries – a narrative of U.S. ruggedness, individuality, and youthful Aryan manliness. He provides accounts of his father "[i]n the first flower of his manhood" (11), when "[i]t must have been a good time for him[,] ... when he did not yet have a wife and children or the obligations that always come with them" (12). Nevertheless, in a world in which "[w]ounds or scars give an awesome credibility" (21) to stories celebrated by white men, Crews's imagination fails him when he is faced with "Auntie [who] had been born in the time of slavery. She had told [him] all about it a long time ago, but it never meant very much to [him]. It was hard to imagine what a slave might be, and it was impossible to think of people like [his] daddy and mama owning people like Willallee's daddy and mama. It still is" (84). Value in the world Crews describes is assured, well-rehearsed, and, by classic U.S. standards, easily predictable. It unfolds with exceptional constancy.

In many ways, it is precisely this exceptional constancy that comes increasingly under interrogation in a post-1960s academy and U.S.

landscape generally. This is also to say that to a significant degree the provocative enabling liberty taken by Crews, which centers his narrative and premises its constancy, begs to be constituted as a focus or a point of concern for any decentering strategy of knowing. Crews's discursive prerogative, so much in keeping with the disposition of material and psychic prerogatives in the U.S. landscape, is fixed in place by an imaginative insularity easily understood in terms of race and gender, just as analogously in Poe's short story, one recognizes that, despite all exclusive appeals to reason, violence holds the circulating letter in place. What is lacking in the two narratives, to draw a very broad picture, is the same matter: an open account of the difference cum utility of the Other. What is lacking are crucial and indispensable points of "undesignation" that remain the obverse of repeated self-regard.

6

SIGNS OF THE VISIBLE: (RE)MOVING PICTURES IN THE NARROWS

The film scholar Anne Friedberg and the historian Donald Lowe in separate projects argue for the paramount role of the scopic as a cultural imperative in the social and epistemological systems of the modern West. Concerned in *History of Bourgeois Perception* with "the society of Western Europe, especially Britain and France, from the last third of the eighteenth to the first decade of the twentieth century" (17), Lowe claims that the ascendancy of typographic media and the scopic define the dominant field of perception for this period then are extrapolated into the historical period after 1910. The typographic, the scopic, and "the epistemic order of development-in-time" (17), Lowe argues, define the nature of perception and come to stand for the rational. In *Window Shopping: Cinema and the Postmodern*, Anne Friedberg argues that modern and postmodern subjectivity emerged in terms of "the increased centrality of the mobilized and virtual gaze as a fundamental feature of everyday life" (4). Defining the virtual gaze as "a *received* perception mediated through representation" and the mobilized gaze as any "that travels . . . through an imaginary elsewhere and an imaginary elsewhen" (2; emphasis in original), Friedberg details how particular organizations of looking are fundamental to constructing social subjectivity in "late eighteenth- and early nineteenth-century industrialization and urbanization" (13) and, as Lowe does, in the cultural order proceeding from that period. Both studies propose that a politics and socialization of looking are rudimentary to the establishment and culture of the modern West. No matter how seemingly sedimented in the fabric of the quotidian and, therefore, seemingly beyond political instrumentation, the "interestedness" and "resourcefulness" of the scopic are overwhelming. Any communities within the West managing to monopolize by concerted means these social technologies and sensory hierarchies monopolize considerable terms of value, considerable cultural resources.

Thus, if considering the cultural logic of racial blackness in the New World entails articulating socially and historically powerful conceptions of literacy, it also entails articulating peculiar monopolizations, deployments, and countercultural dispellings of the sensory modality of vision – or, in the words of Martin Jay, "the tacit cultural rules of different scopic regimes" ("Vision" 9), for African Americans find themselves disqualified from "the Enlightenment view of innate human equality" (Forsman 100) and the attendant material rewards of industrial capitalist economies as the result of the "sight" of us. It is the skin colors, the textures of hair, the shapes of skulls and noses, the placements of cheekbones, the thicknesses of lips, the contours of buttocks that visibly define those in the African diaspora and, accordingly, the enduring social, political, and economic oppressions of the African diasporia. Diasporic populations find themselves in circumstances in which the sense-making capacity of vision, the significance of vision, is monopolized from a hostile perspective. Inasmuch as the fundamental circumstances of poverty and violence in which populations metonymically represented by singing voices find themselves do not change, the fundamental predicament of African Americans is a sensory one. Visual reflexes, in the same way literacy determines in large part the logic of racial blackness, aim to hypostasize racial blackness.

Judgments of individual and cultural legitimacy based on literacy propose abjected Otherness for African Americans; visual evidence proposes the same; and so do the protocols by which these separate proposals function in tandem. For these reasons, although generally unacknowledged, the exemplarity of the poststructuralist debate around "The Purloined Letter" exceeds the insularity of frames or boundaries. Concerning, in fact, guileful investments in the utility of a present absence, the narrative and debate around it highlight a particular disposition of reason, a scopic order of reason uncontested in both. The implicit and unchallenged opticism of Dupin's version of events is no incidental element of "The Purloined Letter" or his claims to authority. It allows a celebrated *vision* of Dupin that does not wholly disclose the intrigue and interest of the plot even as it purports to do so, in the same way that one can contend that the scopic is harnessed within the dynamics of the New World to allow and maintain a vision of African Americans that opposingly dismisses them for the most part from reason, intellect, and the material boons of Western modernity. Oculocentricism is embraced fiercely by Enlightenment and post-Enlightenment cultural logics in which "a basic metaphorical understanding of vision . . . leads to the connection of vision with intellectual activity" (Mark Johnson 108). The scopic – by means of which the world is apparently most faithfully known, understood, and assimilated – comes to stand (like literacy) for reason, intellect, and perhaps even consciousness. For Western modernity – which one can date from the peculiar coincidence of Enlightenment thought and the ambitious pursuit of trade in and enslavement of Africans and African Americans – the scopic is a preeminent cultural matrix of power and order.

What has already been proposed as the racialized opposition of singing and signing voices also confirms this state of affairs. Whereas the singing voice prioritizes the sonority of vocal communication, presenting the voice primarily as a phonic phenomenon, the signing voice slights the audible dimension of voice in order to re-present other material. When spoken, the signing voice appears "immaterial" in its representations. Only when it is most fixed and seemingly made permanent in the form of alphabetic script does it appear to materialize visibly. The signing voice, then, not only refuses the phonic condition of the singing voice but attains the scopic as a position of value in its paramount instantiation as script. Appearing either entirely immaterial or overwhelmingly and visibly present, the signing voice is given credibility foremost in its latter formation as overwhelmingly and visibly present, credibility granted by systems of exchange indispensable to Western economic, legal, and geopolitical ascendancy. When it renders visible the information it presents, it holds greatest value and, insofar as it is taken to emblematize racial whiteness, it monopolizes in its most prized form the scopic for that racial position. Conversely, insofar as it stands as an emblem of racial blackness, the singing voice situates blackness within the phonic. This is to say, the reciprocal interests of the scopic and the phonic are indices of unequal cultural positions and resources, an important element of "The Purloined Letter" generally neglected.

Nonetheless, in order to understand the paramount position, the unquestionable centrality, of visual evidence in assigning hostile meaning and rank to African Americans in the New World, recall Thomas Jefferson's objection in *Notes on the State of Virginia* to "incorporat[ing] the blacks into the state," which rests unabashedly on his reaction to "the black of the negro [which] resides in the reticular membrane between the skin and scarf-skin, or in the scarf-skin itself" (138). Jefferson proposes that the sight of African Americans foremost justifies exclusion from the American republic and from recognition as fully human:

> Is [color] not the foundation of a greater or less share of beauty in the two races? Are not the fine mixtures of red and white, the expressions of every passion by far greater or less suffusions of colour in the one, preferable to that eternal monotony, which reigns in the contenances of, that immoveable veil of black which covers all the emotions of the other race? Add to these, flowing hair, a more elegant symmetry of form. (138)

"[T]he circumstances of superior [visual] beauty," as Jefferson imagines them, prove the ultimate gauge of greater or lesser humanity. His tortured but consequential reasoning, the reasoning of a representative U.S. Enlightenment thinker, concludes that notions of beauty are "thought worthy of attention in the propagation of our horses, dogs, and other domestic animals; why not in that of man?" (138).

Given this situation – because African Americans are in this way disbarred from meaningful participation in the sense-making activity of vision, are confronted with vision as a hostile realm of significance – one might argue that the priority of a musical legacy attests to African American populations' turning earnestly, ingeniously, and with marked success to the less privileged sense-making medium of sound. Sound, one might argue, gains especial importance for those who remain visibly outside the designation of most fully human. Since "[m]usic is intimately connected with African custom and practice" (Lovell 37), this particular cultural negotiation of a sensory predicament seems almost inevitable.

African Americans, barred from the privileged affirmation afforded by vision, the primary means of conceptualizing systems that define the world and one's place in it, refine and invigorate those resources with which they are left – the less apparent power of audition and, in particular, the voice. Still, issues of sound and the voice are not trivial and, left undisturbed, may prove as disbarring as those of vision. The speaking, or signing, voice remains, like vision, claimed by the dominant community in substantial ways.

Within the logocentricism of Western thought the signing voice stands as an emblem of full, originary, celebrated self-presence, self-presence marking mind and spirit, the effulgence of human self-hood. Although the voice, like vision, is not directly accessible to African Americans, neither is it as closely guarded. As argued earlier, the African American appropriation of voice and the privileging of its sense-making capacity are marked by indirection, the indirection of song.

In its disturbance of the already scripted significance of vision and speaking, the singing voice reopens the very issue of making sense in the New World, undertaking the moving and "removing" of visual evidence in a confrontation in which racial whiteness ideally is read as the human, as the visible, and as the essential meaning of the human and the visual. The singing voice, in this way of under-standing matters, registers resistance to hostile dominant regimes in commensurate ways to, say, the violence of confrontation, escape from enslavement, or establishment of maroon communities. Fur-thermore, one might even say the contraventions of the singing voice prove more telling than these other forms, because they redact the perceptual point of conflict defined by oppressed and dominant cultures. These contraventions codify not only a virtually ubiquitous African American response[1] to important cultural circumstances of New World existence but the particular grounds on which these hostile circumstances "make sense." They prove a point of cathexis at which the premises of New World racialism and improvisational resistance converge. More than the relations of industrialization and mass commodification, more than claims for burgeoning democra-tization, more than claims for unprecedented knowledge of and dominance over the physical environment, the contraventions of the singing voice represent, one might say, the inaugural and endur-ing premises of U.S. and European world dominance. This – em-phatically – is not to say that an embattled African American self-expression is most representative of the terms of New World civilization by dint of some essential message, but to say – very dif-ferently – that this embattled self-expression is representative insofar as it redacts insistent violence grounded in scopic evidence that is with equal insistence refunctioned in other terms. The singing voice and its populations, in effect, disturb the terms on which knowledge and dominance, democratization, and industrial wealth would rou-tinely be understood and distributed.

Ann Petry's last published novel *The Narrows* (1953) subtly and clearly appreciates this state of affairs. It instructively documents vexed ratios of sight and sound. The seemingly incidental *singing* voices in *The Narrows*, as they do in *The Street*, appear as casual, almost fleeting elements in the intricately intertwining events, characters, desires, and oppressions forming the narrative, while their function, in fact, belies their seeming insignificance. As already suggested, both within and without Petry's fiction, singing voices are points of cathexis in a context that, in Petry's own words, remains remarkably stable: "The sad and terrible truth," Petry writes in a 1987 autobiographical essay, "is that now forty-one years [after writing *The Street*] I could write that same book about Harlem or any other ghetto. Because life hasn't changed that much for black people" ("Petry" 265).

Whereas *The Street* concerns itself with fantastic visual images in terms of which the United States would see itself – such as the advertised "miracle of a kitchen" with which Lutie Johnson is fascinated (28) or matinee images of police, spies, and other agents of U.S. law and order with which Bub is enthralled – *The Narrows* interrogates visual images of African Americans that U.S. culture manufactures. These pervasive and consequential images are challenged in the narrative by African American voices calling attention to themselves "as though something important depended on ... not losing the sound" (*Narrows* 124) – especially the alluring voice of the sensual and perpetually singing Mamie Powther; the novel is haunted by "Mamie Powther's voice, voice lifted in song, voice ascending and descending the outside back stairs, voice increasing in volume, voice diminishing, almost disappearing" (124). Conversely, the primary agents of a hostile scopic regime in the narrative are Camilo Treadway, her very wealthy mother, and Bullock, editor of the *Monmouth Chronicle*, the local newspaper.

The climax of *The Narrows* is precipitated by and rehearsed in terms of the startling clash of scopic and phonic registers. The murder of the sometimes wayward Link Williams, who possesses "a perfectly beautiful speaking voice ... [that] belonged to a colored man" (88) forms the climax of the novel. The sound of Link's voice, as does his physical attractiveness, seems to belie the meaning that would be assigned to his racial blackness, for "the clean, clear enunciation, the resonance, the timbre" (88) of his voice launch him into the central intrigue of the novel, an affair with the married, wealthy, and white Camilo Treadway. Similarly, these qualities of his voice shape the final moments of his abduction by Treadway's mother and husband. When he speaks for the first time in their presence, Mrs. Treadway is so taken aback she has to sit down, and Link muses to himself:

> If she'd had a gun, she would have shot me, right then, at that moment. But why? Voice. It's the sound of your voice, Bud. You hadn't spoken before and she took it for granted you would sound like AmosAndySambo, nobody in here but us chickens. And it has for the first time occurred to her that you and Camilo were making the beast with two backs. An old black ram has been tupping her white ewe. She will never let you get out of this room alive. (401)

The sound of Link's voice disturbs the scopic evidence of his racial blackness. It asserts what Mrs. Treadway understands as fully rational and perceptive personhood, which she, as does U.S. culture, most routinely equates with racial whiteness. In these moments, sound disrupts a system of cultural and racial representation premised foremost on the scopic. The stark binarism of racial blackness and racial whiteness, which should be confirmed by plain perception, is so effectively dislocated when Link speaks that for Mrs. Treadway the situation demands dramatic, unequivocal violence to reinstate that binary opposition. Mrs. Treadway realizes from the sound of Link's voice that the publicized claims of Link's raping Camilo are certainly false. She is forced momentarily to view otherwise, in the words of Sandra Gunning, "[t]he black male body, hypersexualized and criminalized, [which] has always functioned as a crucial and heavily overdetermined metaphor in an evolving national discourse on the nature of a multiethnic, multiracial American society" (3).

The murder of Link draws together the diverse array of narrative threads the narrative comprises. Whereas Petry's genius in *The Street* has much to do with her intricate and dexterous handling of narrative chronology, in *The Narrows* it more fully concerns the construction of a narrative architecture that holds in very delicate balance the memories, passions, appetites, boredoms, jealousies, insecurities, blindnesses, and greed of an impressively diverse array of characters. No one character in *The Narrows*, not even Link Williams, stands as so central a figure as does Lutie Johnson in *The Street*. The intrigue of *The Narrows* involves the rippling network of actions formed by a large cast of characters: the very proprietary Abbie Crunch, who owns her own home but is forced to take in boarders; Link Williams, her attractive and carefree nephew; Malcolm

SIGNS OF THE VISIBLE

Powther, the very proper butler to the wealthy Treadways and boarder of Abbie Crunch; Mamie Powther, his sensual and unpredictable young wife; J. C., their incorrigible youngest son; Camilo Treadway, bored and adventurous socialite; Bill Hod, owner of the Last Chance saloon and surrogate family to Link; and others. Nellie McKay, in her introduction to the 1988 Beacon Press reprint of the novel, states that Petry's "focus is on the physical and psychological havoc that lies at the intersection of capitalism and patriarchy, where the most vulnerable are black people (people of color) and women" (xii). Much of this havoc recapitulates the racialized power of visual imagery and the predicament in which this situation places African American communities. Not until the final one hundred pages or so of the more than four hundred pages of the novel does a conventional narrative rhythm overwhelm Petry's very patient storytelling. This belated, conventional pacing leads to Link's murder, which serves not only as the denouement of the plot and its intrigue, but as the climax for the well-established dissonance between scopic and phonic registers in the narrative.

The intensity of this dissonance bears noting. The predicament arising for African American communities from the monopolization of the scopic is a profound one, since investigators of the physiology of sensory perception agree – to quote, for example, Ian Gordon's *Theories of Visual Perception* – that "we are a species in whom visual sense is strikingly dominant" (10). Indeed, the uniqueness and very sophistication of the modality of visual perception attest to its status among the five senses: The organs of vision are "photosensitive," whereas the organs of hearing and touch share a "mechanosensitive" modality and those of taste and smell a "chemosensitive" modality (Marks 182). The historian Martin Jay also rehearses some of the case for the primacy of visual sensory modality:

> Having some eighteen times more nerve endings than the cochlear nerve of the ear, its nearest competitor, the optic nerve with its 800,000 fibers is able to transfer an astonishing amount of information to the brain, and at a rate of assimilation far greater than that of any other sense organ. In each eye, over 120 million rods take in information on some five hundred levels of lightness and darkness, while more than seven million cones allow us to distinguish among more than one million combinations of color. The eye is also able to accomplish its tasks at a far greater remove than any other sense,

hearing and smell being only a distant second and third. (*Downcast* 6)

The biological priority of scopic activity does not alone account for the cultural peculiarities structuring the dynamic between vision and race. The preeminence of vision in human experience and world making is also acknowledged by scholars in nonscientific fields. The intellectual John Berger begins his influential *Ways of Seeing* by reminding us that "[s]eeing comes before words. The child looks and recognizes before it can speak," and he continues, "[i]t is seeing which establishes our place in the surrounding world" (7). In an essay in which he aims to detail "the plurality of scopic regimes now available to us" (20), Martin Jay writes: "Whether we focus on 'the mirror of nature' metaphor in philosophy with Richard Rorty or emphasize the prevalence of surveillance with Michel Foucault or bemoan the society of spectacle with Guy Debord, we confront again and again the ubiquity of vision as the master sense of the world" ("Scopic" 3). The phenomenologist Don Ihde, in a study dedicated to pointing up the neglect of auditory phenomena in philosophical investigation, remarks upon "the close association of reason and [visual] perception" (82). Mark Johnson, succinctly summarizing the work of his fellow philosopher Eve Sweetzer, enumerates reasons for the all-important parallel between vision and intellection:

> (i) Vision is our primary source of data about the world. It typically gives us far more information than any of the other senses, and it appears that children rely most heavily on visual features in their early categorization. In other words, vision plays a crucial role in our acquisition of knowledge. (ii) Vision involves the remarkable ability to focus at will on various features of our perceptual array, to pick out one object from a background, or to differentiate fine features. All these operations have parallels in intellectual acts. (iii) Furthermore, vision is more or less identical for different people who can take up the same viewpoint. It thus seems to provide a basis for shared, public knowledge. (108–109)

It is very easily imaginable that – in response to biological, psychological, and cultural imperatives – those attempting to construct themselves as most fully human necessarily monopolize the significance of sight.

Needless to say, however, this monopolization of vision, like the racial schematization in the service of which it is placed, is perpetually troubled, and the trouble, as Mrs. Treadway is forced to acknowledge, can be overwhelming. Although racial division ideally would be marked in terms of a simple polarization, the case is, in fact, much more involved, for race is fundamentally a reproductive issue, which is to say it is invested in the preservation and perpetuation of a particular set of phenotypical traits. This serialization paramount to race is realized only through sexual congress, so that sexual congress becomes a cultural and racial performance requiring very careful scripting and management. Yet, as confirmed by the dazzling array of potential sexual unions and activities – not necessarily limited to any particularly racially inscribed participants, nor for that matter to any particular number of participants, nor to any form of gender symmetry – sexual congress is only by tenuous fiat reduced to and conflated with the issue of reproduction. What is at issue, then, in racialization, more than any reproductive imperative, is the conscripting of desire and the most intimate of phantasms. In other words, racialization is doomed to complications never quite reducible to ordered dualities, because "[d]esire is the site in which demand and need are never reconciled, and this makes of desire a permanently vexed affair" (Butler, "Desire" 381). It is neither fully calculable nor formulaic and, insofar as racialization attempts to measure out and formalize the unruliness of desire in strict accordance with calculable oppositions, its task is overwhelming.

Mrs. Treadway has this revelation, to her dismay, when Link speaks for the first time after his abduction. Rather than the ultimate reliability of the scopic in substantiating racial polarizations, she is faced, on the contrary, with her daughter's vexing, unruly, and unimaginably reckless desire. The sexual congress of Link and Camilo violates a social/sexual/disciplinary complex that the scopic is trained to produce and rationalize, and it is violated again in Mrs. Treadway's recognition of the *consensual* nature of their sexual congress. Whereas her abduction of Link is intended only to wrest a public confession of attempted rape from him, it ends abruptly in his murder.

Significantly, then, the most consequential meeting in the narrative, the unexpected encounter of Link and Camilo at night on the Monmouth dock, occurs, in a fog "so thick now it was like smoke from a fire that had water poured on it, clouds of it, white, thick, visibility zero, ceiling zero" (57). The deep fog, like Mrs.

Treadway's epiphany, abrogates the scopic so completely that normative social codes depending on it are set in abeyance. Link and Camilo are unaware of each other on the dock until Link hears "a kind of frenzy that suggested that [Camilo] was literally running for her life" (57). He shouts, "This way! This way!" (58). Camilo is fleeing the voyeuristic (or perhaps even physical) advances of Cat Jimmie, and, thus, from the very beginning, contact between Link and Camilo is fraught with the sexual tension and danger that openly define their relationship when abeyant racial markers "dependent on culturally inflected visual practices" (Jay "Vision" 3) are recognized and reinstated – not only by themselves but, eventually, by the entire community of Monmouth. At these moments, however, the deep sexual uneasiness is rendered in the grotesque form and virtual sexual hysteria of Cat Jimmie, who prowls the docks on his little flat cart with only stumps for legs, "a fullgrown male, with all the instincts and urges of the male left, and no way in the world of satisfying them ... [except to] lie flat on his homemade cart and moan like an animal as he looked up under a woman's skirts" (61).

Because he pursues Camilo in the fog, under conditions denying him any chance of his usual voyeuristic pleasures, the intensity of Cat Jimmie's compulsive behavior at this fateful moment of the novel warrants particular notice: Whether the virtual blindness brought on by the fog exacerbates the blindness of his urges and prompts him to attempt physical assault is unclear. What is clear, however, is the terrific figure of untamable perversion and desire he seems to represent. He is the counterpart of Jones, the building superintendent in *The Street*, for both formalize the damaged racial subject in terms of violently skewed libidinal economies. Barbara Christian at the conclusion of *Black Women Writers* proposes that

> [t]he racism that black people have had to suffer is almost always presented in peculiarly sexist [and sexual] terms. That is, the wholeness of a person is basically threatened by an assault on the definition of herself or himself, as female or male. The literature suggests that this holds true not only for black women but for black men as well. (252)

One very important element of this assault is the assumption from the dominant perspective that all African Americans are, in fact or *potentia*, lewd, dangerous, or phenomenal sexual beings – codified, for example, by U.S. lore aimed at justifying ritual acts of lynching.

This lore forwards "a characterization of blacks as nomadic savages [and] denie[s] the possibility of imagining African Americans – especially African American men – as viable contributors to communities black or white, or as themselves members of respectable domestic units" (Gunning 49). Cat Jimmie and Jones are paramount figures of such a characterization. They stand in the African American literary canon among a group of black male figures forged, in part, by dominant discourse to confirm and embody the role of the sexual predator (a group of which some notable figures are enumerated by Farah Griffin in her study *"Who set you flowin'?"*). Expectations that all black men are sexual predators or potentially so and that all black women are perpetually sexually available are entrenched tenets of U.S. racialization, and, in their respective narratives, Cat Jimmie and Jones most completely represent such damaged and mythical racial figures.

The ugliness of Cat Jimmie's wayward and aggressive sexual appetite is matched by his physical deformities, deformities in regard to which even Link, to whom Cat Jimmie is a familiar fixture on the dock, does not disguise his distaste:

> Everything about him was repulsive – the flesh on the stumps that had once been arms was red, angry, covered with scar tissue, purposely revealed, because he covered them with leather pads when he propelled himself along on his homemade cart; his shoulders were tremendous, overdeveloped. He was legless from the thighs down, and the same rawlooking angrylooking flesh was exposed to view on the stumps that were his legs. This red rawlooking flesh of the arms and legs formed a shocking contrast to the dark brown skin of his face and neck. His eyes were straight out of a nightmare – there was a red glare in them, there was excitement in them, and hate. (61)

Cat Jimmie is an African American man who is reprehensible as well as visually repulsive, an African American man in whom the two conditions – as U.S. lore would have it – strictly coincide. The perversion he embodies and represents is a perversion to be associated with blackness: He is a seemingly permanent fixture of the dock and the black section of town in which it is located, the part of Monmouth called "The Narrows. The Bottom. Little Harlem. Eye of the Needle. Sometimes they just say Dumble Street" (62). Cat Jimmie is a figure who confirms the distressing view of the "unsightly" guaranteed by U.S. monopolizations of the visual in the name of racial whiteness. He is, as suggested by his obsessive voyeurism, an early and profound emblem of the scopic in the novel.

It is strikingly ironic, then, given Cat Jimmie's symbolization of the mythologized libidinal and visual repulsiveness of blackness, that Camilo in the blinding fog flees from one African American man by running directly to another. She is misled by the sound of her rescuer's voice; she "could not see [Link] because of the fog but she headed straight toward the sound of his voice, reaching for him, close now, grabbing at him, holding on to him, clutching at his hand, his arm, her hand with a tremor in it, tremor all over" (58). In the disorientation of the fog – beyond the broad assurances of the scopic – the irony of her escape is not yet recognized, and, even when it is, it is ultimately translated into sexual attraction, not repulsion or dismissal. The tension between what is and is not seen and what is heard resolves itself in even greater irony. In these moments of sensory dislocation, not only is the artifice of racializing regimes apparent, but so too the sexual premises of race are glaring, and they become even more so as the novel moves toward its violent conclusion.

As Barbara Christian suggests, and Cat Jimmie symbolizes, to think, speak, and act in deference to race amounts necessarily and already to thinking, speaking, and acting in terms of sexuality. The sexual terms of the meeting of Link and Camilo are not incidental. Nor do these terms merely forecast the couple's precarious affair. As does the dissonance of the scopic and phonic, the sexual tension of their meeting uncovers a set of contingencies requiring strict regulation lest the self-regard of race be lost altogether. These sexual premises of race, their dangers, and their necessary regulation constitute an insistent strain of the narrative powerfully exposed and recapitulated in the events leading to Link's murder.

One must keep in mind that in the same passage in which Link understands the disruptive force that the sound of his voice holds for Mrs. Treadway, he equally broaches her greatest fears concerning her daughter's recklessness. He states to himself: "And it has for the first time occurred to her that you and Camilo were making the beast with two backs. An old black ram has been tupping her white ewe. She will never let you get out of this room alive" (401). Beyond the way the Shakespearean posturing of Link's self-reflections – "the beast with two backs," "[a]n old black ram . . . tupping her white ewe" – confirms the jarring meaning of "the clean, clear enunciation" (88) of his voice, it highlights the manner in which the "co-dependent structures of race and sex converge" (Doyle 21). Race is guaranteed only through sexual means and, accordingly, Link's reflections highlight the significance of a public understanding of rape as the only possible sexual interaction "conceivable" between him and Camilo. Of this public understanding of rape and its implications in marking racial positions, Jane Gaines writes:

> We can never again use the concept of "rape" quite so abstractly in its generic or metaphorical sense, after we have considered the way "white" or "black" has historically modified, or shall we say "inflamed", the act and the term. During slavery, white male abuse of black women was a symbolic blow to black manhood, understood as rape only within the black community. With the increase in the sexual violation of black women during Reconstruction, the act of rape began to reveal its fuller political implications. After emancipation, the rape of black women was a "message" sent to black men. . . . Simultaneous with the actual violation of black women, the empty charge of rape hurled at the black man clouded the real issue of black (male) enfranchisement, by creating a smokescreen through the incendiary issue of interracial sexuality. (23)

In this historical formation around the concept of rape, heterosexual miscegnation between a black man and white woman, ingeniously, seems to stabilize racial meaning even as the act itself might very likely destablize actual racial bodies. In the invidious cultural turn given the concept, one recognizes aspects of violence, libido, gendered positions, and rights of citizenship converging within processes of racialization and rationalization that only by the grossest misrepresentation might be understood as binary.

In this vein, Link's reflections redact what the philosopher Noami Zack terms the existential (rather than biological) "reality" of racial blackness.[2] They redact race as an assuredly libidinal complex, as a series of prohibitions on social desire and sexual practice determining an "asymmetrical kinship system" (Zack 27). More assiduously than scopic or phenotypical evidence, and in ways more complicated than a binary scheme suggests, it is family membership that determines the animus of racial blackness and whiteness and, in doing so, exposes the cathected ground of race, gender, and sexuality. Zack reasons:

Designated black physical racial characteristics are genetic. The mechanism of human genetics is heterosexual sexual intercourse. That fact alone is enough to account for much of the obscenity, fear, fascination, lust, scorn, degradation, and both real and pseudo-revulsion with which white people have considered the sexuality of black people. Individuals who are designated black have the ability, through the mechanism of their heterosexuality, to destroy the white identity of families, and because race of kin determines race of individuals, to destroy the white identity of the relatives of their descendants. Thus the asymmetrical kinship system of racial inheritance in the United States not only is intrinsically racist in favor of white people, but it defines black people as intrinsically threatening and dangerous to white families. (27)

At bottom, the danger is a sexual one so that, stated even more plainly, race amounts foremost to a set of fundamental prohibitions on the discharge of sexual energies, to prohibitions aiming to stabilize and ensure the transmission of identifying phenotypical traits from generation to generation. If, in this way, race is a set of practices worrying over the coding and dissemination of visible but unstable physical traits, then it is, finally, a system strictly rationalizing libidinal energies.

In the same way the sound of Link's voice disturbs a scheme monopolizing the scopic, his unthinkable liaison with Camilo and the images he calls up in his soliloquy profoundly disturb the basis of racialized order, an order in which "the interracial struggle over the terrain of the public would always be figured finally within the terms of the domestic – the privatized expression of the nation's political anxieties" (Gunning 21). This order is intimately and intuitively known in the United States, and Camilo instinctively invokes it in her desperate but mistaken jealousy of Link and Mamie Powther, which sets off the chain of events leading to his murder. Back on the dock late one night, when Link dismisses her and her jealousies, Camilo vows, "I'll get even . . . I'll hurt you just like you've hurt me" (319). As she attempts to slap him across the face for a second time, Link pinions her arms and pushes her away, and, with the thoughtlessness of reflex, Camilo broaches the center of the sexual prohibitions on which racialization in the United States is maintained:

She screamed suddenly. He looked at her in astonishment, not believing that fullbodied sound, born of terror, came out from her throat, unrehearsed, that it had always been there, waiting to be called forth, terror, outrage, fury, all there in the throat, emerging when needed. He winced, listening to her, thinking, Now I understand all of them, this Dumble Street sound is in all their throats, the potential is there, and when the need arises they emit this high horrible screaming. (319)

Even the refuge or alterity of sound, usually exploited by the singing voice, is denied in these moments that witness the power of the U.S. racial paradigm and reflexes invoking it. In her charade, Camilo produces a sound that seems to overwhelm all else. Whereas in the terror of the actual attack by Cat Jimmie she is "apparently so frightened that she could not scream . . . [is] too exhausted to scream" (57–8), her calculated invocation of race and its scripted violences provides her the opportunity to find her voice with an ease and gusto almost rendering it palpable. She reacts as though the horror of Cat Jimmie were grossly magnified. She fully understands and internalizes gender and sexual prescriptions and proscriptions underwriting racial communities, despite the fact she has ignored or chafed against them for most of the narrative. Her intuitive knowledge of these cultural protocols, as played out in her charade, is detailed and dramatic:

> Camilo screamed and screamed. He heard the thud of feet, on the sidewalk, feet running toward them, coming down Dumble Street. He stood, not moving, watching her open the expensive mink coat, watched her wrench at the front of her dress, give it up, reach inside, wrench at her slip, the lovely delicatelooking hands strong from tennis, golf, badminton, trying to tear the fabric, and the fabric not giving, the fabric used in the clothes made for a multimillionairess not easy to tear, impossible to tear. The hands gave it up, the hands were now rumpling the pale yellow hair. Hair disordered, disarranged, but the clothes intact. (320)

The rape of a white woman by a black man is a paradigmatic racial signifier in the U.S. imagination for several reasons. The violence of this kind of sexual congress stands in for the villainy, bestial instincts, and, therefore, perpetual danger understood to characterize blackness. Moreover, the sexual appetites and reproductive possibilities of this congress abrogate for white communities the role of their "mothering women [as] a defensive border . . . so that they may stand strong against contamination" (Doyle 27) from the moral degeneracy and various and sundry threats of racial Otherness. To propose rape as the only and villainous mechanism allowing one to imagine in tandem black sexuality and the reproductive responsibilities of white women is, reminiscent of Mrs. Treadway, to imagine the impossibility of desire or consent marking such sexual congress.

It is extremely important to understand that this impossibility extends, in fact, to all forms of interracial sexual contact – whether heterosexual or not (and this is the reason for designating black sexuality in general and not simply black male sexuality). In a revealing question, Judith Butler broaches this issue: "How might we understand homosexuality and miscegnation to converge at and as the constitutive outside of a normative heterosexuality that is at once the regulation of a racially pure reproduction?" (Bodies 167). Normative heterosexuality, Butler's question implies, is that which respects the imperatives of race, since race is tied ineluctably to reproduction. Race is a sexual scheme conscripting desire in absolute ways, absolute ways positioning gay and lesbian sexuality (whether interracial or intraracial) not simply as a breach of normative gender citations but, moreover, like miscegnation, a breach of, a challenge to, and the antithesis of racialization itself. The libidinal logic of homosexuality, in another version of the villainous unreasonableness of rape, defies the premises of racialization – villainous and unreasonable because it is not implicated in the idea of reproduction (always, in turn, racially conscripted). Race – and rape as a paradigmatic signifier of race – forecloses the question of desire. Rather than merely marking a criminal encounter involving two individuals, the paradigmatic signifier of a black man raping a white woman remains a part of symbolic mechanisms aimed at disciplining every member of the population. The image forwards the assurance that its aberrant sexual congress is not desired, but violent and coerced. Conversely, homosexuality is aberrant precisely because it is so *plainly* about desire, to the point of displacing reproduction altogether and thus, to the point of placing desire dangerously out of control. In these and other cases the purity and perpetuation of the race – the production and reproduction of a particular "strain" of the human species (most especially, dominant racial whiteness) – are jeopardized.

Racialization entails that the sexual congress subsequent to the chance meeting, flirtations, and emotional attachments of Link and Camilo be, emphatically, a moment policed, forestalled, rejected.

Camilo's charade fully depends on and asserts this intuitive knowledge. She can be assured that her charade will be immediately and unmistakably accredited, because the only possible understanding of their encounter will be a breach of racial etiquette for which, by rote, the responsibility will fall to Link. Because desire is overdetermined within the schematics of race, Link will be criminalized by virtue of his visible blackness and Camilo will be rescued from the sight of that danger.

Still, no matter how potent, the force of racial specification is not inviolable. Camilo's reputation as all too reckless and the subsequent dissemination of Link's picture in a regional newspaper confound these idealized understandings of race and official reports of attempted rape on the dock. Bullock, the editor of the *Monmouth Chronicle*, when he sees the picture of Link printed in a New York tabloid, thinks to himself:

> So here was this Negro standing on the dock, lordlylooking bastard, leaning against the railing, head slightly turned, profile like Barrymore, sunlight concentrated on his left side, so that the head, the shoulders, the whole length of him had the solidity of sculpture, the picture damn near had the three-dimensional quality of fine sculpture. There was an easy carelessness about the leaning position of his body, controlled carelessness, and the striped T-shirt, the slacks, the moccasins on the feet suited his posture. (365)

Bullock fearfully recognizes that "[e]very woman who saw this nigger's picture would cut it out, clip it out, tear it out, drool over it. Every white man who saw it would do a slow burn" (365). He fully understands and, given his way, would reinforce further, by the broad means available to him as a newspaper editor, the intuitive knowledge and cultural cues drawn on by Camilo in feigning sexual assault. His sympathetic understanding of Camilo's charade is structured, though, through an ultimately irksome set of scopic moves so that the scopic appears once again as an unreliable register, regardless of how insistently it may be enlisted by racial designs. In his sympathetic gaze, Bullock is forced to make spectatorial moves contravening the deepest principles of racialization and drawing him into a complex of libidinal possibilities that, precisely, must be rejected in order to reinforce the racial binarism he is so eager to valorize and the reading of Camilo's actions he is so anxious to validate.

Although reluctantly, he is even willing to sacrifice professional integrity for his sympathies, for he withholds from his paper a subsequent story that Camilo ran down a child while driving intoxicated on Dock Street only a few days after her alleged attack. "Is it a matter of morality?" he asks himself. "No, it's a matter of what will people say – what will people think – public opinion" (358). The additional story placing Camilo on the docks so soon after the reported attack by Link would unduly compound public perception of her recklessness, "would, in fact, polish off what was left of" (357) her reputation. It would raise too many questions about her presence in "The Narrows" at midnight with Link, with the result that interest in an all too intriguing local news story would increase exponentially. Accordingly, when Mrs. Treadway goes to his office to request that he suppress the story, he reluctantly complies. More than any concern for Camilo, however, his compliance is coerced by the fact that Mrs. Treadway accounts for an immense amount of the advertising in and revenue for his paper. What he is faced with, then, when he not only glances at the picture of Link but also reads in the New York paper the story he withholds from the *Monmouth Chronicle,* are the consequences of a long series of overweening investments in the prescriptives of race. Indeed, rather than racial protocols, he is faced with outlines of Camilo's – and potentially many others' – desire for Link, not to mention his own curious speculative desire in imagining that "[e]very woman who saw this nigger's picture would cut it out, clip it out, tear it out, drool over it" (365).

Whereas the unnerving dislocation of the visual is clearly evident in Mrs. Treadway's shocked response to Link's voice, it is most fully and dramatically articulated in the structure of Bullock's disconcerted gaze. Laura Mulvey's well known essay "Visual Pleasure and Classic Cinema" is helpful in illuminating this structure, because Mulvey theorizes the scopophilic principles of classic cinema in terms of ambivalent or competing masculine impulses, impulses very much operative in Bullock's gaze. Drawing on Lacan and Freud, Mulvey proposes a series of overlapping tensions determining spectatorship in classic cinema. These tensions include: pleasure derived from erotic stimulation through sight but complicated by narcissistic reinforcement of the ego, viewing of the feminine concomitantly as an erotic object within the diegesis and as an erotic object for the spectator in the theatre, viewing of the feminine as passive spectacle while understanding the masculine as active bearer of the look, pleasure in viewing the feminine complicated by castration anxiety implicit in recognizing feminine difference, and sadistic or fetishistic responses to this anxiety. Always alternating between pleasure and displeasure in this way, classic narrative film continually negotiates these tensions, which, as a result, "act as formations, mechanisms which would mould this cinema's formal attributes" (25). The masculinized pleasures of the "heterosexual division of labour" (20) in classic cinema must be formally (not merely diegetically) allayed.

These formulations characterize cinematic scopophilia as unmistakably about men even though driven most patently by heteroerotic display: The primary concern of the gaze that cinema trains on women is the production of masculine pleasure and allaying of masculine anxieties. As assuredly, one can easily imagine that the spectacle of racial blackness analogously requires a series of negotiations of the pleasures and anxieties of those understanding themselves as racially white, all this even as whiteness never patently presents itself as an object of scrutiny: "The colourless multi-colouredness of whiteness secures white power by making it hard, especially for white people and their media to 'see' whiteness . . . [as well as] hard to analyze" (Dyer 46). Any congruence between the management of the spectacles of femininity and racial blackness is far from complete, however. Employing the concept of gender difference but never imagining how it must be complicated by racial difference, the women Mulvey understands as the objects of cinematic scopophilia are implicitly white. For the dynamics of blackness dramatically alter important aspects of her scheme.

First, whereas the scopic enterprise of classic cinema wrestles with forms of pleasure that skirt displeasure, the scopic enterprise concerned with racial blackness wrestles with predisposed forms of displeasure and repudiation that, as delineated in *The Narrows,* may often provoke pleasure or interest. Second, as "the place of the look defines the cinema, the possibility of varying it and exposing it" (25), it is the fixing and immobilizing of the look that guarantee the meaning of racial blackness; the classic cinematic gaze must roam among various points of identification, but the gaze trained on blackness must, in order to guarantee its spectacle, be strictly fixed. Third, and perhaps most consequentially, whereas the sexual interest of cinematic scopophilia is most aligned with titilation, the sexual interest of the gaze on blackness is necessarily extrapolated into and determined by the ends of reproduction. The sexual interest of the racialized scopic field always takes the phantasmatic "heterosexual division of labor" to its extreme.

For these reasons, some of Linda Williams's observations in *Hard Core: Power, Pleasure, and the "Frenzy of the Visible"* on heterosexual pornographic cinema are useful for reconsidering Mulvey's scheme, even though Williams too pays little to no attention to matters of race. As the ultimate spectacle of titilation, heterosexual pornography captures the "originary" events of heterosexual reproduction, but it does so, according to Williams, and reminiscent of Mulvey, problematically from a male heterosexual vantage since its "attempt to capture the hard-core 'truth' of pleasure [apparently cannot] countenance any vision of female difference when representing the orgasmic heights of its own pleasure" (116). Evolving over its history to enshrine the money shot, images of "external penile ejaculation" (73), mainstream pornography in its most spectacular moments renders the scopophilic enterprise unmistakably about men even though driven most patently by heteroerotic display. Sexual satisfaction premised on a heterosexual phallic gaze is made curious, homoerotic, ambiguous:

> [S]eeing from the single perspective of the phallus and the male orgasm is not to see woman at all but to see only, as Irigaray tells us, the one and the same of man against the more or less of woman. . . . [T]his very blindness, this inability to make the invisible pleasure of woman manifestly visible and quantifiable, is the hard-core text's most vulnerable point of contradiction. (56–7)

To acknowledge the homoerotics of the singularly important money shot is to contradict the significance of heterosexual display, to challenge its preeminence and, therefore, to challenge phallic masculinity. Thus, troublesome masculine self-regard is at issue in Williams's formulations as it is in Mulvey's formulations.

Negotiation of the trouble depends strictly on the type of scopic mobility Mulvey aims at documenting in her essay. Mulvey observes that in classic cinema "the woman displayed [functions] on two levels: as erotic object for the characters within the screen story, and as erotic object for the spectator within the auditorium" (19), and, in this way, tension and movement arise between the perspectives "of the spectator in direct scopophilic contact with the female form displayed for this enjoyment (connoting male fantasy) and . . . of the spectator fascinated with the image of his like set in an illusion of natural space, and through him gaining control and possession of the woman within the diegesis" (21).

Interracial sex (especially between a black man and white woman) deeply complicates this matrix, because it in large part confounds identification between the phallic male spectator and a projected self in the representational image. The male gaze of classic cinema, insofar as it is implicitly white, is necessarily disrupted by images of an averred sexual moment offered for rapacious consumption. In the image of the sexual congress of a black man and white woman, whiteness is removed from the position of phallic masculinity. In fact, it is nullified – as fixed by the asymmetrical kinship system outlined by Naomi Zack – precisely because it is denied by the reproductive configuration of the engagement. Plainly stated, this form of sexual congress nullifies the *person* of the phallic white male inhabiting the classic cinematic gaze, because the reproductive upshot of the congress, by definition, would not be a white subject. There can be no more vivid representation of Robyn Wiegman's insight that "[i]f the phallic lack characteristic of the feminine must be physically and psychologically inscribed in order to deny the black male the primary signifier of power in partriarchal culture, then his threat to white masculine power arises not simply from a perceived racial difference, but from the potential for masculine sameness" (90). Insertion of the black penis in the white vagina is the hyperbolic representation of that threatening masculine sameness. Rending the grounds of classic scopophilic identification, this particular representation of the "potential for masculine sameness" articulates the very possibility of negating that scopophilic gaze in the first place insofar as it further articulates the possibility of abrogating the *person* understood to be doing the looking.

It is key to recognize that the irksome disruption occurs not simply in spectatorial terms, but also in social and historical terms, for beyond frustrating the classic gaze, the scene frustrates the viewer's "proper" sense of a noncinematic or "nonrepresentational" world awaiting his return at the conclusion of the spectacle. Writing in particular of the work of Stephen Heath, Laura Mulvey, and Christian Metz, Manthia Diawara codifies (with the consequences for racial blackness in mind) the unacknowledged importance of the larger, neglected field in which the spectator is always situated:

> The position of the spectator in the cinematic apparatus has been described by recourse to the psychoanalytic account of

the mirror phase. Suggesting that the metapsychology of identification (with the camera or point of enunciation) entails a
narcissistic form of regression which leads to a state similar to
the infant's illusion of a unified ego. But since spectators are
socially and historically as well as psychically constituted, it is
not clear whether the experiences of black spectators are included in this analysis. (66)

The dynamics of the gaze, as they are generally laid out, leave unaccounted social and historical contingencies to which racial blackness is closely tied.

There is in Bullock's reaction much of the psychological and per-
spectival mobility Mulvey sees as foundational to the classic scopophilic enterprise: "So here was this Negro standing on the dock,
lordlylooking bastard, leaning against the railing, head slightly
turned, profile like Barrymore. . . . Every woman who saw this nigger's picture would cut it out, clip it out, tear it out, drool over it.
Every white man who saw it would do a slow burn" (365). Yet it by
no means follows the trajectory she delineates. Bullock makes sense
of the picture only from perspectives he reluctantly takes up. In his
response, he inhabits initially and foremost a feminized position
rather than a phallic one. Speculatively, he enacts fantasies proscribed for white women, which, in turn, deeply challenge his prerogatives as a white man and cast a significant element of his
speculations in homoerotic terms.

These perspectives he takes up articulate a series of threats to
racialization that, ironically, are threats he is always intent to vanquish. To articulate the fantasies of a white woman for a black man
is to articulate a libidinal site from which he himself is excluded (in
more ways than one); it is a libidinal site that confounds the reproductive charge of race usually invested in him (as a white male) both
psychologically and sexually. To make these imaginative moves is
also, as it were, to articulate through his person – even if ultimately
attributed to another agent – desires for another man, desires registering a further abrogation of racialization insofar as it defies the
gender symmetry and reproductive foundations on which racialization is forged. What becomes most visible in these spectatorial identifications ultimately aimed at maintaining the racial categorization
and devaluation of Link is a faltering racial economy. In the place
of stable racial categories one witnesses cultural conventions inhering in problematic heterosexist rationalizations. Displacing classic,

familiar scopophilic transactions are "social prohibitions against the black man's [and white woman's] sexual glance, the interracial intermingling of male 'looks', and other visual taboos related to sanctions against interracial sexuality" (Gaines 21).

In the same way that Mulvey proposes the inability of the phallic cinematic economy to attain visual satisfaction unproblematically, and Williams discusses an apparently hyberbolic instance of the same issue, the psychosexual complex of Bullock's glance is complicated by its homosocial and homoerotic dimensions. A troublesome masculine self-regard is once again at issue. Similarities end here, however. Whereas the mobility of the gaze is not itself the problem in the instances outlined by Mulvey and Williams, the complications of Bullock's scopic situation arise precisely from this mobility and the shifting points of identification it signals. As Bullock moves from perspective to perspective, the tensions of his situation are not allayed or negotiated but exacerbated. His shifting scopic identifications distort black and white racial prescriptions usually secured by duplicitous recourse to repulsion and attraction, vilification and innocence. They yield frustrating psychodramatic identifications that fail to produce, despite all effort, one of the most intuitive narratives of race, "the projection of feminized whiteness in danger . . . as a primary argument of white supremacists to justify terrorism against black communities" (Gunning 7). In relation to blackness, the scopic enterprise should hold a singular spectatorial position confirming that the sexual congress Bullock is forced to imagine is only conceivable as a sign of black sexual aggression and white victimization. Any deviation from this position undermines the significance of race.

Racialization demands foreclosing the mutability of the gaze, and the profundity of this reversal of usual spectatorial principles cannot be underestimated. The dislocation upsets not only classic scopophilic impulses but, as Anne Friedberg outlines it, modern subjectivity itself, subjectivity born and confirmed in large part in posing "imaginary mobility as psychic transformation" (xi). Most rightfully, these spectatorial transactions serve as spurs to consumption in an urban and industrial order. The modern subject comprehends the world and her or his place in it through the "imaginary mobilities" (37) of visual pleasure, not least of which is as a consumer in a capitalist political economy. Thus, the portability of the gaze – which is abandoned in the manufacture and certainty of black undesirability – turns into a liability one of the defining resources of the modern subject. Cinema and modern/postmodern life refine, in Friedberg's elaborations, the activities of the nineteenth-century flaneur, "a 'street person' at home in the public realm of urbanity" (74). This world is one of the consumerist gaze and bourgeois sensibility – one to and in which racial blackness is most often figured in the cultural imagination as a threat or rupture, a rupture so great it skews fundamental protocols of looking and spectatorial identification.

Bullock, with immense frustration, most completely makes sense of the picture of Link from the vantages of proscribed female desire and homoerotic desire, although the racialization he seeks to confirm must brook neither. His dilemma is unrelenting. To undertake a series of scopic moves that have been conventionalized is profoundly dissatisfying; equally, to refuse scopic mobility altogether is seemingly to dismiss paramount reflexes of modern subjectivity. Given these unavoidable dissatisfactions, it seems inevitable that, in his estimation, "[e]very white man who saw [the picture] would do a slow burn" (265).

All this is to say that from the vantages of the primary agents of racial whiteness in the novel, Camilo, Mrs. Treadway, and Bullock, the accumulating abrogations of race in the narrative are overwhelming. Camilo's recklessness underscores the certainty that desire does not necessarily reinforce the divisions of race but, on the contrary, is quite capable of forgoing them. Rather than foreclosed by race, desire is implicated in it and may, all too easily, contest racial perscriptives (or in other circumstances those of gender). Mrs. Treadway's ultimatum to Bullock highlights the deep implications of race in technologies of literacy, implications contesting the apparent neutrality of these technologies and the certainty that their meaning is "in the last analysis . . . civic and emancipatory" (Warner 3), as is the staunch belief fostered by post-Enlightenment sensibilities. On the contrary, these technologies underwrite a highly consequential "way of being white" (15). They provide a means of publicizing and entrenching many idealizations of whiteness. In Bullock's professional embarrassment, one understands that the entanglements of race reach into the most unlikely of fiscal arrangements. The financial stability of the *Monmouth Chronicle* rests finally on a covert agreement to counterfeit the appearance of white racial propriety in circumstances denying it. These expositions document complicated refractions of race never quite reducible to simple binary formulae, all of which converge glaringly in the seductive "picture" of Link.

Thus, it is key to note that the final blow to Camilo's reputation and all concerted efforts to save it occurs, ironically, in pictorial form. The picture of Link violates the usual significance of vision, just as the complicated intrigues of the narrative violate racial perscriptives. Advertising his desirability and undermining his criminalization, the picture of Link presents a disposition to racial blackness that is untenable, since it would in profound ways unsettle black and white racialization. If, as already outlined, routine dispositions of the scopic and phonic codify and shape the way one recognizes race, it is the failure of such strict rationalizations that accounts for the frustrations of Camilo, her mother, and Bullock.

Deeply challenging the strict rationalization of sexual energies presupposing race, the picture of the disturbingly attractive Link, in conjunction with Camilo's reckless reputation, for all intents and purposes exposes the falsehood of Camilo's story of an attack. Because the widely circulated image abrogates customary visual representations and characterizations of African Americans, Bullock attempts to counteract it, insofar as it is in his power, by placing in the *Monmouth Chronicle* one such customary image two weeks later. He aims, in his own words, "to offset, counterbalance, outweigh" (378) the earlier picture of Link with the photograph of an escaped black convict set beneath the headline NEGRO CONVICT SHOT. The lurid picture

> showed the convict not as a man but as a black animal, teeth bared in a snarl, eyes crazy, long razor scar like a mouth, an open mouth, reaching from beneath the eye to the chin, the flesh turned back on each side, forming the lips of this dreadful extra mouth.... [E]veryone who saw that picture would remember it and wake up in the middle of the night covered with sweat. (377)

The racialized power of visual imagery – its power to disenfranchise and often to criminalize – remains crucial here, as it does in *The Street*. For this second picture functionally represents the criminalization of Link, and one is reminded of the climax of *The Street* when Lutie is criminalized by her bludgeoning of Boots so that, more dramatically than ever, she is excluded from the suburban images and life she cherishes and pursues. Equally, the actions of Lutie's son Bub, his misguided pursuit of glamorous cinematic plots, effects his own criminalization and incarceration. Like these events in the earlier novel, the criminal transformation of Link is implicated with the overwhelming potency of visual imagery. Bullock supplants one visual image with another, effectively revising and monopolizing the significance of vision for those whom the wealthy Treadways represent, for those (like him) in the position to manipulate mass media representation of U.S. social circumstances, and, in short, for all those who are not "niggers." Indeed, Bullock's supplanting of Link's photo with the picture of the dead convict foreshadows Link's own death.

It is part of the crucial insight of Petry's novels that they comprehend this contestation played out across vision and sound. The climax of *The Narrows*, like that of *The Street*, is marked by a controversion of the customary significance of visual imagery. The phonic proves the medium by means of and in relation to which the visual falters, and, notwithstanding Link's possession of a disarming speaking voice, the primary agent of the phonic in the narrative is Mamie Powther, the sensual and unconventional wife of the very proper Treadway butler. Mamie is forever singing and, moreover, in a manner that makes her voice often seem not just a voice "but the woman, too" (124). Like her riveting voice, Mamie's presence in the novel seems always a seductive alternative to the overwhelming and complex chain of events in which the other characters find themselves consumed. Indeed, it is the happenstance of Mamie's presence in the Last Chance Saloon, in tandem with an offhand comment, that causes Camilo mistakenly to believe that Link has left her for Mamie. In the rippling, eccentric network of events it is Mamie Powther and her seemingly ubiquitous singing that remain the most settled, the most assured, the most accountable elements in the frenzied circulation of characters in the economies of race, gender, and capitalist inequalities. In *The Street* and *The Narrows*, the phonic operates in important ways to redact the nature of the oppressive contest in which their African American characters are caught. The distinctions between black and white, human and subhuman, entitled and disenfranchised, value and valuelessness, that vision is made to underwrite are interrogated or controverted by the efficacy and currency of the phonic.

Part of what this sensory contestation discloses is that the cultural binarism continually troubled by the narrative events is anything but settled and anything but binary. There is much more than a simple dualism at issue. Aside from the way in which racial classification is determined through the asymmetrical workings of kinship, the much less reliable trajectories and eccentricities of desire (especially as they may be transmuted into violence) dismiss entirely the simplicity of an orderly dualism. Part of the reassuring illusion of value – and of race as a prime exemplum of the dynamics of value – is precisely its binary simplicity; however, the sexually charged drama of Link and Camilo's meeting as well as their final encounter shatter binary racial codifications into a multiplicity of terms. These terms include gendered positions that would be ideally differentiated along racial poles, which, as it turns out, hold their racial significance solely by recourse to a heterosexist paradigm always extrapolated into a procreative paradigm. Any attempt to reduce this skewed, looping multiplicity to a simple binarism is an impossible and disingenuous task.

Indeed, these asymmetrical cultural dynamics of racialization are registered in the very figure of the newspaper Bullock holds. One recognizes in it the curious overlapping convergence of scopic economies and economies of literacy. Yet they do not parallel or mirror one another; their relation is neither synchronous nor regularized, since the very public services they render do not follow commensurate cultural paths, institutional or otherwise. They represent only related but not identical monopolizations of sense in the service of a plain accounting of race. The literacy of print media, even though closely bound to the scopic, insinuates itself into a contractual, legal, juridical, bureaucratic, and proprietary fabric of U.S. society with a precision, efficiency, and objectivity to which more diffuse scopic economics simply cannot aspire.

Economies of literacy affirm that

> [r]ace in particular was one of the social meanings of the difference between writing and speech by racial division in the reproduction of literacy, and by the consequent overlap between determinant features of the medium and traits of the race. Black illiteracy was more than a negation of literacy for blacks; it was the condition of a positive character of written discourse for whites. By extension, printing constituted and distinguished a specifically white community; in this sense it was more than a neutral medium that whites simply managed to monopolize. (Warner 12)

Differently, visual economies, according to Kim Hall, confirm "the very *language* of color . . . [as] encod[ing] racial, political ideologies; the inclusion of Africans in Western [schemes of representation] in many cases merely serves to demonstrate their exclusion from Western culture" (214; emphasis added). The fateful image of Bullock examining the photograph of Link in the newspaper, which he, no doubt, rustles in annoyance, suggests the conflated spaces and dynamics of visual economies and economies of literacy.

The asymmetrical, incongruous convergence as well as the reflexive gaze registering it describe an elusive center of value and of racialization. The point that would act as an incontrovertible center must, oddly, always be created and recreated by whatever means or opportunities present themselves. That is, if literacy and the visual converge to fix racial blackness, they do not do so in an easy, unremarkable convergence but, rather, a complex, errant improvisation that yields in addition to the abjected figure of value its inextricability from opposing valued figures. Rather than fixed figures or processes, there only emerges the force by which figures and processes are fixed. The improvisation, concomitantly exposing and repairing mechanisms of value and racialization, is always revealed at some point as violent.

Whatever certainty race as an index of value would seem to provide is a false certainty dearly bought. The binary of race and the binary of value (which, contrary to appearances, are at least tripartite) are such compound falsehoods. In this way, because of the insistent misapprehension of at least tripartite configurations as twofold, one is left to assume that there may be very little "of value" in a culture that so enduringly mystifies race as a simple value. Indeed, one is left to assume – and the irony is profound – that there may be much less than one imagines "of value" in value.

NOTES

VIOLENCE AND THE UNSIGHTLY
Figures of Violence

1 In his introduction to *For a Critque of the Political Economy of the Sign*, Charles Levin summarizes Baudrillard's contestation of Marx in this way: "Baudrillard's argument boils down to the insight that the articulation of binary terms must always privilege one side of the opposition, as the means of setting the system in motion. Thus, in the commodity system, it is exchange value that is privileged over use value precisely because exchange value is the system's principle of circulation. Thus it is this very *structural* logic that allows Marx to imagine that use value is not itself structurally implicated in the 'logic' of political economy. His critique thus stops short at grasping the form of the commodity, failing to seize its cultural implications" (17; emphasis in original).

2 See the discussion of Mary Douglas.

3 Violence is understood here as the forcible disrupting and altering of Otherwise established forms. This understanding of violence I take away from conversations with and the work of Laura E. Tanner. See *Intimate Violence: Reading Rape and Torture in Twentieth-Century Fiction* (Bloomington: Indiana University Press, 1994).

4 Jacques Derrida, "From Restricted to General Economy: A Hegelianism Without Reserve," in *Writing and Difference*, trans. Alan Bass (Chicago: University of Chicago Press, 1978), p. 259. The negative, recuperated and made logical in a restricted economy, is the enabling absence of meaning, of presence (of value, for my purposes) – Hegel's insight. Obversely, the unrestricted negative, the unrecuperable expenditure – Georges Bataille's "sovereignty" – is the absence of that presencing

243

dialectic, the unbounded betrayal of that dialectic – an unrestricted confounding of value and its correlate authority. The positive can only be the positive by restricting the negative. Once that transaction is set in abeyance or interfered with, the entire production of value is rendered problematic.

5 At the beginning of the sixth chapter of her study "Powers and Dangers," Douglas writes: "Granted that disorder spoils pattern; it also provides the materials of pattern. Order implies restriction; from all possible materials, a limited selection has been made and from all possible relations a limited set has been used. So disorder by implication is unlimited, no pattern has been realised in it, but its potential for patterning is indefinite" (*Purity and Danger* 94). Echoing these observations later in the book, she also writes, "Each culture must have its own notions of dirt and defilement which are contrasted with its notions of the positive structure which must not be negated" (159).

6 See Eric Foner, *Nothing but Freedom: Emancipation and Its Legacy* (Baton Rouge: Louisana State University Press 1983). Foner's project is comparative. Examining slavery chiefly as the control and exploitation of cheap black labor, he compares emancipation in the Caribbean, the American South generally, and South Carolina rice plantations in particular. He begins his project with the statement "Among the revolutionary processes that transformed the nineteenth-century world, none was so dramatic in its human consequences or far-reaching in its social implications as the abolition of chattel slavery" (1).

7 See Alan Bass, Translator's Introduction. *Writing and Difference*, by Jacques Derrida (Chicago: University of Chicago Press, 1978). Bass explains, "The counterviolence of *solicitation*, which derives from the Latin *sollicitare*, meaning to shake the totality (from *sollus*, 'all,' and *ciere*, 'to move, to shake'). Every totality, [Derrida] shows, can be *totally shaken*, that is, can be shown to be founded on that which it excludes, that which would be in *excess* for a reductive analysis of any kind. (The English *solicit* should be read in this etymological sense wherever it appears.)" (p. xvi; emphasis in original).

8 This understanding of violence I take away from conversations with and the work of Laura Tanner. See *Intimate Violence: Reading Rape and Torture in Twentieth-Century Fiction* (Bloomington: Indiana UP, 1994).

9 Even more maddening is the assurance that the second term of value – the devalued, the violated – in any specification of value can be and, of course, often is multiple (many Others, not a single Other).

10 It must be noted that this instance of self-distanciation, of the disruption of value from itself, is not the same moment of self-contestation or self-distanciation that characterizes the movement of value as force to value as form. This new moment of rupture is a moment of self-

disruption that subsumes the earlier, anterior moment in the way concentric circles embed one another. That is to say, it is the same but not the *same*.

11 That is, finds its responsibility in infinite arbitration.

12 For a sample of some important extended considerations of the drama of the "self" endemic to autobiography, see Georges Gusdorf, "Conditions and Limits of Autobiography," in *Autobiography: Essays Theoretical and Critical*, ed. James Olney (Princeton N.J.: Princeton University Press, 1980), pp. 28–48; James Olney, "Autobiography and the Cultural Moment," in *Autobiography: Essays Theoretical and Critical*; Candace Lang, "Autobiography in the Aftermath of Romanticism," *Diacritics* 12.4 (Winter 1982); as well as the essay by Julia Watson cited above.

13 See Elaine Scarry, *The Body in Pain* (New York: Oxford University Press, 1985). The prolonged analyses of pain Scarry sets forth treat intricately and subtly the certainty of physical pain and many of its interactions with unanchored, immaterial issues. Indeed, Scarry's book is an extensive charting of the present and the absent, their juxtapositions and their incongruities. Scarry writes, for example, "In death the body is emphatically present while the more elusive part represented by the voice is so alarmingly absent that heavens are created to explain its whereabouts" (49). Scarry does not investigate violence per se; however, as violence and pain are often so closely allied that the two prove virtually indistinguishable, many of Scarry's descriptions and analyses of pain prove illuminating for considerations of violence.

14 Such claims would be equivalent to what Perry Anderson laments as the "exorbitation of language"; see *In the Tracks of Historical Materialism* (Chicago: University of Chicago Press, 1984), pp. 40–45. Anderson presents as an unacknowledged disqualification of many structuralist and poststructuralist theories the fact that the structure–subject relation of various phenomena often does not accord to the *langue–parole*, or other relations, of Saussurian linguistics. Anderson summarizes, "The opening move of structuralism, in other words, is a speculative aggrandisement of language that lacks any comparative credentials" (45). To my mind, this objection is not relevant here.

15 One might think that this displacing action of the sign is only characteristic of it when considered along the paradigmatic axis, that is, along an axis where similar signs might take its place in a signifying sequence; however, the same is true of the activity of the sign along the syntagmatic axis. That is, even in its sequential consideration, the sign must eclipse all Other signs for the moment when it takes its place in the sequence, as will be suggested presently.

16 Of course, from the vantage of the subordinated or unauthorized, authority is diminishing rather than aggrandizing. It is an imminent

threat, an immediate power that can forcibly inscribe itself upon one. Rather than aggrandizing, authority is belittling.

17 A very close and extensive exposition of such a resemblance is Edward Said's *Orientalism* (New York: Vintage, 1979).

18 In an opposing way this is true even for the victim. In submitting to a threatening and imposing authority, the victim preserves the preeminence of her or his own form. That is, submission to authority in its forcible imposition, especially in the instance of pain, may be equivalent to the preservation of the preeminence of one's own form.

19 The violence of value and the violence within the violence of value are most strictly prevented from displaying themselves within the form of value and the form within the form of value. That is, the privilege terms of these valuative binarisms most fully and beguilingly dispense with the underprivileged terms.

Figuring Others of Value

1 The geography of the New World is not taken as merely the geography contained by the hemisphere of the Americas, but as all geographies in which the racial history of the Americas stands as a hyperbole.

2 The singing voice and its revisionary African American operations provide the primary means of participation in a hostile economy of value. To speak for a moment in terms of Western popular culture: The *singing voice*, as opposed to the *signing voice*, initiates the a capella rhythmics of Ladysmith Black Mambazo, the West Indian calypso abandon of Sparrow, the staccato reggae invectives of Bob Marley and the Wailers, the insinuating riffs of a blues and jazz tradition, the technopop funk of Karen White and Bobby Brown produced by Babyface, and the haunting dynamics of the African American gospel choir. Indeed, one need only remember the overpowering sound of such a choir to understand the immediate, material dimension of the singing voice.

3 DuBois writes more extensively: "[T]he human spirit in this new world has expressed itself in vigor and ingenuity rather than in beauty. And so by fateful chance the Negro folk-song – the rhythmic cry of the slave – stands to-day not simply as the sole American music, but as the most beautiful expression of human experience born this side of the seas. It has been neglected, it has been, and is, half despised, and above all it has been persistently mistaken and misunderstood; but notwithstanding, it still remains, as the singular spiritual heritage of the nation and the greatest gift of the Negro people" (265).

4 Derrida attempts to show that, paradoxically bracketed in Husserl's theory of the sign, the sign disappears in its derivation from self-sufficient

self-presence, and, in an attendant homology, writing is understood as a mundane derivation of speech. The voice, like Husserl's transcendental intentional "expression," is conceived as "an object whose showing may be repeated indefinitely, whose presence to *Zeigen* [defined as "the space, visibility, field of what is ob-jected and pro-jected" (*Speech and Phenomena* (72)] is indefinitely reiterable precisely because, freed from [anterior to, both temporally and spatially,] all mundane spatially, it is a pure noema that I can express without having, at least apparently, to pass through the world" (75). In other words, the voice, or speech, is transcendentally determinative and belies form because it is prior to form. As an idealized object, it is never spatially present; nonetheless, its presence may be spatially captured in writing, a reductive, spatially mundane form.

5 See Jacques Derrida, "From Restricted to General Economy: A Hegelianism Without Reserve," in *Writing and Difference*, trans. Alan Bass (Chicago: University of Chicago Press, 1978).

6 See the discussion of the the violence of the sign and control of the sign in Chapter 1.

7 The geography of the New World is not taken as the area contained only by the hemisphere of the Americas, but that of all regions in which the racial history of the Americas stands as a hyperbole.

8 "Signing" as used here should not be mistaken for the "signifyin(g)" central to the theories of Henry Louis Gates, Jr. "Signifyin(g)" and "singing," however, are not opposites. Indeed, "signifyin(g)" is a form of the "singing" performance, as the "singing" performance is understood here. The newest correlate of "signifyin(g)," rap music, is similarly an extension of the "singing" performance.

9 For a book-length contextualization of the most recent cries of alarm concerning a form of African American musical production see Tricia Rose, *Black Noise: Rap Music and Black Culture in Contemporary America*. Rose studies musical, cultural, and political dimensions of rap.

10 See the first five chapters of Russell Sanjek and David Sanjek, *American Popular Music Business in the 20th Century* (New York: Oxford University Press, 1991).

11 Of course, this is not to say that such a performance cannot be commodified and placed in the marketplace.

12 Painter's next statement reads, "As workers and as the basis of the economy in which they toiled, slaves circulated like legal tender."

(Further) Figures of Violence

1 *The Street* was originally published in 1946 by Houghton Mifflin and reissued in 1985 by Beacon Press.

2 These violences, moreover, are obscured by their very significance, because as transcendence "takes place" in the United States or any other landscape it inevitably "provid[es] an alibi for the historical violence of light: a displacement of technico-political oppression in the direction of philosophical discourse" (Jacques Derrida, "Violence and Metaphysics: An Essay on the Thought of Emmanuel Levinas," in *Writing and Differences*, trans. Alan Bass [Chicago: University of Chicago Press, 1978], p. 92).

3 There is, of course, no "the voice" in the first place.

4 It is important to see that in a very dramatic manner the singing voice supersedes the antithesis rehearsed by Husserl's idealization and Derrida's gainsaying deconstruction of the *signing voice*. That is, in addition to providing a critique of the *signing voice*, somewhat analogous to an antinomian Derridean critique, the *singing voice*, unlike an antinomian Derridean critique, massively figures, refigures, and *capitalizes* upon the dominant metaphysics of presence in the American landscape.

5 Fredika Bremer, *America of the Fifties: Letters of Fredika Bremer*, ed. Adolph B. Benson (New York: Oxford University Press, 1924), p. 275, as quoted in Sterling Stuckey, *Slave Culture* p. 54.

6 See, for example, C. Vann Woodward, *The Strange Career of Jim Crow* (New York: Oxford University Press, 1974).

7 See Derrida, "Violence and Metaphysics: An Essay on the Though of Emmanuel Levinas," in *Writing and Difference*. "It can be said only of the other that its phenomenon is a certain nonphenomenon, its presence (is) a certain absence" (91).

8 Renewing the irony underscoring the opening episode, the narrative chronology is speciously characterized by a more fortunate chronology – though still fraught with shifting perspectives and relapses. Fortunately Bub raids mailboxes and is apprehended by the authorities, and a misguided Lutie, believing she must hire a lawyer, turns to Boots for the two-hundred-dollar fee; she meets Boot at his apartment to receive the money and discovers he uses the meeting as an opportunity to procure her for Junto. In other words, a progressive "and then, and then" ironically effects its most sustained appearance during a sequence of events that precipitates the novel's ultimate transformation of spacelessness in time into timelessness in space, the voice into the dead body. The *fortunate* chronology effects its absence. It reveals the *misfortune* of time recast as obdurate materiality, time removed from the condition of time.

9 "Even though the captive flesh/body has been 'liberated,' and no one need pretend that even the quotation marks do not matter, dominant symbolic activity, the ruling episteme that releases the dynamics of nam-

ing and valuation, remains grounded in the originating metaphors of captivity and mutilation so that it is as if the subject is 'murdered' over and over again by the passions of a bloodless and anonymous archaism, showing itself in endless disguise" (Spillers "Mama's Baby, Papa's Maybe" 68).

10 *Get Smart, Again*, with Don Adams and Barbara Feldon. ABC. WPVI, Philadelphia. 26 February 1989.

REASONING AND REASONABLENESS
De-Marking Limits

1 Lietch, in this passage, is quoting Cleanth Brooks's *The Well Wrought Urn* (New York: Harcourt, Brace, 1947), abbreviated *WWU,* and Allen Tate's *Essays of Four Decades* (Chicago: Swallow Press, 1968), abbreviated *EFD.*

2 My purpose here is not to elide the important distinctions between such leading New Critical figures as Cleanth Brooks, John Crowe Ransom, I. A. Richards, Allen Tate, and W. K. Wimsatt; nevertheless, neither does an extended rehearsal of the various distinctions of New Critical theories at the height of their celebrity much serve my point. For a more attentive unpacking of the varieties of New Criticism one might look to vol. 6 of René Wellek's *A History of Modern Criticism.*

3 See especially p. 4–5. For example: "[D]eeply ingrained ideologies are no more easily escaped when they are aesthetic than when they are political, and New Criticism remains a pedal point beneath our literary studies" (4).

4 See, for example, Henry Louis Gates, Jr., "Literary Theory and the Black Tradition" in *Figures in Black* (New York: Oxford University Press, 1987), pp. 3–58. For an incisive reconsideration of Gates's position, see Ronald A. T. Judy's *(Dis)Forming the American Canon: African–Arabic Slave Narratives and the Vernacular* (Minneapolis: University of Minnesota Press, 1993), chaps. 2 and 3.

5 Violence is understood here as the forcible disrupting and altering of Otherwise established forms. This understanding of violence I take away from conversations with and the work of Laura E. Tanner. See *Intimate Violence: Reading Rape and Torture in Twentieth-Century Fiction* (Bloomington: Indiana University Press, 1994).

6 In the volume in which this essay appears, as elsewhere, black feminist critics enumerate their suspicions of the avidness with which writings and criticisms by black women are being acknowledged with growing frequency by various other critics, as well as otherwise embraced by the academy. Such suspicions are well founded and certainly apply to my own references in this essay and elsewhere to the work of black feminist

critics and writers. Notwithstanding the acumen of such suspicions, the very necessity of such caution among black feminist critics points up the singularity of the times in which the literary academy finds itself. It is in this capacity that I refer with some frequency to the work of black women writers and feminist critics. I look to their work as the clearest markers of the singularity of the present time in the academy. Equally, I must note here that the intent of these suspicions, as rehearsed by Valerie Smith, is not "to reclaim the black feminist project from those who are not black women; to do so would be to define the field too narrowly" (39). On the contrary, and appropriately, it seems to me, the suspicions arise in regards to the machinations of what Deborah E. McDowell terms "an unacknowledged jostling for space in the literary marketplace" ("Reading Family Matters," 83).

7 *The Chronicle of Higher Education*, March 6, 1991, A13. According to this report the current distribution of Ph.D.s among various nonwhite groups stands as follows: American Indian, 0.4 percent; Hispanic, 2.7 percent; Black, 3.8 percent; Asian, 5.1 percent; Other, 1.8 percent, (racial designations are reproduced as they appear). Men constitute 63.5 percent of Ph.D. recipients and women 36.5 percent.

8 A page earlier, Cornell West writes: "[I]t is impossible to grasp the complexity and multidimensionality of a specific set of artistic practices without relating it to other broader cultural and political practices at a given historical moment" (199).

9 I have in mind, particularly, the volume *Deconstruction and Criticism.*

10 Walter J. Ong, in an endeavor very different from that of Graff or Rabinowitz, states: "By the 1930s the New Criticism was under way, a spin-off from the new academic study of English, the first major vernacular criticism of English-language literature to develop in an academic environment" (163).

11 Notwithstanding the fact that he also demonstrates that a profound crisis has been variously and repeatedly diagnosed in literary criticism for as long as the study of literature has been institutionalized in the American academy, William Cain argues in 1984 in *The Crisis in Criticism* that there is "evidence to suggest that the disturbances in [the] discipline are especially serious at the present time" (72). I have replaced in this quotation Cain's use of the possessive pronoun *our* with the more open-ended article *the*, and, it seems to me, the "especially serious" nature of the post-1960s crisis in criticism arises precisely from the necessity to make such a substitution.

12 Hooks continues, "The idea that there is no meaningful connection between black experience and critical thinking about aesthetics or culture must be continually interrogated" (23).

13 See James Baldwin's "Stranger in the Village" in *Notes of a Native Son* (Boston: Beacon Press, 1984) for an analysis of the difference between European and American soil in terms of African American presence: "Europe's black possessions remained – and do remain – in Europe's colonies, at which remove they represented no threat whatever to European identity. If they posed any problem at all for the European conscience, it was a problem which remained comfortingly abstract: in effect, the black [person], *as a [person]*, did not exist for Europe. But in America, even as a slave, [the African American] was an inescapable part of the general social fabric and no American could escape having an attitude toward him [or her]" (171; emphasis in original).

14 Of course, similar claims can be made about Indian bodies, Asian bodies, gay and lesbian bodies, and so on.

15 Hegel continues: "In Negro life the characteristic of point is the fact that consciousness has not yet attained to the realization of any substantial objective existence, – as for example, God, or Law, – in which the interest of man's volition is involved and in which he realizes his own being" (97).

16 African Americans are nonetheless, however, human absences.

17 Jefferson, *Notes on the State of Virginia*, ed. William Peden (New York: Norton, 1954), p. 138.

18 In a curious rewriting of American history, Hirsch writes elsewhere in *Cultural Literacy: What Every American Needs to Know* (Boston: Houghton Mifflin, 1987): "[Martin Luther] King [Jr.] envisioned a country where the children of former slaves sit down at the table of equality with the children of former slave owners, where men and women deal with each other on their characters and achievements rather than their origins. *Like Thomas Jefferson*, he had a dream of a society founded not on race or class but on personal merit" (12, emphasis added).

19 See "The Concrete Universal" in W. K. Wimsatt and Monroe Beardsley, eds., *The Verbal Icon: Studies in the Meaning of Poetry* (Lexington: University of Kentucky Press, 1954), pp. 69–83.

20 See p. 134–143.

21 See, for example, *The Origins of Literary Studies in America: A Documentary Anthology*, ed. Gerald Graff and Michael Warner (New York: Routledge, 1989).

22 In his introduction to *The Verbal Icon*, W. K. Wimsatt writes, for example, that "rhetoric in the full classical sense means a pragmatic art of discourse. But there is nothing in the nature of the verbal act to prevent us from looking at the same features not in a pragmatic, but in a dramatic, light, and if we do this we are looking at a given discourse as a literary work" (xv). In "The Domain of Criticism," and in *The Verbal*

Icon, Wimsatt writes: "A verbal composition, through being super-charged with significance, takes on something like the character of a stone statue or a porcelain vase. Through its meaning or meanings the poem *is*" (231; emphasis in original).

23 J. C. Ransom in his introduction to *I'll Take My Stand* claims: "The capitalization of the applied sciences has now become extravagant and uncritical; it has enslaved our human energies to a degree now clearly felt to be burdensome" (xxi).

24 See, for example, James Weinstein, *The Corporate Ideal in the Liberal State* (Boston: Beacon, 1968), or Robert H. Wiebe, *The Search for Order* (New York: Hill & Wang, 1967). For a related study that does not, however, extend its examination into the twentieth century, see Alan Trachtenberg, *The Incorporation of America: Culture and Society in the Gilded Age* (New York: Hill & Wang, 1982).

25 Marable summarizes the "democratic" history of the West as follows: "The 'Great Ascent' of the West since the sixteenth century was fundamentally a process of growing capital accumulation, the endless drive to control the human and material resources of the world's people" (*How Capitalism Underdeveloped Black America* [Boston: South End Press, 1983], p.

26 See "The World, the Text, and the Critic" in *The World, the Text, and the Critic* (Cambridge: Harvard University Press, 1983), 31–53. In the essay, Said argues for a perception of the text "as significant form, in which – and I put this as carefully as I can – worldliness, circumstantiality, the text's status as an event having sensuous particularity as well as historical contingency, are considered as being incorporated in the text, an infrangible part of its capacity for conveying and producing meaning." In short, Said insists that the text has "a specific situation . . . [that] exists at the same level of surface particularity as the textual object itself" (39).

27 See Weber's distinction between *granting* and *taking for granted* in *Institution and Interpretation*.

SCOPIC AND PHONIC ECONOMIES
Signs of Others

1 JanMohamed and Lloyd edited two special issues of *Cultural Critique*, spring and fall 1987, "The Nature and Context of Minority Discourse." The essay quoted here is the introduction to the second of the two issues. Barbara Christian's essay "The Race for Theory" appears in the first issue.

2 "The Frame of Reference: Poe, Lacan, Derrida" in John P. Muller and William J. Richardson, eds., *The Purloined Poe: Lacan, Derrida and Psycho-*

analytic Reading (Baltimore: Johns Hopkins University Press, 1988), p. 219.

3 Lacan, to be fair, does take notice early in his seminar of the same nuances of difference between the two scenes of robbery – even of the orchestrated commotion in the street during the second robbery, which in my reading is understood as central to the narrative. Nonetheless, Lacan proceeds in his analysis to emphasize only "the similarity of these two sequences" (31).

4 Cf. the discussion of the anecdote of the map on p. 210.

5 Poe, *Purloined Poe*, pp. 15–16.

6 Cf. the concluding moments of the discussion of *The Street* on pp. 127–128.

7 The play is "*Atré et Thyeste* (1707), 5.4.13, [*Atreus and Thyestes*] by Prosper-Joylet de Crébillion (1674–1762)" (27, n. 27).

8 See "Mama's Baby, Papa's Maybe: An American Grammar Book," *Diacritics* 17.2 (Summer 1987): 65–81.

9 Hayden White, *The Content of the Form: Narrative Discourse and Historical Representation* (Baltimore: Johns Hopkins University Press, 1987), p. 57. In the sentence I am quoting, White defines narrative as follows: "Narrative is at once a mode of discourse, a manner of speaking, and the product produced by the adoption of this mode of discourse."

10 Johnson, *Purloined Poe*, p. 240.

11 Two studies that immediately come to mind and that suggest unspoken intrigues presupposing the possibility of any such game on a map are Thomas Pakenham's *The Scramble for Africa* (New York: Random House, 1991) and Walter Rodney's *How Europe Underdeveloped Africa* (Washington, D.C..: Howard University Press, 1972). Considering that Poe writes "The Purloined Letter" in 1845, a time when Western interests are very busily construing and reconstruing maps and those names appearing on maps, this anecdote and its game are perhaps more telling than intended. The unspoken narratives behind all maps are, to say the very least, never very plain.

12 Neither this statement nor this analysis should be understood as an individual attack on any or all of these authors, or the bodies of their work. Such an assessment would miss the point of this essay by a wide margin. The essay interrogates hermeneutical and institutional postures that the exchange between these authors, I contend, has come in a way to represent. In the poststructuralist academic climate, "The Purloined Letter" and the critical exchange over it warrant collection in one volume in order "to make available essential moments of this debate and dialogue" (John P. Muller and William J. Richardson, "Preface," *Purloined Poe*, p. viii), and it is the antinomian values of this representative debate and dialogue that form the objects of my interrogation.

Signs of the Visible

1 As the term "response" is used here it is meant to include both or either/or an African American preoccupation with the production and consumption of music.

2 See Anthony Appiah's *In My Fathers House* (pp. 34–37) for an elegant summation of race as a genetic and, therefore, biological fiction.

BIBLIOGRAPHY

Adorno, Theodor W. "On the Fetish-Character in Music and the Regression of Listening." *The Essential Frankfurt School Reader*. Ed. Andrew Arato and Eike Gebhardt. New York: Continuum, 1993, 270–299.

Aijaz, Ahmad. "Jameson's Rhetoric of Otherness and the 'National Allegory.' " *Social Text* 19 (Fall 1987): 3–25.

Allison, David B. "Translator's Introduction." *Speech and Phenomena and Other Essays on Husserl's Theory of Signs*. By Jacques Derrida. Evanston, Ill.: Northwestern University Press, 1973. xxxi – xlii.

Althusser, Louis. "Ideology and Ideological State Apparatuses (Notes Toward an Investigation)." *Video Culture*. Ed. John G. Hanhardt. Rochester, N.Y.: Visual Studies Workshop Press, 1986, 56–95.

Andrews, William. *To Tell a Free Story: The First Century of Afro-American Autobiography*. Urbana and Chicago: University of Illinois Press, 1986.

Aronowitz, Stanley. *Science as Power: Discourse and Ideology in Modern Society*. Minneapolis: University of Minnesota Press, 1988.

Bahktin, Mikhail. *Rabelais and His World*. Bloomington: Indiana University Press, 1984.

Baldwin, James. *Notes of a Native Son*. Boston: Beacon Press, 1984.

Bannet, Eve Tavor. *Structuralism and the Logic of Dissent: Barthes, Derrida, Foucault, Lacan*. Urbana: University of Illinois Press, 1989.

Barlow, William. *"Looking Up at Down": The Emergence of Blues Culture*. Philadelphia: Temple University Press, 1989.

Baudrillard, Jean. *The Mirror of Production*. Trans. Mark Poster. St. Louis: Telos Press, 1975.

For a Critique of the Political Economy of the Sign. St. Louis: Telos Press, 1981.

Bentham, Jeremy. *Deontology, Together with a Table of the Springs of Action and*

255

an Article on Utilitarianism. Ed. Amnon Goldworth. Oxford: Clarendon Press, 1983.

Berger, John. *Ways of Seeing.* New York: Penguin, 1977.

Berman, Art. *From the New Criticism to Deconstruction: The Reception of Structuralism and Post-Structuralism.* Urbana: University of Illinois Press, 1988.

Bhabha, Homi K. "The Commitment to Theory." *New Formations* 5 (Summer 1988): 3–23.

Blassingame, John. *Slave Testimony.* Baton Rouge: Louisiana State University Press, 1977.

Bloom, Allan. *The Closing of the American Mind: How Higher Education Has Failed Democracy and Impoverished the Souls of Today's Students.* New York: Simon & Schuster, 1987.

Bourdieu, Pierre. *Distinction: A Social Critique of the Judgment of Taste.* Cambridge, Mass.: Harvard University Press, 1984.

Bové, Paul A. *Intellectuals in Power: A Genealogy of Critical Humanism.* New York: Columbia University Press, 1986.

Bowles, Samuel, and Gintis, Herbert. *Democracy and Capitalism.* New York: Basic Books, 1987.

Brenkman, Jonathan. *Culture and Domination.* Ithica, N.Y.: Cornell University Press, 1987.

Brodhead, Richard H. "After the Opening: Problems and Prospects for a Reformed American Literature." *Yale Journal of Criticism* 5.2 (1992): 59–71.

Brooks, Cleanth. *The Well Wrought Urn.* San Diego: Harcourt Brace Jovanovich, 1947, 1975.

Bruss, Elizabeth. *Beautiful Theories: The Spectacle of Discourse in Contemporary Criticism.* Baltimore: Johns Hopkins University Press, 1982.

Burnim, Mellonee V. "The Black Gospel Music Tradition: A Complex of Ideology, Aesthetic, and Behavior." *More than Dancing: Essays on Afro-American Music and Musicians.* Ed. Irene V. Jackson. Westport, Conn.: Greenwood Press, 1985.

Butler, Judith. *Bodies That Matter: On the Discursive Limits of "Sex."* New York: Routledge, 1993.

"Desire." *Critical Terms for Literary Study.* Ed. Frank Lentricchia and Thomas McLaughlin. Chicago: University of Chicago Press, 1995.

Cain, William E. *The Crisis in Criticism: Theory Literature and Reform in English Studies.* Baltimore: Johns Hopkins University Press, 1984.

Carby, Hazel. *Reconstructing Womanhood: The Emergence of the Afro-American Woman Novelist.* New York: Oxford University Press, 1987.

Caygill, Howard. *Art of Judgment.* Oxford: Basil Blackwell, 1989.

Chernoff, John Miller. *African Rhythm and African Sensibility: Aesthetics and Social Action in African Musical Idioms.* Chicago: University of Chicago Press, 1979.

Childers, Joseph, and Hentzi, Gary, eds. *The Columbia Dictionary of Modern Literary and Cultural Criticism.* New York: Columbia University Press, 1995.

Christian, Barbara. *Black Women Writers: The Development of a Tradition, 1872–1976.* Westport, Conn.: Greenwood Press, 1980.

——— "But What Do We Think We Are Doing Anyway: The State of Black Feminist Criticism(s) or My Version of a Little Bit of History." *Changing Our Own Words: Essays on Criticism, Theory, and Writing by Black Women.* Ed. Cheryl A. Wall. New Brunswick, N.J.: Rutgers University Press, 1989, 58–74.

——— "The Race for Theory." *Cultural Critique* 6 (Spring 1987): 51–63.

Collins, Patricia Hill. *Black Feminist Thought: Knowledge, Consciousness, and the Politics of Empowerment.* New York: Routledge, 1991.

Condorcet. "Sketch for a Historical Picture of Progress of the Mind." *The Enlightenment.* New York: John Wiley & Sons, 1972.

Conkin, Paul K. *The Southern Agrarians.* Knoxville: University of Tennessee Press, 1988.

Cornelius, Janet Duitsman. *When I Can Read My Title Clear: Literacy, Slavery, and Religion in the Antebellum South.* Columbia: University of South Carolina Press, 1991.

Crenshaw, Kimberlé. "Whose Story Is It, Anyway? Feminist and Antiracist Appropriations of Anita Hill." *Race-ing Justice, En-gender-ing Power: Essays on Anita Hill, Clarence Thomas, and the Construction of Social Reality.* Ed. Toni Morrison. New York: Pantheon, 1992, 402–440.

Crews, Harry. *A Childhood: The Biography of a Place.* New York: Quill, 1983.

Cunningham, Noble E. *In Pursuit of Reason: The Life of Thomas Jefferson.* Baton Rouge: Louisiana State University Press, 1987.

Davidson, Basil. *The African Slave Trade.* Boston: Little, Brown, 1961.

de Man, Paul. *The Resistance to Theory.* Minneapolis: University of Minnesota Press, 1986.

de Saussure, Ferdinand. *Course in General Linguistics.* Ed. Charles Bally and Albert Sechehaye, with Albert Riedlinger. New York: McGraw-Hill, 1966.

Derrida, Jacques. "Structure, Sign, and Play in the Discourse of the Human Sciences." *The Structuralist Controversy: The Languages of Criticism and the Sciences of Man.* Eds. Richard Macksey and Eugenio Donato. Baltimore: Johns Hopkins University Press, 1970, 247–264.

——— *Speech and Phenomena and Other Essays on Husserl's Theory of Signs.* Trans. David B. Allison. Evanston Ill.: Northwestern University Press, 1973.

——— *Of Grammatology.* Trans. Gayatri Chakravorty Spivak. Baltimore: Johns Hopkins University Press, 1974.

——— *Writing and Difference.* Trans. Alan Bass. Chicago: University of Chicago Press, 1978.

Limited Inc. Evanston, Ill.: Northwestern University Press, 1988.

"The Purveyor of the Truth." Trans. Alan Bass. *The Purloined Poe: Lacan, Derrida and Psychoanalytic Reading.* Ed. John P. Muller and William J. Richardson. Baltimore: Johns Hopkins University Press, 1988, 173–212.

Diawara, Manthia. "Black Spectatorship: Problems of Identification and Resistance." *Screen* 29.4 (Autumn 1988): 66–76.

Douglas, Mary. *Purity and Danger.* London and New York: Ark, 1984.

Douglass, Frederick. *Narrative of the Life of Frederick Douglass, an American Slave.* Ed. Benjamin Quarles. Cambridge Mass.: Harvard University Press, 1960.

Doyle, Laura. *Bordering on the Body: The Racial Matrix of Modern Fiction and Culture.* New York: Oxford University Press, 1994.

Du Bois, W.E.B. *The Souls of Black Folk.* New York: New American Library, 1969.

Dyer, Richard. "White." *Screen* 29.4 (Autumn 1988): 44–64.

Eagleton, Terry. *The Ideology of the Aesthetic.* Oxford: Basil Blackwell, 1990.

Ellison, Ralph. *Shadow and Act.* New York: Vintage, 1972.

Epstein, Dena. *Sinful Tune and Spirituals.* Urbana: University of Illinois Press, 1981.

Erenberg, Lewis. *Steppin' Out: New York Nightlife and the Transformation of American Culture, 1890–1930.* Chicago: University of Chicago Press, 1981.

Fabian, Johannes. *Time and the Other: How Anthropology Makes Its Subject.* New York: Columbia University Press, 1983.

Feyerabend, Paul. *Against Method.* London: Verso, 1988.

Fitzhugh, George. *Cannibals All! Slaves Without Masters.* Ed. C. Vann Woodward. Cambridge: Belknap Press, 1960.

Foucault, Michel. *The Archaeology of Knowledge and the Discourse on Language.* New York: Pantheon, 1972.

Language, Counter-Memory, Practice: Selected Essays and Interviews by Michel Foucault. Ed. Donald F. Bouchard. Ithaca, N.Y.: Cornell University Press, 1977.

Discipline and Punish. Trans. Alan Sheridan. New York: Vintage, 1979.

Freud, Sigmund. *The Interpretation of Dreams.* Trans. Dr. A. A. Brill. New York: Random House, 1978.

Friedberg, Anne. *Window Shopping: Cinema and the Postmodern.* Berkeley: University of California Press, 1993.

Gaines, Jane. "White Privilege and Looking Relations: Race and Gender in Feminist Film Theory." *Screen* 29.4 (Autumn 1988): 12–27.

Gates, Henry Louis, Jr. *Figures in Black.* New York: Oxford University Press, 1987.

ed. *"Race," Writing, and Difference.* Chicago: University of Chicago Press, 1986.

Gearhart, Suzanne. *The Open Boundary of History and Fiction: A Critical Approach to the French Enlightenment.* Princeton, N.J.: Princeton University Press, 1984.

Genovese, Eugene. *The World the Slaveholders Made.* Middletown, Conn.: Weslyan University Press, 1987.

Goings, Kenneth W. *Mammy and Uncle Mose: Black Collectibles and American Stereotyping.* Bloomington: Indiana University Press, 1994.

Gordon, Ian. *Theories of Visual Perception.* New York: John Wiley & Sons, 1989.

Gould, Stephen Jay. *The Mismeasure of Man.* New York: Norton, 1981.

Goux, Jean-Joseph. *Symbolic Economies: After Marx and Freud.* Trans. Jennifer Curtiss Gage. Ithaca, N.Y.: Cornell University Press, 1988.

Graff, Gerald. *Professing Literature: An Institutional History.* Chicago: University of Chicago Press, 1987.

Graff, Gerald, and Warner, Michael. *The Origins of Literary Study in America: A Documentary Anthology.* New York and London: Routledge, 1989.

Graff, Harvey J. *The Literacy Myth: Literacy and Social Structure in the Nineteenth-Century City.* New York: Academic Press, 1979.

The Legacies of Literacy: Continuities and Contradictions in Western Culture and Society. Bloomington: Indiana University Press, 1987.

Griffin, Farah Jasmine. *"Who Set You Flowin'?": The African American Migration Narrative.* New York: Oxford University Press, 1995.

Guillory, John. *Cultural Capital: The Problem of Literary Canon Formation.* Chicago: University of Chicago Press, 1993.

Gunning, Sandra. *Race, Rape, and Lynching: The Red Record of American Literature.* New York: Oxford University Press, 1996.

Gusdorf, Georges. "Conditions and Limits of Autobiography." *Autobiography: Essays Theoretical and Critical.* Ed. James Olney. Princeton, N.J.: Princeton University Press, 1980, 28–48.

Guttman, Allen. *The Conservative Tradition in America.* New York: Oxford University Press, 1967.

Hall, Kim. *Things of Darkness: Race, Gender, and Power in Early Modern England.* Ithaca, N.Y.: Cornell University Press, 1995.

Handel, Stephen. *Listening: An Introduction to the Perception of Auditory Events.* Cambridge, Mass.: MIT Press, 1989.

Haraway, Donna. *Primitive Visions: Gender, Race, and Nature in the World of Modern Science.* New York: Routledge, 1989.

Harding, Vincent. *There Is a River: The Black Struggle for Freedom in America.* New York: Vintage, 1981.

Haskell, Thomas L. "Capitalism and the Origins of Humanitarian Sensibility, Part 1." *The Anti-Slavery Debate: Capitalism and Abolition as a Problem in Historical Interpretation.* Ed. Thomas Bender. Berkeley: University of California Press, 1992, 107–35.

Hegel, G.W.F. *Lectures on the Philosophy of History.* Trans. J. Sibree. London: G. Bell and Sons, 1914.

Herrnstein Smith, Barbara. *On the Margins of Discourse: The Relation of Literature to Language.* Chicago: University of Chicago Press, 1978.

Contingencies of Value. Cambridge, Mass.: Harvard University Press, 1988.

Hirsch, E. D. *Cultural Literacy: What Every American Needs to Know.* Boston: Houghton Mifflin, 1987.

Holiday, Billie (with William Dufty). *Lady Sings the Blues.* New York: Penguin, 1988. Originally published 1956.

hooks, bell. *Yearing: Race, Gender, and Cultural Politics.* Boston: South End Press, 1990.

Ihde, Don. *Sense and Significance.* Pittsburgh: Dusquesne University Press, 1973.

Jacobs, Harriet. *Incidents in the Life of a Slave Girl.* New York: Harcourt Brace Jovanovich, 1973.

Jameson, Frederic. *The Political Unconscious: Narrative as a Socially Symbolic Act.* Ithaca, N.Y.: Cornell University Press, 1981.

JanMohamed, Abdul R., and Lloyd, David. "Introduction: Minority Discourse – What Is to Be Done?" *Cultural Critique* 7 (Fall 1987): 5–12.

Jay, Martin. "Vision in Context: Reflections and Refractions." *Vision in Context: Historical and Contemporary Perspective on Sight.* Ed. Teresa Brennan and Martin Jay. New York: Routledge, 1996, 1–14.

Downcast Eyes: The Denigration of Vision in Twentieth-Century French Theory. Berkeley: University of California Press, 1993.

"Scopic Regimes of Modernity." *Vision and Visuality.* Ed. Hal Foster. Seattle: Bay Press, 1988.

Jefferson, Thomas. *Notes on the State of Virginia.* Ed. William Peden. New York: Norton, 1954.

Johnson Barbara. "Introduction." *Dissemination.* Chicago: University of Chicago Press, 1981, vii – xxxiii.

"The Frame of Reference: Poe, Lacan, Derrida." *The Purloined Poe: Lacan, Derrida and Psychoanalytic Reading.* Ed. John P. Muller and William J. Richardson. Baltimore: Johns Hopkins University Press, 1988, 213–51.

Johnson, James Weldon. *God's Trombones.* New York: Penguin, 1976.

Johnson, Mark. *The Body in the Mind: The Bodily Basis of Meaning, Imagination, and Reason.* Chicago: University of Chicago Press, 1987.

Jones, LeRoi. *Blues People: The Negro Experience in White America and the Music That Developed from It.* New York: Morrow Quill, 1963.

Judy, Ronald A.T. *(Dis)Forming the American Canon: African–Arabic Slave Narratives and the Vernacular.* Minneapolis: University of Minnesota Press, 1993.

Julien, Eileen. *African Novels and the Question of Orality.* Bloomington: Indiana University Press, 1992.

Kant, Immanuel. "Lectures on Pedagogy." *The Educational Theory of Immanuel Kant.* Ed. Edward Franklin Buchner. Philadelphia: J. B. Lippincott, 1904.

The Kerner Report: The 1968 Report of the National Advisory Commission on Civil Disorders. New York: Pantheon, 1968.

Klotman, Phyllis R. " 'Tearing a Hole in History': Lynching as Theme and Motif." *Black American Literature Forum.* 19:2 (Summer 1985): 55–63.

Krieger, Murray. *Theory of Criticism: A Tradition and Its System.* Baltimore: Johns Hopkins University Press, 1976.

Kuhn, Thomas. *The Structure of Scientific Revolutions.* Chicago: University of Chicago Press, 1970.

Lacan, Jacques. *The Four Fundamental Concepts of Psycho-Analysis.* New York: Norton, 1978.

"Seminar on 'The Purloined Letter.' " Trans. Jeffrey Mehlman. *The Purloined Poe: Lacan, Derrida and Psychoanalytic Reading.* Ed. John P. Muller and William J. Richardson. Baltimore: Johns Hopkins University Press, 1988, 28–54.

Laclau, Ernesto, and Mouffe, Chantal. *Hegemony and Socialist Strategy: Towards a Radical Democratic Politics.* New York: Verso, 1985.

Lauter, Paul. *Canons and Contexts.* New York: Oxford University Press, 1991.

Lentricchia, Frank. *Criticism and Social Change.* Chicago: University of Chicago Press, 1983.

Leitch, Vincent B. *American Literary Criticism: From the 30s to the 80s.* New York: Columbia University Press, 1988.

Levin, Charles. "Introduction." *For a Critique of the Political Economy of the Sign.* By Jean Baudrillard. St. Louis: Telos Press, 1981.

Levine, Lawrence. *Black Culture and Black Consciousness: Afro-American Folk Thought from Slavery to Freedom.* New York: Oxford, 1977.

Lincoln, Abraham. "First Joint Debate, Ottawa, August 21: Mr. Lincoln's Reply." In *The Lincoln–Douglas Debates.* Ed. Robert W. Johannsen. New York: Oxford University Press, 1965.

Livingston, Paisley. *Literary Knowledge: Humanistic Inquiry and the Philosophy of Science.* Ithaca, N.Y.: Cornell University Press, 1988.

Lovell, John, Jr. *Black Song: The Forge and the Flame.* New York: Macmillan, 1972.

Lowe, Donald M. *History of Bourgeois Perception.* Chicago: University of Chicago Press, 1982.

Lubiano, Wahneema. "Foreword." *(Dis)Forming the American Canon: African–Arabic Slave Narratives and the Vernacular.* By Ronald A. T. Judy. Minneapolis: University of Minnesota Press, 1993, xv – xxiii.

Macaulay, Thomas Babington. *Prose and Poetry.* Ed. G. M. Young. Cambridge, Mass.: Harvard University Press, 1952.

Macpherson, C. B. *The Political Theory of Possessive Individualism: Hobbes to Locke.* New York: Oxford University Press, 1962.

Marable, Manning. *How Capitalism Underdeveloped Black America.* Boston: South End Press, 1983.

Marks, Lawrence E. *The Unity of the Senses: Interrelations Among the Modalities.* New York: Academic Press, 1978.

Martin, Sella. "Sella Martin." *Slave Testimony.* Ed. John W. Blassingame. Baton Rouge: Louisiana State University Press, 1977.

Maultsby, Portia K. "West African Influence and Retentions in U.S. Black Music: A Sociocultural Study." *More Than Dancing: Essays on Afro-American Music and Musicians.* Ed. Irene V. Jackson. Westport, Conn.: Greenwood Press, 1985.

"Africanisms in African-American Music." *Africanisms in American Culture.* Ed. Joseph E. Holloway. Bloomington: Indiana University Press, 1990.

Marx, Karl. *Das Kapital.* Washington D.C.: Regnery, 1996.

McDowell, Deborah. "Boundaries: Or Distant Relations and Close Kin." *Afro-American Literary Study in the 1990's.* Ed. Houston A. Baker, Jr., and Patricia Redmond. Chicago: University of Chicago Press, 1989.

McKay, Nellie Y. "Introduction." *The Narrows.* By Ann Petry. Boston: Beacon Press, 1988, vii – xx.

Morrison, Toni. "Unspeakable Things Unspoken: The Afro-American Presence in American Literature." *Michigan Quarterly Review* 28.1 (Winter 1989): 1–34.

Muller, John P., and Richardson, William J. "Lacan's Seminar on 'The Purloined Letter': Overview." *The Purloined Poe: Lacan, Derrida and Psychoanalytic Reading.* Ed. John P. Muller and William J. Richardson. Baltimore: Johns Hopkins University Press, 1988, 55–76.

Mullin, Gerald W. *Flight and Rebellion: Slave Resistance in Eighteenth-Century Virginia.* New York: Oxford University Press, 1972.

Mulvey, Laura. *Visual and Other Pleasures.* Bloomington: Indiana University Press, 1989.

Nelson, Cary D. *The Word in Black and White: Reading "Race" in American Literature 1683–1867.* New York: Oxford University Press, 1992.

Nelson, Dana. *The Word in Black and White.* New York: Oxford University Press, 1992.

Noonan, F. Thomas. *The Dark Side of the Enlightenment: An Exhibition on the Occasion of the Fifteenth Meeting of the American Society of Eighteenth-Century Studies.* Cambridge, Mass.: Harvard University Library, 1984.

Nowotny, Helga. *Time: The Modern and Postmodern Experience.* Cambridge: Polity Press, 1994.

Nranjana, Tejaswini. "Brokering English Studies: The British Council in India." *The Lie of the Land: English Literary Studies in India.* Ed. Rajeswari Sunder Rajan. Dehli: Oxford University Press, 1993. 130–55.

Ogren, Kathy. *The Jazz Revolution: Twenties America and the Meaning of Jazz.* New York: Oxford University Press, 1989.

Olney, James, ed. *Autobiography: Essays Theoretical and Critical.* Princeton, N.J.: Princeton University Press, 1980.

O'Malley, Michael. "Specie and Species: Race and the Money Question in Nineteenth-Century America." *American Historical Review* 99.2 (April 1994): 369–95.

"Response to Nell Irvin Painter." *American Historical Review* 99.2 (April 1994): 405–8.

Ong, Walter J. *Orality and Literacy: The Technologizing of the Word.* London: Methuen, 1982.

Painter, Nell Irvin. "Race Relations, History, and Public Policy: The Alabama Vote Fraud Cases of 1985." *American in Theory.* Ed. Leslie Berlowitz, Denise Donoghue, Louis Menard. New York: Oxford University Press, 1988.

"Thinking About the Languages of Money and Race: A Response to Michael O'Malley, 'Specie and Species.'" *American Historical Review* 99.2 (April 1994): 396–404.

Pakenham, Thomas. *The Scramble for Africa: The White Man's Conquest of the Dark Continent from 1876 to 1912.* New York: Random House, 1991.

Pattison, Robert. *On Literacy.* New York: Oxford University Press, 1982.

Peden, William. "Introduction." *Notes on the State of Virginia.* By Thomas Jefferson. New York: Norton, 1954, xi – xxv.

Petry, Ann. "Ann Petry." *Contemporary Authors: Autobiographical Series,* vol. 6. Ed. Adele Sarkissia. Detroit: Gale Research, 1986.

The Narrows. Boston: Beacon Press, 1988.

The Street. Boston: Beacon Press, 1985.

Pocock, J. G. A. *Virtue, Commerce, and History: Essays on Political Theory and History Chiefly in the Eighteenth Century.* Cambridge: Cambridge University Press, 1985.

Poe, Edgar Allan. "The Purloined Letter." *The Purloined Poe: Lacan, Derrida and Psychoanalytic Reading.* Ed. John P. Muller and William J. Richardson. Baltimore: Johns Hopkins University Press, 1988, 3–27.

Rabinowitz, Peter. *Before Reading: Narrative Conventions and the Politics of Interpretation.* Ithaca, N.Y.: Cornell University Press, 1987.

Ransom, John Crowe. "Introduction." *I'll Take My Stand.* New York: Harper & Row, 1930.

The New Criticism. Westport, Conn.: Greenwood Press, 1979.

"Reconstructed but Unregenerate." *I'll Take My Stand.* New York: Harper & Row, 1930.

Richards, I. A. *Poetries and Sciences.* New York: Norton, 1970.

Robson, John M. "Mill's Theory of Poetry." *University of Toronto Quarterly* XXX (1960): 420–38.

Roberts, John W. *From Trickster to Badman: The Black Folk Hero in Slavery and Freedom*. Philadelphia: University of Pennsylvania Press, 1989.

Rodney, Walter. *How Europe Underdeveloped Africa*. Washington D.C.: Howard University Press, 1974.

Roediger, David R. *The Wages of Whiteness: Race and the Making of the American Working Class*. New York: Verso, 1991.

Rose, Tricia. *Black Noise: Rap Music and Black Culture in Contemporary Culture*. Hanover, N.H.: University Press of New England, 1994.

Ross, Marlon B. "Authority and Authenticity: Scribbling Authors and the Genius of Print in Eighteenth-Century England." *The Construction of Authorship: Textual Appropriation in Law and Literature*. Ed. Martha Woodmansee and Peter Jaszi. Durham, N.C.: Duke University Press, 1994, 231–58.

Rowe, John Carlos. " 'To Live Outside the Law, You Must Be Honest': The Authority of the Margin in Contemporary Theory." *Cultural Critique* 2 (Winter 1985–6):

Rubin, Gayle. "Thinking Sex: Notes for a Radical Theory of the Politics of Sexuality." *The Lesbian and Gay Studies Reader*. Ed. Henry Abelove, Michèle Aina Barale, and David M. Halperin. New York: Routledge, 1993.

Ryan, Michael. *Marxism and Deconstruction: A Critical Articulation*. Baltimore: Johns Hopkins University Press, 1982.

Said, Edward. *The World, the Text, and the Critic*. Cambridge, Mass.: Harvard University Press, 1983.

Saint Augustine of Hippo. *The Confessions of St. Augustine*. Trans. Rex Warner. New York: New American Library, 1963.

Sanjek, Russell, and Sanjek, David. *American Popular Music Business in the 20th Century*. New York: Oxford University Press, 1991.

Smith, Barbara Herrnstein. *Contingencies of Value: Alternative Perspectives for Critical Theory*. Cambridge, Mass.: Harvard University Press, 1988.

"President's Column: Curing the Humanities, Correcting the Humanists." *MLA Newsletter* 20.2 (Summer 1988).

Smith, Valerie. *Self-Discovery and Authority in Afro-American Narrative*. Cambridge, Mass.: University Press, 1987.

"Black Feminist Theory and the Representation of the 'Other.' " *Changing Our Own Words*. Ed. Cheryl A. Wall. New Brunswick, N.J.: Rutgers University Press, 1989.

Southern, Eileen. *The Music of Black Americans: A History*. New York: Norton, 1971.

Snead, James A. "Repetition as a Figure of Black Culture." *Black Literature and Literary Theory*. New York and London: Methuen, 1984, 59–80.

Spillers, Hortense J. "Cross-Currents, Discontinuities: Black Women's Fiction." *Conjuring: Black Women, Fiction, and Literary Tradition*. Ed. Marjorie Pryse and Hortense Spillers. Bloomington: Indiana University Press, 1985.

"Mama's Baby, Papa's Maybe: An American Grammar Book." *Diacritics* 17.2 (Summer 1987): 65–81.

Spivak, Gayatri Chakravorty. "Translator's Preface." *Of Grammatology*. By Jacques Derrida. Baltimore: John Hopkins University Press, 1974, ix – xc.

In Other Worlds: Essays in Cultural Politics. New York and London: Methuen, 1987.

Stallybrass, Peter, and White, Allon. *Politics and Poetics of Transgression*. Ithaca, N.Y.: Cornell University Press, 1986.

"The Making of Americans, the Teaching of English and the Future of Culture Studies." *New Literary History* 21.4 (Autumn 1990): 781–98.

Starling, Marion Wilson. *The Slave Narrative: Its Place in American History*. Washington, D.C.: Howard University Press, 1988.

Steiner, Wendy. *The Colors of Rhetoric*. Chicago: University of Chicago Press, 1980.

Strauss, Gerald. "Techniques of Indoctrination." *Literacy and Social Development in the West: A Reader*. Ed. Harvey J. Graff. Cambridge: Cambridge University Press, 1981.

Stuckey, Sterling. *Slave Culture*. New York: Oxford University Press, 1987.

Tanner, Laura E. *Intimate Violence: Reading Rape and Torture in Twentieth-Century Fiction*. Bloomington: Indiana University Press, 1994.

Taylor, Mark. *Erring: A Postmodern A/Theology*. Chicago: University of Chicago Press, 1984.

Tirro, Frank. *Jazz: A History*, 2d ed. New York: Norton, 1993.

Tise, Larry E. *Pro-slavery: A History of the Defense of Slavery in America, 1701–1840*. Athens: University of Georgia Press, 1987.

Torgovnick, Mariana. *Gone Primitive: Savage Intellectuals, Modern Lives*. Chicago: University of Chicago Press, 1990.

Viswanathan, Gauri. *Masks of Conquest: Literary Study and British Rule in India*. New York: Columbia University Press, 1989.

Walker, Alice. "In Search of Our Mothers' Gardens." *In Search of Our Mothers' Gardens*. New York: Harcourt Brace Jovanovich, 1983, 231–43.

Wall, Cheryl A. "Introduction: Taking Positions and Changing Words." *Changing Our Own Words: Essays on Criticism, Theory and Writing by Black Women*. Ed. Cheryl A. Wall. New Brunswick, N.J.: Rutgers University Press, 1989, 1–15.

Warner, Michael. *The Letters of the Republic: Publication and the Public Sphere in Eighteenth-Century America*. Cambridge, Mass.: Harvard University Press, 1990.

Warren, Robert Penn. "The Briar Patch." *I'll Take My Stand*. New York: Harper, 1930.

Watkins, Evan. *Work Time: English Departments and the Circulation of Cultural Value*. Stanford Calif.: Stanford University Press, 1989.

Watson, Julia. "Towards an Anti-Metaphysics of Autobiography." *The Culture of Autobiography: Constructions of Self-Representation*. Ed. Robert Folkenflik. Stanford, Calif.: Stanford University Press, 1993, 57–79.

Weber, Samuel. *Institution and Interpretation*. Minneapolis: University of Minnesota Press, 1987.

Weiss, Nancy J. *Farewell to the Party of Lincoln: Black Politics in the Age of FDR*. Princeton, N.J.: Princeton University Press, 1983.

Wellek, René. *The Attack on Literature and Other Essays*. Chapel Hill: University of North Carolina Press, 1982.

West, Cornell. "Minority Discourse and the Pitfalls of Canon Formation." *Yale Journal of Criticism* 1:1 (Fall 1987).

White, Deborah Gray. *Ar'n't I a Woman? Female Slaves in the Plantation South*. New York: Norton, 1985.

White, Hayden. *The Content of the Form: Narrative Discourse and Historical Representation*. Baltimore: Johns Hopkins University Press, 1987.

Wiegman, Robyn. *American Anatomies: Theorizing Race and Gender*. Durham, N.C.: Duke University Press, 1995.

Williams, Linda. *Hard Core: Power, Pleasure, and the "Frenzy of the Visible."* Berkeley: University of California Press, 1989.

Williams, Sherley Anne. "The Blues Roots of Contemporary Afro-American Poetry." *Afro-American Literature: The Reconstruction of Instruction*. Ed. Dexter Fisher and Robert Stepto. New York: MLA Press, 1978, 71–87.

Williams-Jones, Pearl. "Afro-American Gospel Music: A Crystallization of the Black Aesthetic." *Ethnomusicology* 19.3 (September 1975): 373–85.

Williamson, Joel. *A Rage for Order: Black–White Relations in the American South Since Emancipation*. New York: Oxford University Press, 1986.

Wilson, Olly. "The Significance of the Relationship Between Afro-American Music and West African Music." *The Black Perspective in Music* 2.1 (Spring 1974): 3–22.

Wimsatt, W. K., and Beardsley, Monroe. "The Affective Fallacy." *The Verbal Icon: Studies in the Meaning of Poetry*. Ed. W. K. Wimsatt. Lexington: University of Kentucky Press, 1954, 21–40.

"The Intentional Fallacy." *The Verbal Icon: Studies in the Meaning of Poetry*. Ed. W. K. Wimsatt. Lexington: University of Kentucky Press, 1954, 3–20.

Winterford, W. Ross. *The Culture and Politics of Literacy*. New York: Oxford University Press, 1989.

Wish, Harvey. *George Fitzhugh: Propagandist of the Old South*. Baton Rouge: Louisiana State University Press, 1943.

Woodward, C. Vann. *The Strange Career of Jim Crow*. New York: Oxford University Press, 1955.

Wright, Richard. "Introduction: How 'Bigger' Was Born." *Native Son.* New York: Harper & Row, 1966.
Zack, Naomi. *Race and Mixed Race.* Philadelphia: Temple University Press, 1993.

INDEX

academy, 6, 48, 131–3, 139–40, 212–13
    see also literary criticism
Adorno, T. W., 89–92, 112
Agrarianism
    see Southern Agrarians
Aronowitz, Stanley, 176, 178, 181
Augustine, Saint, 35–6
autobiography, 35–8, 46

Baraka, Amiri, 80–1
Barlow, William, 74
Barthes, Roland, 140, 143
Baudrillard, Jean, 13–16
Beardsley, Monroe, 134, 145, 170–1
Berman, Art, 171, 175
Bhabha, Homi, 208, 209
binarism, 18, 238, 240–2
Bloom, Allan, 53, 168–9
Bloom, Harold, 141
bla(n)ckness, 137–9, 148–50, 172, 206
borders
    see boundaries
boundaries, 6, 11–12, 16, 19–20
    and discrete literary text, 165–76, 181–2
    in the literary academy, 49–51, 135–7
    see also value, anatomy of
Bremer, Fredrika, 63

Brooks, Cleanth, 181
Burnim, Mellonee V., 81
Butler, Judith, 223, 230

Cain, William E., 134–5, 141–2
capitalism, 72, 89–92, 153–6, 158–9, 170, 179–80
Carby, Hazel, 119
Christian, Barbara, 187–8, 224, 226
Collins, Patricia Hill, 119
Condorcet, Marquis de, 68, 73
Crenshaw, Kimberlé, 119
Crews, Harry, 212–3

dance, 87–8
deconstruction, 3
de Man, Paul, 141, 167
Derrida, Jacques, 7, 71–2, 78, 108, 140, 142–3, 185
    critique of Husserl, 83–5
    reading "The Purloined Letter," 187–200, 203, 206–9, 211–12
de Saussure, Ferdinand, 41–2
desire
    see race as sexual paradigm
Diawara, Manthia, 235
Douglas, Mary, 2, 20–2, 26
Douglass, Frederick, 37–8, 46–7, 60–1
Doyle, Laura, 227, 230
Du Bois, W. E. B., 81